A TO Z OF CAREERS & JOBS

THE TIMES

A TO Z OF CAREERS & JOBS

NINTH EDITION

KOGAN PAGE

About the Editor

Sandhya Sharma has worked in the area of vocational education for over 10 years and has experience of advising businesses on training initiatives.

Acknowledgements

The editor would like to thank all those organisations who offered updated information for inclusion in this edition.

NVQs/SVQs/GNVQs

Scottish readers should be aware that, in order to simplify the text, the editor has referred only to NVQs. In nearly every respect, these are the same as their Scottish equivalent, SVQs. Relevant Scottish abbreviations and sources of further information have been included. GNVQs differ from NVQs in that they measure attainment whereas NVQs are based upon a statement of competence. They are also more broadly based than NVQs.

First published in 1984
Ninth edition 2000

Kogan Page Limited
120 Pentonville Road
London N1 9JN

British Library Cataloguing in Publication Data

A CIP record for this book is available from the British Library.

ISBN 0 7494 3210 1

Typeset by Kogan Page Ltd
Printed and bound in Great Britain by Thanet Press Ltd, Margate, Kent

INTRODUCTION

This book aims to provide information on a wide range of career and job opportunities for young people who are still at school, and for young adults in further education colleges or in training. It should also prove to be a useful source of information for teachers and career advisers.

It is a book that will help the reader gain more information on an area of current interest or develop a new interest that will need further investigation.

The information gives the reader an overview of the job or career, the qualifications, training and personal qualities needed, and an indication of starting salaries. The further information section gives the names, addresses and contact numbers of organisations that can offer more specific and detailed information. In order to meet the skills and needs of readers, Web site and e-mail addresses have been added wherever possible. The book is laid out in alphabetical order with an index that aims to provide easy referencing. A list of abbreviations and useful addresses can also be found on page vi.

Specific areas in this edition have needed updating due to changes at national level. For example, the area of Social Work and Social Care has altered radically, with new qualifications and new job roles. Basic information has also been added on certain aspects of growth areas such as Information Technology and E-commerce.

The job market is in a constant stage of change and the aim has been to reflect its changes as far as is reasonably possible. Starting salaries can only be approximate, as there are inevitable variations dependant upon the sector, the size of an organisation and the geographical location of the job.

Should you have any comments on the information included in this edition or if there are any major omissions from the book, please contact the editor at the publishers.

Sandhya Sharma

ABBREVIATIONS

A level	Advanced level
AS level	Advanced Special level
CAM	Communication, Advertising and Marketing Foundation
CCETSW	Central Council for Education and Training in Social Work
Edexcel (BTEC)	Comprises of ULEAC (University of London Examination and Assessment Council) and BTEC (Business and Technology Educational Council).
Edexcel	Edexcel Foundation
GCE	General Certificate of Education
GCSE	General Certificate of Secondary Education
GNVQ	General National Vocational Qualification
GSVQ	General Scottish Vocational Qualification
H grade	Higher grade (SCE)
HNC/HND	Higher National Certificate/Higher National Diploma
HTC	Higher Technical Certificate
NC/ND	National Certificate/National Diploma
NVQ	National Vocational Qualification
QCA	Qualifications and Curriculum Authority
SCE	Scottish Certificate of Education (equivalent to GCSE)
SNC/SND	Scottish National Certificate/Scottish National Diploma
SQA	Scottish Qualifications Authority
SVQ	Scottish Vocational Qualification
TEC	Training and Enterprise Council

USEFUL POINTS OF CONTACT

Qualifications and Curriculum Authority, 29 Bolton Street, London W1Y 7PD; 020 7509 5556; e-mail: www.qca.co.uk

National Training Organisation National Council, 10 Meadowcourt, Amoss Road, Sheffield, S9 1BX; 0114 261 9926

TEC National Council, Westminster Tower, 3 Albert Embankment, London SE1 7SX; 020 7735 0010

Scottish Qualifications Authority, Hanover House, 24 Douglas Street, Glasgow, G2 7NQ; 0141 242 2214; www.sqa.org.uk

A

ACCOUNTANT

Accountants are trained to examine, interpret and plan all types of financial transaction. Those who work in accountancy firms deal with such matters as auditing, analysing, verifying and interpreting clients' accounts, advising on taxation, executorship and trusteeship, and liquidations. Accountants employed in industry and commerce or by local authorities are concerned with financial planning and the allocation of funds. After qualifying, some Accountants specialise in such areas as taxation, auditing or management consultancy. They may also specialise in clients from a particular field, for example, music or the theatre.

Qualifications and Training

Accountants must obtain membership of one of the many professional bodies. Minimum educational requirements are five GCSE/SCE passes to include English language and maths, two at A level, or an Advanced GNVQ plus at least three GCSEs or, in Scotland, three at H grade and three ordinary grades. The majority of entrants for The Institute of Chartered Accountants in England and Wales are graduates, but it is possible to enter through the A level route. For The Institute of Chartered Accountants of Scotland, all entrants must hold a degree. It is generally compulsory for students to undertake a period of practical training – of three to four years' duration – in addition to taking professional examinations before being admitted as a professional Member of an Institute.

Personal Qualities

Numeracy, careful attention to detail, and a logical and analytical mind are all required. Good interpersonal skills and management potential are equally important.

£ The national average salary is £14,500, and can be as high as £28,000 in London. The salary often doubles after graduation.

i The Association of Cost and Executive Accountants, Tower House, 3rd Floor, 139 Fonthill Road, London N4 3HF; 020 7272 3925
www.icea.enta.net

The Chartered Association of Certified Accountants, Student Recruitment and Training, 29 Lincoln's Inn Fields, London WC2A 3EE; 020 7396 5800

The Chartered Institute of Management Accountants, 63 Portland Place, London W1N 4AB; 020 7637 2311
www.cima.org.uk

The Chartered Institute of Public Finance and Accountancy (CIPFA), 3 Robert Street, London WC2N 6BH; 020 7895 8823

The Institute of Chartered Accountants in England and Wales, PO Box 433, Chartered Accountants' Hall, Moorgate Place, London EC2P 2BJ; 020 7920 8100

The Institute of Chartered Accountants of Scotland, 27 Queen Street, Edinburgh EH2 1LA; 0131 225 5673

The Institute of Company Accountants, 80 Portland Place, London W1N 4DP and 40 Tyndalls Park Road, Bristol BS8 1PL; 0117 973 8261

Careers in Accountancy (Kogan Page)

Account Executive*, see *Advertising

ACCOUNTING TECHNICIAN

Accounting technicians work in a variety of roles alongside professionally qualified Chartered Accountants. They are involved in the day-to-day practical work of accountancy and finance, including the preparation of information and accounts and the interpretation of computer information, such as audit tax and payroll. Accounting technicians are widely employed in public finance, industry and commerce, and private practice. A growing number of accounting technicians provide a range of services direct to the public and manage their own practice. Many go on to qualify with the senior chartered accountancy bodies.

Qualifications and Training

The Association of Accounting Technicians' (AAT) Education and Training Scheme offers open access, although candidates must demonstrate numeracy and literacy skills. The scheme, which usually takes three years part-time, is competence-based and accredited at NVQ levels 2 to 4. Central assessments are combined with relevant work-based assessments during the training period. The three stages of the scheme are Foundation (NVQ level 2 in Accounting), Intermediate (NVQ level 3 in Accounting), and Technician (NVQ level 4 in Accounting).

Personal Qualities

The job requires a methodical, systematic approach and the ability to work with figures. Computer skills are an advantage.

£ With experience £13,000 in London, £7,500–£13,000 outside London; fully qualified £18,000 in London, £13,000–£14,000 outside London.

i The Association of Accounting Technicians, 154 Clerkenwell Road, London ECIR 5AD; 020 7837 8600
www.aat.co.uk

'Improve Your Prospects – Quality with AAT' (The Association of Accounting Technicians)

ACTOR

(see also Theatre)

Acting involves the interpretation of someone else's work and the communication of it to an audience. Actors are employed in various types of theatre (commercial, subsidised, community and fringe theatre, theatre-in-education), and also in television, film, radio, and television and radio commercials. Competition is keen and, because it is such a precarious profession, those entering it must be prepared for long periods of unemployment.

Qualifications and Training

Most potential actors attend drama school. The National Council for Drama Training is a useful source for information on accredited courses. A good general education is important and some schools require GCSEs and/or A levels. Training courses at established schools usually last two or three years. Entrance is by audition and is competitive. Further experience may be gained from working in a repertory company or in fringe theatre. This may be an alternative way of entering the profession, but it is becoming increasingly difficult to enter solely by this method.

Personal Qualities

Acting requires a combination of intelligence, sensitivity and imagination, together with a good memory, determination and physical stamina.

£ Comparatively low: minimum weekly salaries are set by theatre employers after negotiations with Equity (the actors' union) as £260.25 for subsidised repertory, £255 for provincial commercial, £233.10 for small-scale touring and £275 in the West End. Equity has a number of different agreements for television and film work, both of which are more highly paid than stage work.

i British Actors Equity Association, Guild House, Upper St Martin's Lane, London WC2H 9EG; 020 7379 6000

National Council for Drama Training, 5 Tavistock Place, London WC1H 9SS; 020 7387 3650 (*send sae for list of accredited courses*)

Careers in the Theatre (Kogan Page)

Contacts (theatrical directory; from The Spotlight Casting Directory, Charles House, 7 Leicester Place, London WC2H 7BP; 020 7437 7631)

ACTUARY

The work of an actuary is largely concerned with the application of mathematical probability theory, statistical techniques and the theory of compound interest to all kinds of practical problems. It is a small but influential profession, and there are good opportunities to go into management. The majority of actuaries are employed by UK-based insurance companies and consultancies. Opportunities also exist in Government service, on the Stock Exchange, in universities and overseas. Actuaries carry out a vital role within life assurance companies, advise pension funds, work in general insurance and use their unique skills in investment, health care and risk management. Such work offers management opportunities, often at the highest level, with actuaries having a commercial as well as a technical role.

Qualifications and Training

Most trainees have a degree in maths, statistics or economics, although it is possible to enter with two A levels or three H grades in mathematical subjects, providing the grades are good. Proficiency in English, equivalent to GCSE grade C, is also required. Training is on the job, often with an insurance company or firm of consultants, and is combined with part-time study for the examinations of the Institute or the Faculty of Actuaries. On average, it takes five to six years to complete all of the examinations and become a qualified actuary.

Personal Qualities

Prospective actuaries should have an aptitude for maths, a practical outlook and an analytical mind, as well as the ability to express themselves clearly and accurately.

£ Actuarial students earn in the region of £13,000–£25,000, and £30,000+ when qualified. London salaries are higher.

i Institute of Actuaries, Napier House, 4 Worcester Street, Oxford OX1 2AW; 01865 268200; fax 01865 268444 www.actuaries.org.uk

Faculty of Actuaries, Maclaurin House, 18 Dublin Street, Edinburgh EH1 3PP; 0131 240 1300; fax 0131 240 1313

'A Head Start – Your Guide to Careers in the Actuarial Profession' (available from either the Institute of Actuaries or the Faculty)

ACUPUNCTURIST

Acupuncture is a Chinese system of curing many symptoms and relieving pain by inserting fine needles into one or more points of the body. Acupuncture in China is also used to anaesthetise patients, and operations are performed without use of further drugs.

Qualifications and Training

The training of acupuncturists is monitored by the British Acupuncture Accreditation Board (BAAB), an independent body which is allied to the British Acupuncture Council. Graduates of accredited or candidate colleges have automatic right of membership of the Council. For specific information on courses, contact the colleges below. They also offer a list of courses which is updated every 3 months and is available directly from them.

Personal Qualities

In addition to possessing the necessary medical knowledge, acupuncturists must be able to put patients at their ease and to gain their confidence.

£ Salaries vary depending on number of patients and amount charged. After qualifying, acupuncturists may practise on their own, or as they choose.

i British Acupuncture Council, 63 Jeddo Road, London W12 9HQ; 020 8735 0400

The College of Traditional Acupuncture (UK), Tao House, Queensway, Royal Leamington Spa, Warwickshire CV31 3LZ; 01926 422121

The International College of Oriental Medicine UK, Green Hedges House, Green Hedges Avenue, East Grinstead, West Sussex RH19 1DZ; 01342 313106

Traditional Chinese Medicine/Acupuncture, Centre for Community Care and Primary Health, University of Westminster, 309 Regent Street, London W1R 8AL; 020 7911 5082

Working in Complementary and Alternative Medicine (Kogan Page)

ADMINISTRATIVE MANAGEMENT

Administrative management is about managing information through people. Information is central to all management processes, and people are the resources who use that information to add value. Administrative management represents at least an element of all managers' and most professionals' jobs, whether they are employed in finance, personnel, the arts, facilities management, purchasing, marketing or general administration. An organisation's ability to manage its administrative operations effectively in this era, which is so dominated by information technology, is often crucial to its success, or even to its survival. This is a sector that offers potential for people to start in clerical and junior administrative jobs and to proceed to any level according to their capability and qualifications.

Administrative management is a key process in all industries and throughout the public sector. The Institute of Administrative Management (IAM) has 12,000 members throughout the world, in jobs ranging from Administration Officer to Chief Executive; 42 per cent of members are senior executives or board directors.

Qualifications and Training

The Institute of Administrative Management (IAM) offers a range of professional educational qualifications, including the certificate, diploma, advanced diploma and BA (Hons) in administrative management. IAM qualifications are offered through colleges, universities and distance-learning providers.

Personal Qualities

Individuals who enjoy organising and who work cooperatively with other people will find satisfying opportunities in administrative management. They should be numerate, and have effective verbal and written communication skills. An aptitude for using computers will dramatically increase the number of opportunities for a career in this field.

£ Salaries in this diverse field are very varied. Supervisory posts start at around £12,000–£15,000, depending on qualifications, experience and special expertise (eg high levels of skills in IT). Managerial grades start at around £18,000, and the most senior IAM members and fellows are paid at company director levels.

i The Institute of Administrative Management, 40 Chatsworth Parade, Petts Wood, Orpington, Kent BR5 1RW; 01689 875555; fax 01689 870891

ADVERTISING

(see also Artist)

Advertising is a complex industry providing a wide range of openings, mostly with agencies that plan, organise and run advertising campaigns.

On behalf of their clients, advertising agencies study the product or service to be advertised and its market, then plan how it should be sold and distributed and how the media might be used to the best advantage in this process.

Account Executive

Account executives are responsible within the agency for a particular client or group of clients. They interpret the client's wishes; coordinate and supervise the work of others within the agency, such as creatives, account planners, and copy- and scriptwriters; seek advice from other experts such as media executives; and then present the ideas most likely to meet with the client's approval.

Account Planner

Some agencies employ full-time account planners. On the marketing side they are involved in annual planning and in making longer-range plans for the future. They may also plan future campaigns for particular accounts and consider the long-term position regarding media advertising. Apart from knowledge of the activities being planned, account planners need imagination, common sense and an ability with figures.

Market Researcher

The function of market research is to provide information about the needs, likes and dislikes of the client's potential consumer, and to indicate how a particular product should be presented. Information is gathered through interviews, surveys and questionnaires, and considerable skill and knowledge is involved in the interpretation of the results and statistics.

Media Executive

Media executives provide expert advice on the advertising medium – for example, television, cinema, posters, newspapers, journals – that will best suit a particular campaign, and negotiate for the most economical rates.

Copy- and Scriptwriters

The writers in the agency produce headings, text and jingles, copy for articles in journals and scripts for films and commercials. Copywriters often work closely with the Art Editor and visualisers.

Art Editor/Executive
This position involves coordinating the work of the creative department, which converts the client's original intentions into a visual form for approval. Others, including copywriters, may elaborate upon this.

Artist
Agency artists prepare initial visual layouts of adverts, posters and displays, and produce final artwork for printing. Some artists may design their own typography, and others may work with specialists who are responsible for printing and type selection.

Qualifications and Training

Courses in advertising and marketing provide a useful background, but none of them is an automatic passport to a job in the business. The Communication, Advertising and Marketing (CAM) Education Foundation runs certificate and diploma courses. The CAM Certificate in Communication Studies takes an average of two years to complete and provides a background to the business, before specialisation is necessary, in such subjects as marketing, advertising and public relations. Minimum entry requirements for the certificate are passes in five GCSE/SCE subjects, two of which should be at A level or Scottish equivalent. As an alternative, vocational qualifications in business studies or five GCSEs and at least one year's experience of full-time employment in communications are also acceptable. Business studies graduates and postgraduates or holders of a diploma in management or Edexcel (BTEC)/SVQ, HND/HNC business studies may be exempt from the certificate.

The diploma may be studied for in one year by candidates who hold the certificate; it covers international, industrial and consumer advertising and marketing. The Dorset Institute of Higher Education offers a BA degree in creative advertising.

Graduates in relevant subjects or those with vocational qualifications are preferred for market research positions and training is given mostly on the job, starting as a research assistant. The Market Research Society diploma is awarded to entrants with degrees and diplomas who have successfully completed courses of practical training. Creative staff who have attended a recognised college of art or have a degree in art and design are preferred.

Personal Qualities

Advertising account and media executives need to be able to lead and organise; they must be persuasive, critical, enthusiastic, confident and able to get on well with the public. They need boundless drive and stamina and considerable business acumen. Market researchers deal a lot with the public and a pleasant personality is therefore very important. They must be methodical, objective and unbiased. Creative staff require imagination and ingenuity in order to express ideas and concepts accurately and economically, emphasising the most important aspects of a product. Copy- and scriptwriters must have a flair for writing and communication.

£ Trainees' salaries are £12,000+; experienced staff may earn very high salaries.

i Advertising Association, Abford House, 15 Wilton Road, London SW1V 1NJ; 020 7828 2771
www.adassoc.org.uk
CAM Foundation Ltd (address as above); 020 7828 7506
Institute of Practitioners in Advertising, 44 Belgrave Square, London SWIX 8QS; 020 7235 7020
www.ipa.co.uk
Careers in Marketing, Advertising and Public Relations (Kogan Page)
Getting Into Advertising (The Advertising Association)
How to Get On in Marketing (Kogan Page)

Advocate,* see *Barrister

AERIAL ERECTOR

Aerial erectors fix aerials to roof structures along with the necessary cabling to feed equipment such as televisions, VCRs and radio receivers. With the extension of broadcasting methods and the growth of multi-channel viewing, many installers offer cable and satellite-dish installation alongside normal aerial installation. A number of businesses specialise in satellite installation as well as communication aerial installation.

Qualifications and Training

Formal qualifications are not necessary as training is often given on the job by experienced colleagues. Formal training is given in all aspects of aerial and satellite installation through the CAI. The ability to drive is an advantage.

Personal Qualities

A head for heights plus the ability to work in a confined space (aerials and the relevant cabling are sometimes installed in lofts) are essential, as is good colour vision. As all the work takes place in homes or business premises, it is necessary to be pleasant and polite.

£ Low when training, varying according to experience and whether working in a firm. The majority of aerial installers are self-employed, sometimes working on a sub-contract basis to establish a steady income.

i Confederation of Aerial Industries Ltd (CAI), Fulton House Business Centre, Fulton Road, Wembley Park, Middlesex HA9 0TF; 020 8902 8998

Local Jobcentres and Careers Offices

Aeronautical Engineering, **see** *Engineering*

Agent, Literary, **see** *Literary Agent*

Agent, Theatrical, **see** *Theatre*

AGRICULTURAL CONTRACTOR

Agricultural contractors employ experienced workers and managers to provide specific help to farmers at certain times of the year. About 60 per cent of farms use contractors from time to time.

Qualifications and Training

While specific qualifications are not essential, NVQs are available in relevant subjects. These, together with certificates at national or advanced national level in agriculture or agricultural contracting, obtained at a college of agriculture, would considerably enhance chances of employment.

Personal Qualities

Agricultural contractors must have a genuine sympathy with farmers and an appreciation of their needs, combined with efficiency, reliability and a good business sense.

£ Variable, depending on whether or not the contractor is an employee or running his own concern, and the size of the operation.

i Careers, Education and Training in Agriculture and the Countryside, Warwickshire Careers Service, 10 Northgate Street, Warwick CV34 4SR; 01926 401300

Agricultural Engineering, **see** *Engineering*

Agricultural Surveying, **see** *Surveyor, Surveying Technician*

Agriculture, **see** *Farming*

AMBULANCE SERVICE

People employed in the ambulance service spend most of their time working with people – patients, hospital staff and members of other services. The work involves dealing with accidents and emergencies, conveying patients needing regular care to hospitals, and completing the necessary paperwork. All ambulance personnel are skilled in first aid. They work interchangeably in pairs and must act as driver or attendant.

Ambulance Care Assistants

Assistants are mainly concerned with transporting elderly, infirm or handicapped people to hospitals or day centres. They may also do some work in hospital units.

Ambulance Technicians
Technicians respond to accidents and emergencies, including calls by GPs to take seriously ill people to hospital. They are able to use various types of life-saving equipment.

Ambulance Paramedics
Paramedics are technicians with additional training, who are able to use more advanced forms of life-support equipment. For example, they may set up a drip or, in certain circumstances, administer drugs.

Control Room Assistants
These assistants work in ambulance stations or central control units answering calls from GPs and the public, keeping in radio contact with ambulance crews.

Qualifications and Training

Formal educational qualifications are not required. It is necessary to hold a current British driving licence, and experience of driving heavier vehicles is useful. Recruits must complete a trial period as driver/attendant, involving non-emergency work driving mini-buses, cleaning vehicles and helping out at the ambulance station. If considered suitable, they can then apply to train as fully qualified ambulance workers. Applicants must be 18, although in some areas cadet schemes are available at 16 and 17. Academic qualifications vary, but four GCSEs grades A to C (SCE Standard grades 1 to 3) are an advantage.

Technicians have normally trained as care assistants first, but in some cases, with four GCSEs grades A to C (SCE Standard grades 1 to 3), and subjects including English, maths and a science, direct entry is possible.

Technicians take an eight-week residential course followed by 12 months' accident and emergency experience, leading to the National Ambulance Proficiency Certificate.

Paramedics must have a minimum of 12 months' experience in all aspects of ambulance work and may then qualify for a four-week intensive course.

The scope of training is being widened to increase life-saving skills.

Personal Qualities

For this work, tact and sympathy in dealing with people are needed and the ability to cope well in an emergency. Physical fitness is important, since the job is physically demanding and involves heavy lifting.

£ At 18 or over, ambulance persons (non-emergency) receive £10,648, ambulance persons (accident and emergency) £14,641, and control room assistants £9,260–£10,752. London staff receive a London allowance of £1,695.

i Local Department of Health
London: London Ambulance Service Headquarters, 220 Waterloo Road, London SE1 8SD; 020 7928 0333

ANALYST

Analysts work in industry providing a service for research, development and production departments. They analyse the results of experiments and advise what a newly produced substance may be. An analyst may check the quality of raw materials bought in by a company and examine the quality of the company's own products.

Public analysts are employed by local authorities to examine, for example, the state of the water supply; the adequacy of the sewage treatment system; toxic and suspect materials and leachate from landfill sites. They may also be asked to examine food from a suspect restaurant. Public analysts are frequently required to give witness on their findings in courts of law and should be familiar with the law relating to goods and services.

Qualifications and Training

A degree in chemistry, or in some instances an approved equivalent qualification, is necessary. To become a public analyst it is necessary to hold the Mastership in Chemical Analysis (MChemA), a qualification awarded by The Royal Society of Chemistry.

Personal Qualities

A meticulous care for detail and a sense of responsibility are essential.

£ £13,000–£14,000.

i The Royal Society of Chemistry, Burlington House, London W1V 0BN; 020 7437 8656

ANCIENT MONUMENTS INSPECTOR

These inspectors are employed by the Civil Service in the Department of the Environment to preserve ancient monuments and historic buildings. The work involves inspection generally, and particularly when conservation or restoration work is being carried out. Inspectors may also have to write reports and small guidebooks and occasionally attend courts of inquiry.

Qualifications and Training

A relevant degree – in history or archaeology – is necessary, or a non-relevant degree with a postgraduate qualification. All recruits start as assistant inspectors.

Personal Qualities

An ability to concentrate on details plus a sense of responsibility. A liking for being out of doors is also useful.

£ £17,000–£25,000; more in London.

i Royal Commission for the Ancient Monuments of England, 55 Blandford Street, London W1H 3AF; 020 7208 8200

Animal Nursing Auxiliary, **see** *Veterinary Nurse*

ANIMAL TECHNICIAN

This is a job for people who like working with animals, but not for those who are sentimental about them, as it involves looking after the animals kept in laboratories for the purposes of medical research. The law insists that new medical products, and a wide variety of domestic and industrial products, must be tested. It is the responsibility of the animal technicians to observe the effects of experiments, and to act as nurses to the animals, making sure that they are well cared for and that they do not suffer unnecessarily.

Qualifications and Training

Qualifications required are four GCSEs grades A to C (or Scottish equivalents). The subjects should include English, maths and biology, or two subjects in the sciences. Training is generally in-house and trainees may work towards the Certificate in Animal Technology (one year), the Membership diploma (two years), or the Fellowship diploma (two years). City and Guilds also offers NVQs in levels 2 and 3 in related areas.

Personal Qualities

The job requires people who are good with animals and can handle them with confidence, and have an interest in animal welfare. An interest in scientific research is also an advantage. Since the job requires close observation of the animals, the ability to give careful attention to detail is important.

£ First-year trainee, £7,500–£8,000.

i The Association of the British Pharmaceutical Industry, 12 Whitehall, London SW1A 2DY; 020 7930 3477

The Institute of Animal Technology, 5 South Parade, Summertown, Oxford OX2 7JL
www.iat.org.uk

Universities Federation for Animal Welfare (UFAW), The Old School, Brewhouse Hill, Wheathampstead, Hertfordshire AL4 8AN; 01582 831818
www.ufaw3.dircon.co.uk

Careers Working with Animals (Kogan Page)

'Careers with Animals' (from UFAW, 50p per leaflet)

ANTHROPOLOGIST

Anthropologists study the development of human societies, making comparisons between different communities and cultures. This academic discipline is linked with the other social sciences and with evolutionary biology. Much of the work still concerns non-industrial, 'primitive' or rural cultures, but changes brought about by contact with more sophisticated outside influences and pressures from 'modern' societies are an important aspect of study, and many anthropologists now undertake research in urban or industrial societies. The career involves a combination of research, teaching and finding out more about the people being studied by going to live with them over a period of time.

Increasingly, anthropologists are finding employment as consultants, for instance, in the development, health and humanitarian fields, and in such professions as journalism, human resource management, planning, tourism and heritage, museum curatorship and medicine.

Qualifications and Training

A good degree in anthropology. Postgraduate study is usually required.

Personal Qualities

Those wishing to embark on this career must normally be committed to an academic way of life, although there is growing demand for qualified anthropologists outside universities. Most field researchers must be prepared to spend long spells abroad, often in basic conditions. Physical and mental stamina is required, as well as independence and resourcefulness. Anthropologists must be prepared to work on their own for much of the time. However, as the subject matter of anthropology has diversified, so the ways of working life adopted by anthropologists have become more varied too, and they now work in every imaginable setting, from offices and day-care centres to out in the field. Linguistic ability is useful.

£ Salaries are variable, depending on the path chosen.

i Royal Anthropological Institute of Great Britain and Ireland, 50 Fitzroy Street, London W1P 5HS; 020 7387 0455; fax 020 7383 4235
www.rai.anthropology.org.uk

ANTIQUE DEALER

The buying and selling of antiques for profit entails expert knowledge of the field, combined with sound managerial and business sense. Comparatively few people make a living at this trade and many businesses are family concerns. Dealers frequently specialise in particular types of antiques and trade among themselves as well as with private buyers and sellers. Dealers may sell from shops, antiques markets, antiques fairs and from home.

Qualifications and Training

No specific qualifications are required, although a broad artistic background may be useful. The accepted route into the business is via a job with an established antique dealer, which provides an opportunity for learning the trade.

Personal Qualities

A good memory for detail is necessary in order to acquire the expertise required, and good business acumen is also important.

£ Salaries are generally low, but may be more if secretarial skills are also offered.

i British Antique Dealers' Association, 20 Rutland Gate, London SW7 1BD; 020 7589 4128; e-mail *enquiry@bada.demon.co.uk*

Arboriculturist*, see *Horticulturist

Archaeological Surveying*, see *Surveyor/Surveying Technician

ARCHAEOLOGIST

Archaeology – building up a picture of the past – is both an art and a science; its modern practitioners use highly technical and scientific methods of discovery, analysis and identification to reconstruct and study men and women in the past from their material remains. The evidence is collected through field work, including excavations, where clues are sought in objects, their surroundings, the ground itself and remains of living things. The evidence is analysed, subjected to experiment, assessed, identified, catalogued, conserved and possibly exhibited. Archaeologists usually specialise in a particular period, technique or geographical area. Opportunities for full-time, permanent positions are limited, and competition is consequently fierce for the few jobs available, which are to be found in central and local government, museums and universities, independent units and trusts, as well as a variety of positions in commercial operations. Some work will take place abroad.

Qualifications and Training

A good honours degree in archaeology is necessary for a position as a qualified archaeologist. Archaeology is offered at universities both as a single and a combined course. Five GCSE/SCE passes and two A levels or three H grades are the minimum qualification for university entry (20 points). Practical experience of archaeological field work is advantageous.

A postgraduate qualification is highly recommended for work in some areas of archaeology; training in a variety of specialities is available.

The conservation of archaeological, historical and ethno graphical artefacts requires a specialist training of its own. A certificate in conservation is offered by the Museums Association to people working in museums, and the Institute of Archaeology offers a diploma on a block- or day-release scheme. Degrees in conservation are also available.

Archaeological science also holds opportunities: bioarchaeology is the study of animal and plant remains – bones, teeth, grain – found on an archaeological site; materials science allows precise dating of artefacts; geoarchaeology is the study of sediments deposited on a site; forensic archaeology involves the use of archaeological techniques in police investigations.

Personal Qualities

Archaeologists need endless patience. They must pay great attention to detail, and have imagination and an enquiring mind. They must be able to use computers, write reports, plan and administer, work as a team with other academic experts and get on well with their workforce. Languages are useful, as is an ability to negotiate, and a talent for drawing or photography. Archaeologists should be healthy and willing to work in all conditions and environments.

£ £11,000–£13,000 for salaried posts; less for short contracts.

i Council for British Archaeology, Bowes Morrell House, 111 Walmgate, York YO1 2UA; 01904 671417
www.britarch.ac.uk

Institute of Archaeology, University College London, 31-34 Gordon Square, London WC1H 0PY; 020 7380 7495
www.ucl.ac.uk/archaeology

The Museums Association, 42 Clerkenwell Close, London EC1R 0AT; 020 7608 2933
www.museumassociation.org

A job information service is run by the Institute of Field Archaeologists at
www.archaeologists.net/serve.html

ARCHITECT

Architecture is a profession requiring the practical combination of imaginative design with scientific and technological principles, to produce designs for new buildings and for the extension, or renovation, of those already existing. In the first instance, conceptual design is based on information supplied by the client as to the function of the building, the proposed budget and the site. When the design is agreed, working drawings are produced for the builder. These show dimensions and materials and how everything will be put together. On large jobs there will be a team of architects working with engineers and other specialists, and it may take months to prepare all the drawings and schedules. Alternatively, very small jobs take only a few weeks. After the contract documents have been prepared and a builder selected, work begins on the site. The architect visits frequently as the building goes up. This can involve tramping around in boots and a hard hat, and climbing up and down ladders, as well as taking the chair at site meetings.

Opportunities exist for employment in private practice, with local authorities, central Government and in some industrial organisations.

Qualifications and Training

Candidates should have passes in at least two subjects at A level or one A level and two AS levels, together with passes in at least five other subjects at GCSE level. Subjects should be drawn from academic fields of study and include maths, English language and a separate science (physics or chemistry), or a double certification in science.

Training takes a minimum of seven years, but only five of those are spent at a school of architecture. After a three-year degree course, students spend a year in an architect's office. Students often work abroad during this year or work in other parts of the building industry. Another two years' further study to obtain a diploma or higher degree are followed by another year of working in an office, ending with a professional practice exam to become registered as an architect with the Architects' Registration Board. This allows the use of the title Architect in business.

Part-time training is an alternative offered by a few schools for students already working in an architect's office on a day-release basis.

Membership of the Royal Institute of British Architects (RIBA) and Royal Incorporation of Architects, Scotland (RIAS) is open to students while studying and also to those who are fully qualified.

Personal Qualities

Architects must have artistic ability and be imaginative, but at the same time need to be able to understand and apply technical information. They must adopt a practical approach to their work and be able to communicate their ideas and instructions to a variety of people. Business acumen, a professional approach, discretion and willingness to conform to a strict code of practice and professional conduct are very important.

£ While completing their two years' practical training, architectural students may expect to earn between £10,000 and £15,000; when fully registered this will increase to about £18,000, and thereafter will be dependent upon position, experience and employer. £27,000 is the average.

i The Architects' Registration Board (ARB), 73 Hallam Street, London W1N 6EE; 020 7580 5861

Royal Incorporation of Architects in Scotland (RIAS), 15 Rutland Square, Edinburgh EH1 2BE; 0131 229 7545/7205

Royal Institute of British Architects (RIBA), Public Information Line, 66 Portland Place, London W1N 4AD; 0891 234 400 www.riba.net

Careers in Architecture (Kogan Page)

ARCHITECTURAL TECHNOLOGIST

The architectural technologist works alongside an architect and other professionals as an essential part of the building design and construction team. The architectural technologist is concerned primarily with the science of architecture and, as such, could be involved in project management, design presentations, submissions and negotiations to gain statutory approvals, materials selection and specification, coordinating the work of other professionals, contract administration, inspection and certification of construction and application of CAD techniques.

Qualifications and Training

A degree in architectural technology, an HNC/HND in building studies (or a related subject), or an NVQ level 4 in architectural technology leading to Associate Membership of the British Institute of Architectural Technologists (BIAT).

Personal Qualities

Architectural technologists should be able to work both as part of a team and on their own. Attention to detail is necessary, as is the ability to take account of other professionals' needs. Effective communication skills are necessary when working as part of the team, liaising with clients or tendering for contracts.

£ Junior technologists, £8,000–£10,000; qualified technologists with three years' experience, £12,500–£14,000; senior technologists with appropriate educational qualifications and ten years' experience, £19,000.

i British Institute of Architectural Technologists (BIAT), 397 City Road, London EC1V 1NE; 0800 731 5471

ARCHIVIST

Archivists preserve the records of the past, in the form of all types of documents: books, papers, maps, photographs and films. They take charge of the documents in national or local archives, universities, hospitals, businesses or charities. Their job includes the selection of material, indexing and cataloguing, and giving help and advice to archive users.

Qualifications and Training

This is a small profession, requiring a strong academic background. Entrants should have a good degree, and an interest in heritage and information management. The recognised qualification is a postgraduate diploma in archive studies or administration. This is usually taken as a one-year full-time course at one of four universities in the UK.

Personal Qualities

Meticulous attention to detail is very important; archivists should also possess practical ability, since the work requires such skills in the physical care of the records.

£ £13,000+.

i Society of Archivists, Information House, 40 Northampton Road, London EC1R 0HB; 020 7278 8630
www.archives.org.uk

ARMY

The Army is the largest of the three armed forces and offers a wide range of opportunities to both men and women, both in the UK and abroad. Regiments and corps provide opportunities in the Armoured Corps, Royal Artillery, Royal Engineers, Royal Signals, Infantry, Army Air Corps, Royal Logistics Corps, Military Police, in pay and administration, teaching, catering and for qualified doctors, dentists, vets, lawyers and chaplains.

Qualifications and Training

Officers
There are two main types of commission: a regular commission (up to the age of 55) and a short service commission (three to eight years). The minimum entry qualification is five passes at GCSE (grade A, B or C), to include English and maths. Applicants for a regular commission must have two passes at A level.

Sponsorship
Cadetships and bursaries are available for those studying for a recognised first degree. All successful applicants complete 11 months' officer training at the Royal Military Academy, Sandhurst.

Soldiers and Servicewomen
Single entry from age 16 to 25; some apprentice vacancies are also available. Recruits enlist usually on an open engagement by which they agree to serve for 22 years, although it is possible to leave after a minimum of three years and three months' service over the age of 18, provided one year's notice is given.

Personal Qualities
Applicants must be British or Commonwealth citizens, born of British or Commonwealth parents and have been resident in the UK for the past five years. All candidates must be medically fit, intelligent, have the ability to work in a team and show dedication, courage, patriotism and a sense of responsibility.

£ Soldiers: 16–17 £5,720, 17–17½ £6,939, 17½ and over £9,180. Officers: £19,340.

i Officer entry: write for an information pack to Officer Entry, Freepost 4335, Department 0253, Bristol BS1 3YX
Local Army Career Information Offices

ARTIST
(see also Advertising, Interior Decorator, Interior Designer)

Only a very few artists are able to earn a living solely by the sale to clients of original work. Many more work as designers in advertising, industry and publishing, the latter also offering opportunities for illustrators, particularly for covers and jackets and children's books, or teach art in a school or college. Design work includes graphic design concerned with display, lettering, packaging – all aspects of visual communication; fashion and textile design; environmental design – office and shop interiors as well as some museums and galleries; interior design; and product design – the appearance of equipment such as televisions, cars and also more scientific apparatus.

There are limited opportunities for work as a community artist, community arts officer (encouraging art in the community) and artist in residence.

Qualifications and Training

For the majority of artists, academic qualifications are necessary, ranging from two-year foundation courses for 16-year-olds with some GCSEs or equivalents, to one-year courses for older students with at least five GCSEs or equivalents and one A level, and degree courses requiring at least five GCSE passes with two A levels or three H grades. There are vocational qualifications available too, providing both general and specific qualifications (for example, fashion design). Art teachers in schools require appropriate teaching qualifications.

Personal Qualities

The qualities required vary according to the work undertaken. Creativity, talent and imagination are all important, as well as enthusiasm and, in some cases, the ability to work as part of a team and to meet deadlines.

£ Designers £11,000–£12,000, and teachers a minimum of £13,350.

i National Society for Education in Art and Design (NSEAD), The Gatehouse, Corsham Court, Wiltshire SN13 0BZ; 01249 714825

'Creative Futures' (£12.30 inc. p&p from NSEAD)

Careers in Art and Design (Kogan Page)

ARTS ADMINISTRATION

This is the administration and management of theatres, orchestras, opera houses, ballet companies and arts centres. The Arts Council, responsible for the promotion of art throughout the country, has its own administrative staff. The British Council, responsible for displaying British arts abroad, also employs a small number of staff.

Qualifications and Training

Experience is often more important than formal educational qualifications although a good general education is expected. This applies also to courses in administration sponsored by The Arts Council.

The examinations of the Institute of Chartered Secretaries and Administrators are at three levels. To enter the first level, the

Foundation Programme, specific academic requirements are not necessary. This level must be completed before going on to the Pre-Professional Programme and the Professional Programme. Graduates or equivalent have certain exemptions.

Personal Qualities

The ability to communicate and to get on with people is vital. Practical administrative and organisational skills are also required.

£ £11,000+ as an assistant.

i The Arts Council, 14 Great Peter Street, London SW1P 3NQ; 020 7333 0100

ART THERAPIST

Art therapy is used as a treatment for psychological and emotional disorders. Drawing, painting, modelling and sculpture are among the creative activities used. Most art therapists work in hospitals, some in special schools and child guidance clinics and some in prisons, detention centres and community homes. As most posts are part-time, full-time therapists usually work for more than one institution within an area.

Qualifications and Training

A degree in art or design followed by a postgraduate course is the recommended training. The postgraduate qualification is usually a two-year full-time course, or a three-year part-time course.

Personal Qualities

Art therapists should have an interest in teaching and the ability to apply art in a practical way, together with a great deal of patience. A calm disposition is also an asset, as well as one year's relevant work experience.

£ Salaries vary greatly according to the place of employment. Therapists employed by the NHS earn from approximately £13,900 to £20,550.

i The British Association of Art Therapists, 11a Richmond Road, Brighton, East Sussex BN2 3RL (an information folder costs £5; send sae for list)
Careers in Art and Design (Kogan Page)

ASTRONOMER

Astronomers study the sun, planets, stars, galaxies and other objects in the sky analysing the radio, infrared, optical, ultraviolet, X- and gamma-radiations they emit to find out how they work. Some of these radiations do not penetrate the earth's atmosphere, so observations by satellite are necessary as well as from the ground. Modern astronomical detectors are usually based on electronic methods and give results which can be analysed by computer.

Qualifications and Training

To become a research astronomer, a good degree in physics or maths is necessary (some universities offer such courses with astronomy or astrophysics) followed by a doctorate. Various grants are available to support students during their three-year doctoral courses.

Astronomy-related careers at an engineering or technical level are also open to those with skills in applied physics, electronics, computer hardware and software, optics and mechanical engineering. Direct entry with A level or Scottish highers is now unusual and recruits should expect to obtain their initial technical training, leading to at least an HNC, outside astronomy.

Personal Qualities

Astronomers need curiosity and imagination; they must be able to make logical deductions from the available observations. Working long and unusual hours and travelling to remote observatories may also be involved.

£ Post-doctoral salaries start at around £16,000; technical salaries after training are around £13,500-£16,000, depending on qualifications.

i The Library, Royal Astronomical Society, Burlington House, Piccadilly, London W1V 0NL; 020 7734 4582; e-mail *info@ras.org.uk*
www.ras.org.uk/ras

Public Information Officer, Royal Observatory Greenwich, National Maritime Museum, London SE10 9NF; 020 8312 6735; fax 020 8312 6734
www.rog.nmm.ac.uk

AUCTIONEER

(see also Estate Agent, Valuer)

The auctioneer's work involves the sale by auction of property of all kinds, including all types of buildings (houses, farms and estates), livestock, and goods such as furniture, antiques, paintings, glass, toys, carpets and china. The work also entails valuations for various purposes, including investment, insurance, and so on.

Qualifications and Training

An auctioneer's work involves the valuation of land and property, so surveying or valuation qualifications are necessary.

There are two components to qualifying as a Chartered Surveyor or Valuer. First, successful completion of either a Royal Institution of Chartered Surveyors (RICS) or ISVA-accredited degree or diploma, followed by a period of practical training while in employment. Postgraduate conversion courses are also available; full-time one year and part-time two years.

Personal Qualities

The ability to pay attention to detail is important for this job, together with a practical and astute mentality and an aptitude for figures. In fine-art auctioneering, a certain flair and the ability to distinguish a fake from the genuine article are desirable.

£ While qualifying, salaries are in the region of £10,000 for trainees with A levels to £13,000–£14,000 for graduates with a relevant degree. Once fully qualified, salaries can be very high, particularly in London.

i ISVA (Incorporated Society of Valuers and Auctioneers), 3 Cadogan Gate, London SW1X 0AS; 020 7235 2282
www.isva.co.uk

The Institute of Revenues, Rating and Valuation, 41 Doughty Street, London WC1N 2LF; 020 7831 3505

The Royal Institution of Chartered Surveyors, 12 Great George Street, London SW1P 3AD; 020 7222 7000

Audio Assistant, see *Broadcasting*

AUDIOLOGY TECHNICIAN

Audiology technicians carry out tests to assess the presence, nature and extent of a hearing loss, using complex and advanced techniques. They take aural impressions for individual moulded ear inserts, fit and instruct the patients on how to use hearing aids, and review their progress.

Qualifications and Training

Four GCSEs at C grade or equivalent, in English, maths, physics and another science. Training involves two years of combined theory and practice while in employment, leading to an Edexcel (BTEC) qualification in medical physics and physiological measurement, or NVQ equivalent.

Personal Qualities

Candidates must be patient, have a clear speaking voice and the ability to get on with people.

£ Trainee £6,700–£8,000+. Once qualified, depending on grade, £9,000–£27,000+.

i British Society of Audiology, 80 Brighton Road, Reading RG6 1PS; 0118 966 0622; fax 0118 935 1915
www.b-s-a.demon.co.uk

Society of Hearing Aid Audiologists, Bridle Croft, Burgh Heath Road, Epsom KT17 4LF; 01372 725348

Auditor, see *Accountant*

B

BAKER

The baking trainee learns the skills involved in the production of a wide variety of bread and confectionery goods. Master Bakers have traditionally provided, and continue to provide, an ideal environment in which to acquire craft skills, perhaps with a view to eventually setting up a business. Although hours of work can be unsocial, with shifts or early starts, the rewards can include tremendous job satisfaction.

Trainees can also enter the baking industry by working for a supermarket in an in-store bakery or at a large manufacturing plant bakery. In-store bakeries have seen a prolific growth over recent years. Plant bakeries can teach mass-production techniques, with the operation of highly sophisticated, though usually automated, equipment.

In addition, many organisations employ research and quality control staff; normally, specific qualifications will be required for these posts. Local bakery colleges will be able to give more information about exact requirements.

Qualifications and Training

No formal educational qualifications are required to enter the trade. Both large and small firms often operate schemes by which trainees can attend their local bakery college and/or train in the workplace for NVQs in Craft Baking at levels 2 and 3, awarded by City and Guilds or HAB.

Bakery colleges provide a wide variety of other courses, which can be studied on a full- or part-time basis. They include, for example, advanced confectionery and decorating skills. Plant bakers would normally use the NVQs in Food and Drink (Manufacturing Operations) awarded by City and Guilds/FDQC. Advanced bakery management and science-based courses are available from Edexcel (BTEC).

Candidates wishing to pursue an Edexcel (BTEC) or degree course should enquire from their local college about entrance requirements; these are often quite flexible. Modern Apprenticeships are available in craft baking and bakery service. Details of both Modern Apprenticeships and colleges that provide bakery courses can be obtained from the National Association of Master Bakers.

Personal Qualities

Willingness to learn the craft and the ability to work in a team, with an above-average concern for cleanliness and hygiene.

£ Low at 16, when qualified, £150 per week, or higher depending on experience, responsibility, region and overtime.

i National Association of Master Bakers, 21 Baldock Street, Ware, Hertfordshire SG12 9DH; 01920 468061; fax 01920 461632 www.masterbakers.co.uk/masterbakers

Ballet, see *Dancing*

BANKING

Banks provide a delivery point for financial services. The most obvious side of banking is the high-street branches but other work areas in banking include: international (the financing of foreign trade and the provision of a complete overseas banking service for UK customers); corporate finance (dealing with the requirements of large companies); human resources, recruitment, training and staff development; insurance; computer services; selling and marketing (promoting banking services); training; and trust work (when a bank is appointed as executor or joint executor of a will).

High Street or Clearing Banks

These banks provide a complete financial service for their customers: maintaining accounts, making payments, and arranging personal loans and mortgages. They also undertake the safe custody of valuables and act as executors and trustees of wills. Many of the careers in banking are in the high street, or clearing banks. The work involves: general office work, such as dealing with telephone enquiries, using the mechanised accounting systems and computer terminals, and dealing with standing orders; cashier work at the counter; and foreign and securities work. The latter includes the buying and selling of currency and travellers' cheques, and handling import-export documentation. Marketing and selling skills are also required. Specialisation may take place in areas such as investment, a computer centre, an international division, personnel and marketing. To work in a British bank abroad, or for an overseas bank in London, requires specialisation in international business, finance, and development projects. The ability to speak one or more other languages is very useful.

Bank of England

The banker to the Government is the Bank of England. It is also concerned with the financial structure of Great Britain and with other banks in the country as well as operating accounts for overseas central banks. The Bank of England is responsible for the printing, issue and withdrawal of British banknotes and it also controls interest rates and raises short-term Government finance. The monitoring of economic developments at home and abroad provides information for the Bank, the Treasury and other Government departments. It does not offer banking facilities to the general public. Specialists such as economists, statisticians and librarians are recruited in addition to other banking staff.

Investment Banks

These are generally financial houses, which started from trading as merchants and have expanded their role to financing the trading and commercial activities of others, especially in the international marketplace. An investment banking group nowadays includes the following services for its clients: corporate finance and advisory work, banking for governments, institutions and companies, investment management and securities trading.

Qualifications and Training

Each bank has different entry points but there are four main categories: standard, accelerated, graduate and secretarial. For standard entry, banks ask for a range of GCSEs grades A to C and, sometimes, A levels; for accelerated entry, candidates must have a minimum of two A levels or GNVQ Advanced, or equivalent. Those who join as accelerated entry candidates follow a structured training programme leading to senior clerk status. Graduate training schemes are designed for those with the potential to reach management. There are fewer vacancies for secretaries now;

candidates need a range of GCSEs grades A to C, a typing speed of 40wpm and good English grammar and punctuation.

The Chartered Institute of Bankers in Scotland is a separate body; its first-level qualification is the Certificate in Financial Services, which requires no previous qualifications for entry. Students completing the certificate can progress to the Associateship and Membership examinations.

Most investment banks welcome applications from graduates who can have qualified from a range of disciplines such as law, accountancy or business. There are also vacancies for individuals seeking a career in information technology. Although there are some vacancies for individuals with GCSEs or A levels (or equivalent), these are quite limited.

Personal Qualities

Accuracy, integrity, good powers of concentration and a clear mind are essential for success in a banking career. It is important to be able to get on with people and to work as a member of a team.

£ New entrants are paid from £5,675–£6,500 at age 16, to over £14,000 for someone at the top of the clerical scale. An assistant manager earns £14,500–£21,500 a year. Thereafter, salaries are dependent on the job and performance of the individual. Banks operate a job evaluation salary structure and promotion is on a merit basis. Extra allowances are paid to staff serving in London and some other towns and cities.

i London Investment Banking Association (LIBA), 6 Frederick's Place, London EC2R 8BT; 020 7796 3606; fax 020 7796 4345

The Chartered Institute of Bankers, 90 Bishopsgate, London EC2N 4AS; 020 7444 7111

The Chartered Institute of Bankers in Scotland, Drumsheugh House, 38B Drumsheugh Gardens, Edinburgh EH3 7SW; 0131 473 7777
www.ciobs.org.uk

Careers in Banking and Finance (Kogan Page)

BARRISTER

The services of a Barrister are required by solicitors (*see also* Solicitor), who deal with the clients and then 'brief' the Barrister. Barristers plead counsel in the higher courts and may also appear in the lower courts, where they usually begin their careers. They give specialised advice on the law and may advertise their services to the public. Some are employed in the Army Legal Services, giving advice on all aspects of service and civil law that may affect the Army.

In Scotland, the Advocate is the equivalent of the Barrister.

Qualifications and Training

Full details of qualifications required for admission are available from the General Council of the Bar, but generally students are expected to hold a UK law degree with second class honours or better, or a non-law degree at the same standard plus a pass in a special one-year course known as the Common Professional Examination.

Every intending Barrister must join one of the four Inns of Court and complete the necessary dining terms before Call.

Students intending to practise must also attend the one-year full-time vocational course. From 1997, a number of institutions have offered this course (list available from the Bar Council). Students' successful completion of the course is assessed in the practical work, and in tests and examinations carried out during the year. Success in this is followed by Call and one-year pupillage under the personal instruction and guidance of a Barrister. Pupillage may involve researching relevant details of a case, setting them out in detail and drafting documents. During the first six months' pupillage, pupils may attend court but may not accept briefs.

After completing pupillage a Barrister has to find a 'seat' in an existing set of Barristers' chambers. Some may choose to work as employed Barristers and enter the Civil Service, local government or commerce and industry. About 15 years after being established at the Bar a Barrister may apply for a 'patent' as a Queen's Counsel. Although 'taking silk' (as it is known) is usual (but not obligatory) if a Barrister wishes to become a High Court Judge, it can have financial penalties and some Barristers stay 'juniors' throughout their career at the Bar.

In Scotland, Advocates must be admitted to the Faculty of Advocates usually by gaining a degree in law. They must also take a course leading to a diploma in legal practice from a Scottish university. If intending to practise in court, it is necessary to serve 21 months' apprenticeship in a solicitor's office followed by nine months in unpaid pupillage to a practising member of the Faculty, and to pass the Faculty exam in evidence, pleading and practice.

All Advocates practise from the Advocates Library in Edinburgh. Each Advocate is assigned to one of ten clerks.

Personal Qualities

Since the work is confidential, an intending Barrister needs to be trustworthy and discreet. An excellent command of the English language, which ensures the meticulous understanding and use of words, is essential. It will be necessary to understand and interpret complex legal wording in clear basic English. Barristers must understand and talk knowledgeably about technical matters in order to be able to cross-examine the most expert witness, for example, on complex aspects of technology. It is also useful if Barristers can put on a 'good performance' in court and possess certain theatrical qualities.

£ Barristers' earnings relate to the amount and type of their work, their reputation, and, if they share chambers, the apportionment and value of briefs. Barristers may find it a struggle to make a living at the beginning of their profession, but the rewards for those who succeed can be high.

i General Council of the Bar, 2/3 Cursitor Street, London EC4A 1NE; 020 77440 4000

Faculty of Advocates; The Clerk of Faculty, Advocates Library, Parliament House, 11 Parliament Square, Edinburgh EH1 1RF; 0131 226 5071

Careers in the Law (Kogan Page)

BARRISTERS' CLERK/ADVOCATES' CLERK

The Barristers' Clerk is the administrator or manager of the business chambers, deciding which briefs to accept, which of the Barristers in the chamber to give them to, and then negotiating the fees with the solicitor. The Junior Clerk runs errands and makes tea. The accounts, the Barristers' appointment books, and the efficient day-to-day running of the office are all part of the job of an experienced Clerk.

Qualifications and Training

The necessary qualifications are four GCSEs, grades A to C, to include maths and English. Training is on the job and juniors can apply through the Institute to attend a two-year part-time Edexcel

(BTEC) national certificate course studying organisation, finance, management, law, marketing and chambers administration. On obtaining the certificate, juniors may apply after five years' service for qualified Membership of the Institute of Barristers' Clerks.

The Bar in Scotland is divided into ten 'stables', each of which is served by an Advocates' Clerk and a Deputy Clerk employed by Faculty Services Ltd. Training is provided in service. The job of Advocates' Clerk is very similar to that of Barristers' Clerk in England and Wales. Their rates of pay are linked to the Civil Service scale on a level which roughly relates to a comparable post within the courts' administration. The ten Clerks have clerical and secretarial staff back-up.

Personal Qualities

In order to organise efficient chambers and the Barristers who work from them, a Barristers' Clerk needs an orderly mind, and the ability to work in a team, and to get on with the general public. A good command of written and spoken English, and an appreciation of the necessity for absolute confidentiality at all times, are vital to success in this career.

£ £7,000–£8,000. Juniors with two or three years' experience receive £10,000–£15,000, going up to £25,000 for very experienced juniors. Senior Clerks may earn £60,000–£75,000 plus a performance-related bonus. Senior Clerks were traditionally paid a fee which was a percentage of the Barrister's own earnings. Some are still paid in this way and the fee is usually around 5 per cent.

i Institute of Barristers' Clerks, 4a Essex Court, Temple, London EC4Y 9AJ; 020 7353 2699
www.instbclerks.org

Faculty Services Ltd, Advocates Library, Parliament House, 11 Parliament Square, Edinburgh EH1 1RF; 0131 226 5071

Careers in the Law (Kogan Page)

BEAUTICIAN

The beautician is usually either a beauty therapist (who may also be a manicurist) or a sales consultant.

Beauty Therapist
Therapists give treatments ranging from facials, make-up, manicuring and body treatments to electric depilation and waxing (removal of superfluous hair), and the treatment of some skin conditions such as open pores. A fully qualified therapist is capable of using various types of electrical apparatus. Therapists must know when to deal personally with skin complaints and when to refer a client to a doctor. It is usual to treat about eight clients a day in a treatment salon, which may be run by a cosmetic firm, an owner-manager, or occasionally as part of a hairdressing establishment.

Sales Consultant Beautician
Working in the perfumery department of a large store, in a luxury hotel at home and overseas, on a big liner or at airports, sales consultants sell and promote their firm's products, answering questions from potential buyers on skin care and make-up. They occasionally give talks at schools and colleges or to women's organisations, and some may travel for their companies at home and abroad.

Hairdresser/Beautician
The double qualification gives greater scope for employment, and some may work as make-up artists in radio or television. Some progressive psychiatric hospitals employ hairdressers/beauticians in rehabilitation centres and work of this nature plays an important part in treatment and recovery programmes. (*See also* Hairdresser.)

Qualifications and Training
Educational qualifications vary and formal academic qualifications are not always required. However, three GCSEs are needed to take a number of courses. City and Guilds and Edexcel (BTEC) offer awards. NVQs are available in Beauty Therapy, levels 1, 2 and 3. Private schools run courses leading to the award of their own diplomas to candidates who are usually over 18. Most good courses last from five to six months although some are longer. Courses (lasting a few weeks) for sales consultants are usually at schools attached to cosmetic houses, some of which demand a premium, which may be repayable after a period of working for the firm. The minimum age is usually 21, and experience in selling is required.

Personal Qualities

A friendly, confident manner combined with a liking for people of all ages, tact and courtesy, good health and a good skin, a smart and well-groomed appearance are all important. Beauticians need stamina, as they are on their feet for long periods.

£ Trainee beauty therapists' earnings are low and later depend upon the number of clients; consultants earn from £7,500 upwards, plus commission on sales.

i Local Careers Offices and further education colleges
Careers in Hairdressing and Beauty Therapy (Kogan Page)

BIOCHEMIST

Biochemistry is the study of chemical substances and processes which occur in living cells and tissues. Because they practise a practical science, most biochemists work in laboratories. However, some make their careers in education, or industry, where there are opportunities in brewing, food technology, forestry, agriculture, dietetics, pharmaceuticals management and planning.

Many biochemists are employed in hospitals, where they manage and develop the service and carry out research into disease. Pharmaceutical firms also employ biochemists who are concerned with the development of new drugs and their effects on diseases and patients.

Qualified biochemists are also employed in research institutions funded by the Medical Research Council, the National Institute for Medical Research and the Agricultural and Food Research Council, as well as some funded by charities such as the Imperial Cancer Research Fund (ICRF).

Laboratory Technician

Universities, institutes of higher education, hospitals and industry employ Technicians to support the work of biochemists in teaching and research. Technicians are either employed straight from school, in which case they are encouraged to continue their specialist education part-time, or they may be recruited at graduate level.

Qualifications and Training

Most professional biochemists are graduates, usually with an honours degree. Those working in research often have a higher degree. In addition to a degree, entrance qualifications include A level/H grade passes in chemistry and one or two others in biology, maths or physics.

Laboratory Technicians work part-time for Edexcel (BTEC) higher certificates or HNCs in appropriate subjects. Employers prefer to appoint people with GCSE grade A to C or A level passes in maths and science subjects because these qualifications usually gain exemptions from parts of Edexcel (BTEC) courses. Because the routine laboratory work is highly automated, a knowledge of the latest computer and automated systems is most useful.

Personal Qualities

The ability to work independently or as part of a team, patience, accuracy and powers of concentration are the prerequisites of the successful biochemist. Meticulous care of plants and other organisms, and sometimes the sympathetic and careful handling of laboratory animals, are required.

£ Salaries vary with the type of employment and responsibility involved. Graduates start at £12,500–£15,000; Technicians at age 16 from £5,500+. Additional graduate qualifications usually lead to positions of greater responsibility with commensurately higher salaries.

i Association of Clinical Biochemists, 2 Carlton House Terrace, London SW1Y 5AF; 020 7930 3333

The Education Officer, The Biochemical Society, 59 Portland Place, London W1N 3AJ; 020 7580 5530 (*enclose sae*)

The BioIndustry Association, 14–15 Belgrave Square, London SW1X 8PS; 020 7245 9911

A Career for Scientists in Clinical Biochemistry (Association of Clinical Biochemists)

Which Bioscience? (The Biochemical Society)

Biologist, **see** ***Biochemist, Biomedical Scientist, Biotechnologist***

BIOMEDICAL SCIENTIST

Biomedical scientists (including medical laboratory scientific officers in the NHS) investigate specimens of body fluids and tissues, and play an important role in the diagnosis and treatment of diseases. Most are employed in the laboratories of hospitals, in the pathology department, but many also work for the blood transfusion service, in public health laboratories, for veterinary establishments, universities, and pharmaceutical and other manufacturing companies. There are opportunities to assist in research and to teach. There is strong competition among graduates wanting to enter this profession as trainees.

Qualifications and Training

The profession has all graduate entry. A guide to courses can be obtained from the Institute of Biomedical Science. Trainees in the NHS and related bodies have to proceed to state registration and need a degree to do so.

Personal Qualities

Biomedical scientists must be able to work quickly, accurately and methodically. Complicated and new equipment must be used, so technical as well as scientific ability is needed.

£ £7,476–£9,796, depending on qualifications.

i Institute of Biomedical Science, 12 Coldbath Square, London EC1R 5HL; 020 7713 0214

BIOTECHNOLOGIST

Biotechnology is the application of living organisms and biological systems to industrial processes. Various aspects of biological science are involved – biochemistry, microbiology and genetics. At present, the main industrial areas in which biotechnologists are employed are fermentation, waste-systems management, antibiotic production, and animal and human food production.

Qualifications and Training

A degree would be the normal entry route. Degree entry requirements are a minimum of five GCSEs including maths, plus three A levels to include chemistry and two other sciences. (In Scotland, four SCE H grades are needed, to include chemistry, and Standard grade maths.)

Personal Qualities

Those employed in biotechnology need a high degree of accuracy, thoroughness and the ability to check and recheck details.

£ £12,000 upwards for graduates.

i The Education Officer, The Biochemical Society, 59 Portland Place, London W1N 3AJ; 020 7580 5530 (enclose sae)

The BioIndustry Association, 14–15 Belgrave Square, London SW1X 8PS; 020 7245 9911

Institute of Biology, 20–22 Queensberry Place, London SW7 2DZ; 020 7581 8333

BOOKMAKER

Bookmaking and betting shops can be small independent units or part of a large, often international, group of companies operating in the leisure industry. The work is varied and involves counter work and general administration.

Qualifications and Training

Trainee managers need GCSE passes in maths and English and, in addition, most of the well-known companies require them to sit an aptitude test as part of the selection procedure. Trainee managers usually start behind the counter at age 21. Promotion follows basic on-the-job training and counter work.

Personal Qualities

Competence in dealing with cash and with the general public are necessary.

£ Salaries are negotiable in independent shops, with part-time work available.

i National Association of Bookmakers, PO Box 242, East Molesey, Surrey KT8 2WE; 020 8941 8818

BOOKSELLER

In a bookselling career the focus is on knowing the product and on selling it. It is important to keep up to date by reading new books and reviews, in order to assist customers and to display the books to advantage. The ability to find information in catalogues and directories, particularly on computer, is essential. Managers order new stock and endeavour to give their shops an image that will attract regular customers. They may build up mail-order and institutional supply connections and participate in author promotions. Some larger bookshops have their own marketing department.

Qualifications and Training

A good general education is essential. Some bookshops require education to degree level. The industry-recognised qualification, the Diploma in Professional Bookselling, is available through the Booksellers Association of Great Britain and Ireland, together with a number of comprehensive training resources.

Personal Qualities

A liking for books and people, good general knowledge and an interest in reading and handling books are necessary, as are good health and stamina for a job which involves much standing. Customer care is essential to create a friendly and reassuring atmosphere where book buyers know that they are being looked after in an efficient manner by professional, knowledgeable staff.

£ Salaries are usually negotiable in small shops and many booksellers work part-time. Salary ranges are (with London at the top end of each range): sales assistants £9,000–£12,000, senior assistants £10,000–£13,000, managers £14,000–£25,000. Managers of larger chains can earn up to £40,000.

i Booksellers Association of Great Britain and Ireland, Minster House, 272 Vauxhall Bridge Road, London SW1V 1BA; 020 7834 5477
www.booksellers.org.uk

Box Office, **see** *Theatre*

BREWING

Brewing is the complex process of making and packaging beer. Specialist technicians are responsible for the choice of all raw materials – malt, hops, and so on – and plant equipment. Brewing technicians and brewing scientists are required to maintain consistently high-quality products. There are opportunities for non-qualified people to work as plant operators.

Qualifications and Training

No formal qualifications are necessary for non-technical jobs in the brewing industry. For technical jobs, the main demand is for honours graduates in science and engineering, particularly if they have specialised in brewing, biochemistry or chemical engineering. Requirements to enter a degree course are GCSE or equivalent passes in English language, maths and another science and two A levels/three H grades, to include chemistry. Specialist degree courses are offered at Heriot-Watt University in brewing. This degree provides exemption from the Associate Membership examination of The Institute of Brewing.

The Institute of Brewing offers training in the Science and Technology of Brewing and the associated industries. Its internationally recognised qualifications embrace the Foundation Certificate examination, the Associate Membership examination and the Diploma Master Brewer examination.

Personal Qualities

Good health is required for a job that will inevitably involve some night and shift work. The ability to organise and communicate effectively at all levels, and a keen interest in science and engineering, are the hallmarks of successful brewers and brewing scientists.

£ Non-technical staff earn from £8,500 to £9,500; technical trainees £12,000+.

i The Institute of Brewing, 33 Clarges Street, London W1Y 8EE; 020 7499 8144; fax 020 7499 1156; e-mail *enquiries@iob.org.uk*

BROADCASTING

The aim of radio and television is communication. The range of programmes offered is enormous: news, entertainment, sport, music and large number of jobs within the broadcasting industry. The majority of the jobs in radio and television require specialist knowledge, training and experience. A good working knowledge of digital equipment is an asset when applying for jobs. Jobs in the BBC and On-digital are open to new entrants and can be found on their Web site. Other jobs within broadcasting can be found weekly in a number of national newspapers. Broadcasting companies prefer individuals who are multi-skilled and currently skills that are much in demand are the ability to use digital programmes and equipment such as DVD cameras competently. It is important to demonstrate your enthusiasm through practical involvement in relevant activities such as writing for your local newspaper or working behind the scenes at a local amateur theatre.

Journalist/Reporter
Journalists work in all forms of media, reporting on current affairs, events and general items of interest. They carry out research and interviews for newspapers, broadcast news programmes and the Internet. A candidate who is able to script, record and edit their own piece digitally would stand a stronger chance of gaining employment.

Programme Assistant
They work in radio and are responsible for the technical and artistic presentation of programmes. They need to be able to operate the equipment and to be good at dealing with other people in the team and with the people who are interviewed or who work on the programmes.

Producer's Assistant (or Secretary)
They work for the Producer organising all the administrative work. They retype scripts to incorporate any changes which have been made, ready for the next rehearsal or performance.

Floor Manager
Floor Managers work in television doing a similar job to the Stage Manager in the theatre. The broadcasting Floor Manager's job can be strenuous – actors working on different sets cannot see each other and the Floor Manager's function is to cue and coordinate them all. The Floor Manager is also responsible for health and safety in the studio.

Studio Manager
Studio Managers work in radio and are responsible for all issues relating to the artistic and technical operation of a programme. They must know how to interpret the Producer's ideas correctly and how to achieve the best sound effects.

Assistant Floor Manager and Floor Assistant
These people carry out a variety of tasks according to each production. They are often in charge of the prompt book.

Production Assistant
The Production Assistant works as part of the production team. They must have good keyboard and organisational skills, be able to deal with a wide range of contacts and work to deadlines. Part of the job involves sitting in the control gallery timing the programme. In addition, they may do research for programmes.

Director/Producer
Directors and Producers are often specialists in a specific area such as documentary, children's programming, drama, and so on. Both jobs require a good technical knowledge of the media with financial management and budgeting skills as well as the necessary creative ability.

Broadcast Engineer
Engineers are involved in maintaining and testing the equipment used in studios and in outside broadcasts in radio and television, together with operating and maintaining the transmission chain. They may also be involved in project development and research work.

Vision Mixer
Vision mixers are responsible for recording the images from different cameras under the instruction of the director. They must have strong concentration and the ability to work under pressure.

Film Editor/Video Editor

Film and Video Editors increasingly work with both formats. The Editor must be able to visualise the Director/Producer's ideas and make the required creative decisions. Film and Video Editors have usually had experience in a technical/creative capacity before moving to an Editor's position.

Television Make-up and Hairdressing

This is a highly skilled area of work, and competition is keen for any vacancies. It requires a thorough knowledge of period hairstyles and an understanding of the effects of lighting and camera on people's faces. In television, the Make-up Designer/Assistant is responsible for both make-up and hair; in film, the jobs are separate.

Costume Designer

After gaining the relevant diplomas, costume designers should have theatrical experience. The work involves liaison with producers and make-up staff and responsibility, where necessary, for hiring and adapting costumes. They must have had basic training in pattern making, cutting and dressmaking, and have gained practical experience in a fashion house or theatrical costumier.

Costume Dressmaker

The dressmaker carries out necessary alterations and adaptations on hired or existing costumes, as well as making up new designs.

Dresser

Duties involve the maintenance of costumes and the dressing of artists for performances. Requirements are sewing ability, and relevant experience in the theatre, the film industry or as a theatrical costumier.

Camera Operator

Camera Operators work both in studios and on outside broadcasts. They have deep interest in subjects such as photography and lighting. An ability to establish good working relationships with other crew members and the Director is necessary.

Audio Assistant

Audio Assistants work on radio and television programme origination throughout the UK, doing similar jobs to Sound Operators and

Studio Managers. There is a tendency now in BBC regions for the job to split into these two categories.

Sound Operator
They help to set up and operate sound equipment in studios and on outside broadcasts. An understanding of MD recording would be an advantage. They have a deep practical interest in subjects such as hi-fi and sound.

Secretaries and Clerks
There are a large number of administrative jobs available in broadcasting, and there is always the slight possibility of promotion from clerk-typist to secretary, and from secretary to Producer's Assistant.

Qualifications and Training

Many companies offer in-service staff training schemes which are advertised as they occur. Competition for a place on these schemes is fierce. The selection boards are impressed by good all-rounders as well as candidates with specialist knowledge.

In technical areas, Engineers require, at trainee level, at least English GCSE plus A level maths and physics or an Edexcel (BTEC)/SVQ national diploma in electronics. Qualified Engineers need to have a degree or HND in electronic engineering. The BBC also recruits non-electronics graduates and converts them to Engineers via an in-house training scheme.

Technical operators require a good standard of education; at least GCSE grades A to C in English, maths and combined science (preferably physics). To improve their chances, candidates often progress their education further. Evidence of in-depth relevant practical involvement always impresses.

Many training courses, as well as those to an Edexcel (BTEC) standard, now have an equivalent NVQ.

Trainee Studio Managers need to have knowledge of sound equipment together with practical involvement in radio. GCSEs in maths and physics are generally required.

Production trainees must have practical experience of work directly related to production, either professionally or in an amateur capacity. No specific qualifications are asked for but applicants must have a wide range of interests.

Journalism training opportunities require applicants to have a demonstrable interest in news and current affairs, with evidence of practical involvement. Training schemes attract a large response and the standard is high.

Secretarial and clerical staff must have a good education. Qualifications for clerical posts vary, depending on the department – for example, in finance an aptitude for figures is essential. Accurate keyboard skills are required for clerk-typist posts. Secretaries must have accurate typing; shorthand is an advantage.

Make-up trainees need experience in professional or amateur theatre, and must have had formal training in make-up and hairdressing. Applicants should have A levels including art.

Personal Qualities

Qualities vary from job to job but all broadcasting staff must show commitment, enthusiasm, the ability to work as part of a team, and enormous stamina.

£ The range of salaries in broadcasting is vast. Examples include: BBC technical operations trainees £10,000 upwards; direct-entry engineers £12,000 upwards; production trainees £13,500; news trainees £12,500; local radio trainee reporters £13,123. These are basic salaries, and allowances are often paid in addition.

i BBC Recruitment Services, PO Box 7000, London W12 8GJ www.bbc.co.uk

ONdigital plc, 346 Queenstown Road, London SW8 4DG www.ondigital.co.uk

Skillset, 2nd floor, 91–101 Oxford Street, London W1R 1RA; 020 7534 5300; fax 020 7534 5333

Careers in Television and Radio (Kogan Page)

BUILDING

Building is the maintenance and construction of any structure in the UK or abroad. It is allied to civil and structural engineering, building and environmental engineering, municipal engineering, and highway and transportation engineering. Many craftspeople are involved in the building industry, including: carpenters and joiners (*see also* Carpenter and Bench Joiner), formwork erectors, wood machinists, mastic asphalters, bricklayers, painters and decorators, crane drivers and mechanical equipment operators, electricians, refrigeration fitters, thermal insulators, plumbers (*see* Plumber) and gas fitters, plasterers, glaziers, scaffolders, paviours, steel erectors, stonemasons, roofing and wall tilers, floor and ceiling tilers, coiling fixers, heating and ventilation specialists. Each craftsperson is responsible for a specific part of the job but also works as part of a team whose collective responsibility is to produce high-quality work.

Contract Manager
The Contract Manager is the person responsible for the overall control of a building project. This means coordinating the subcontractors and specialist firms, the technical staff and the machine operatives, and making sure that the whole project is completed within the specified time limit and to budget.

Clerk of Works
The Clerk of Works undertakes independent inspection of the works in progress to ensure that they conform to the specification so that the client obtains value for money.

Site Manager
The Site Manager is the person responsible for all operations on a construction site, including the recruitment of skilled and semi-skilled workers. In a large construction company, the Site Manager works in conjunction with the personnel department.

Qualifications and Training

Formal educational requirements are not required. Training is by apprenticeship – usually of three to four years' duration – but may be shortened to 12 months for entrants who have studied building subjects at school or college. Apprentices work towards NVQs awarded jointly by the City and Guilds and the Construction Industry Training Board. SVQs in Scotland are awarded by SBATC and SQA. Technician entrants to the building industry must have a minimum of four GCSEs grades A to C or three standard grades 1 to 3 to include a science, maths and a subject showing the use of English.

Anyone wanting to become a Clerk of Works should have a sound technical education, ideally with a construction trade background. Students can progress through the Institute of Clerks of Works examinations (intermediate and final parts 1 and 2) or gain partial exemption through the HNC/HTC/SQA equivalent routes. Existing Clerks of Works can also gain an NVQ in Site Inspection at level 3 New Works.

Site Managers will have had several years' experience of working on a building site and will probably hold a Building Technician qualification. The Construction Industry Training Board offers an advanced block-release course in scaffolding, with attendance at the employer's discretion. NVQs at levels 2 and 3 are available, awarded jointly by City and Guilds and the Construction Industry Training Board.

Personal Qualities

The construction worker needs to be committed and enthusiastic, able to work accurately from technical drawings using traditional or modern equipment, and to work as part of a team. Some jobs can be physically demanding. Contract Managers need to be well organised in dealing with technical, financial and administrative issues. They must also have the ability to liaise with a variety of clients, from architects (*see* Architect) and planners, to craftspeople and the public.

£ Recommended weekly rates are: £73.90 at 16; £103.46 at 17; £147.81 at 18; when qualified, the craftsman rate is £178.62. Starting salary for a Contract Manager is about £17,500 upwards and for a Site Manager, £15,000 upwards. In Scotland, apprentices' rates are set every year by the SBATC as a percentage of the craftsperson's rate.

i Construction Industry Training Board, Bircham Newton, King's Lynn, Norfolk PE31 6RH; 01553 776677 (ext 2466)

Institute of Clerks of Works of Great Britain Incorporated, 41 The Mall, Ealing, London W5 3TJ; 020 8579 2917

Careers Department, CITB, 4 Edison Street, Hillington, Glasgow G52 4XN; 0141 810 3044

Scotting Building Apprenticeship and Training Council (SBATC), Carron Grange Avenue, Steadhouse Muir, FK5 3BQ, 01324 555 5550

BUILDING CONTROL SURVEYOR

Building control is undertaken by local authorities and Approved Inspectors. The main activities involve the examination and assessment of plans, site visits to inspect work, and liaison with designers, builders, other professionals within the construction team and the fire authorities. A broad knowledge of the many areas of building work, and skill in dealing with people, need to be developed.

Qualifications and Training

The Institute has four levels of qualification. Student membership must be in possession of one of the following academic awards: GCSE or SCE passes in five subjects, including maths, a science subject and a subject requiring the use of descriptive English; two GCSE passes at AS or A level; an appropriate NC or ND; Edexcel (BTEC) national certificate/diploma in building studies or civil engineering; City and Guilds Final or Technical Certificate Parts I and II; or a GNVQ in the Built Environment, level 3.

Associate level membership is attained through an HNC/HND in building studies or civil engineering. Incorporated members are at first-degree level or equivalent, and Corporate membership is obtained by satisfying the requirements of the Institute's incorporated examinations and its Assessment of Professional Competence.

Personal Qualities

A knowledge of construction technology and legislation is necessary, plus the ability to state requirements firmly and to see that they are carried out.

£ Depends on qualifications and experience, and employer.

i Institute of Building Control, 92-104 East Street, Epsom, Surrey KT17 1EB; 01372 745577; fax 01372 748282, e-mail *admin@instobc.demon.co.uk*
www.demon.co.uk/instobc

Building Services Engineering, **see** *Engineering*

BUILDING SOCIETIES

Traditionally, building societies functioned by attracting savings and investments from the public, and then using these funds to make loans for home ownership. The Building Societies Act 1986 allowed societies to enter many new areas, such as insurance, investment, estate agency and unsecured lending, but the savings and loan activities remain the most important. Building societies are among the most highly automated and computerised offices in the UK and are in the forefront of those who offer in-service staff training in the latest office technology. Management and marketing methods in building societies are aggressive and these areas offer good career prospects.

Qualifications and Training

Four GCSE passes including English and maths, and two A levels (necessary for entry to professional career training) are the basic requirements. Time off may be allowed to study for Edexcel (BTEC)/SVQ national and higher awards in business studies, and the examinations of The Chartered Institute of Bankers. Edexcel (BTEC)/SVQ higher awards gain exemption to some parts of the Institute examinations. In-service training tends to be spread over two to five years.

To gain admission to a course leading to the Associateship examinations of The Chartered Institute of Bankers, a recognised UK degree or a professional qualification is required. One pass at A level or two AS levels plus GCSE English language, A to C, is sufficient to gain admission to the foundation course (known as the Pre-Associateship Route). The Institute also offers a vocational level qualification, the Certificate in Financial Services Practice. No academic qualifications are necessary for entry to this, which is aimed at clerical staff who want to learn more about how building societies work. The certificate is a recognised qualification in its own right.

NVQs levels 2 to 4 are available in some building societies. NVQs at level 2 are predominantly aimed at branch staff. Levels 3 and 4 are aimed at supervisory and managerial staff.

Personal Qualities

Since the funds come from the general public, personal honesty and discretion as well as verbal and mathematical skills need to be combined with an ability to make decisions and work methodically. A sympathetic and understanding manner with people is a definite asset.

£ Salaries vary from society to society, but a new entrant could expect £6,500+ and a graduate £12,500.

i The Building Societies Association, 3 Savile Row, London W1X 1AF; 020 7437 0655

The Chartered Institute of Bankers, 90 Bishopsgate, London EC2N 4AS; 020 7444 7115
Careers in Banking and Finance (Kogan Page)

Building Surveying*, see *Surveyor, Surveying Technician

BUS AND COACH COMPANIES

About 65 per cent of personnel working in passenger transport on the roads are drivers and conductors. Many work on routes within one town or city, but some are employed by coach companies taking passengers from one town to another, across the country, or on international journeys. Other staff are employed as engineers, administrators, or managers.

Engineering work includes vehicle maintenance and repair in mechanical work, electrical and electronic systems and body structures, as well as technical research and design. Increasingly, companies are looking for employees with multiple skills or the willingness to undertake training in other occupational areas.

Administration covers route planning, traffic surveys, publicity, fare scales, computer operation, legal work and financial management.

Qualifications and Training

Modern Apprenticeship and National Traineeship schemes are available for engineers; some formal qualifications may be required, depending on the scheme offered. NVQs are available at levels 1 to 5, providing a career progression route within the industry.

Semi-skilled engineers, and engineers from other occupational areas are often recruited, and in-service training is provided.

Passenger-carrying vehicle (PCV) licence driver training is provided by all companies. This may be supported by NVQs at levels 2 and 3 in Transporting Passengers by Road. Formal qualifications are not required.

School leavers and graduates are eligible for training in administration and management. In-service training is an integral part of all careers with bus and coach companies.

Personal Qualities

The work of bus drivers and conductors means dealing constantly with the general public, and a customer-friendly attitude is appropriate. Tact and good humour are essential, as well as a liking for the elderly and for young people, who form the majority of the bus-travelling public. Drivers and conductors also need to be willing to operate early and late shifts.

For engineering occupations, a sound mechanical ability and aptitude are preferred.

A variety of skills is required within administration; information on these occupations is best sought from the individual companies.

£ Salaries vary and applicants should enquire of the individual companies. London salaries are higher than those in the regions.

i Local bus and coach companies

The Passenger Transport Forum for Employee Development (TRANSfED), Regency House, 43 High Street, Rickmansworth WD3 1ET; 01923 896607 www.transfed.org.uk

BUTCHER

(see also Meat Industry)

Career prospects are varied in the meat industry, extending from work in a small retail shop through to supermarkets; from meat buying for large organisations such as hotels and caterers, to the manufacture of meat and poultry products.

Qualifications and Training

A good general education is necessary but there are no formal educational requirements. Training is on the job and courses are available at further education establishments and technical colleges, leading to examinations of the Meat Training Council. NVQs are available at levels 1, 2, 3 and 4, and higher national diploma/certificate qualifications. Modern Apprenticeships are also available. Further training, appropriate to the relevant sector of the industry, in management, meat technology, or small business ownership, may follow an apprenticeship.

Personal Qualities

An above-average attitude to hygiene is vital, as in all the food industries, plus a real interest in people and their eating habits, so that the meat products may be geared to the customers' needs.

£ Around £60 per week at 16, £250 when trained.

i Meat Training Council, PO Box 141, Winterhill House, Snowdon Drive, Milton Keynes MK6 1YY; 01908 231062 www.meattraining.co.uk

National Federation of Meat and Food Traders, 1 Belgrove, Tunbridge Wells, Kent TN1 1YW; 01892 541412

Scottish Federation of Meat Traders Association, 8 Needless Road, Perth PH2 0JW; 01738 637472

BUYER

(see also Purchasing Officer)

The retail price of any product or service depends to a great extent on the cost of raw materials and of labour. Buying departments in manufacturing industries are consequently engaged in the discussion and planning of all projects so that they may buy wisely the raw materials and, in some cases, the services required to supply the manufacturing process.

Buyers in the retail trade, for example, may work in the fashion department of a large multiple store. Their work requires a knowledge of the latest fashion trends ahead of the season, and may involve travel at home and abroad. They will also be involved in transactions with manufacturers and will place orders and chase deliveries.

Buying careers exist in all large organisations – whether profit-making or not. Hospitals in the NHS, local authorities and Government departments are all concerned to keep the prices of supplies at a reasonable level and ensure continuity of supplies, particularly when installing new technology and equipment. The function of the buying – or purchasing, as it is sometimes called – department is to shop around for the best value for money.

Qualifications and Training

Although some companies do not ask for GCSEs, the majority prefer applicants with four or five GCSEs. Graduates, and those with GCE A level passes, usually enter as trainee Buyers working with experienced personnel and continuing their training in-service. To take the examinations of the Chartered Institute of Purchasing and Supply, five GCSE passes are necessary, to include English and a quantitative subject, and two A levels or three H grades. Vocational qualifications are acceptable. All-round experience in organisations of all types is a sound base.

Personal Qualities

Buyers need to be able to think clearly, accept responsibility, and to express themselves concisely and pleasantly. They need to display a measure of determination when negotiating prices, and patience when dealing with colleagues in other departments. They should be willing to travel and to devote some of their own time to the job.

£ Starting salaries for trainee buyers are £10,000–£11,000+ for graduates, but may be much less, in the region of £8,000–£9,000+, for less qualified applicants.

i The Chartered Institute of Purchasing and Supply, Easton House, Easton-on-the-Hill, Stamford, Lincolnshire PE9 3NZ; 01780 56777

Careers in Retailing (Kogan Page)

C

CALL CENTRE

A call centre is a real or virtual function within an organisation. A real function is when the organisation has a call centre in-house, that is like any other department. A virtual function exists when the organisation contracts out the call centre. The main function is to provide customer service and support for organisations. Most call centres are computer automated. It is estimated that there are between 500 and 2,000 call centres in the UK, and there is huge growth potential. The work essentially involves working on the telephone to identify new business opportunities and deal with queries from customers.

i www.callcentre.co.uk
www.cca.org.uk

Cardiac Clinical Scientific Officer, see *Medical Technical Officer*

CAREERS ADVISER

Careers advisers work in a variety of settings, including careers service companies, further and higher education institutes and adult guidance services. They give guidance, careers information and advice about employment opportunities, both local and national, and about further education and training, by means of talks, discussion groups, displays and individual interviews. Advisers working in careers service companies also work closely with careers teachers in schools and colleges and with local employers and training organisations. Visits are made to many different workplaces and educational establishments to gain first-hand knowledge of what is involved.

Many careers advisers specialise, working, for example, with people who have learning difficulties, with sixth-form and college students, with the unemployed or with adult clients.

Qualifications and Training

A degree or equivalent is generally required, although some mature entrants may be accepted on the basis of suitable experience rather than formal qualifications, providing they can show ability in meeting the academic standard required. A background in teaching, industry or personnel work can be an advantage. Candidates can follow a one-year full-time course leading, after a year's supervised experience, to the diploma in careers guidance. Some careers service companies employ trainees who follow a diploma course on a full- or part-time basis over a two-year period. Flexible arrangements for training and qualifying are being steadily extended and NVQs up to level 4 are now available. A new qualification in careers guidance has been piloted in a small number of centres from 1999.

Personal Qualities

An ability to communicate sympathetically with people of all ages and from varied backgrounds is required, as well as the capacity to assimilate and organise a large amount of constantly changing information. Careers advisers must be able to work on their own initiative, or as part of a team.

£ From £14,000.

i The Institute of Careers Guidance, 27a Lower High Street, Stourbridge, West Midlands DY8 1TA; 01384 376464; fax 01384 440830
www.icg-uk.org

Improvement and Development Agency, Local Government Management Board, Layden House, 76–86 Turnmill Street, London EC1M 5QU; 020 7296 6600

DfEE Careers and Information Division
www.dfee.gov.uk

'A Career in Careers Guidance' (Institute of Careers Guidance)

'Training for the Careers Service' (Local Government Management Board)

CARPENTER AND BENCH JOINER

Traditionally, joiners were responsible for smaller, more intricate jobs, and carpenters for larger jobs such as laying floorboards. Nowadays, the terms are synonymous. The work involves making and fitting doors, windows, staircases, cupboards and shuttering; fitting structural joists, roof timbers, door frames, skirting boards, doors, handrails, wardrobes, and so on. Carpenters may also be called upon to wall up excavations and erect shoring during demolition. Opportunities exist with a wide range of employers of all sizes such as building and civil engineering contractors, specialist carpentry and joinery firms, local authorities, in industrial and commercial maintenance, shipbuilding, shopfitting and vehicle manufacture, or as a self-employed craftsman.

Cabinet Maker

Cabinet makers use traditional hand skills to make, finish or restore high-quality items of wooden furniture. They may work in factories for furniture manufacturers or be self-employed in small workshops.

Qualifications and Training

A general education to secondary level is the only academic requirement, although some arithmetical ability is useful. Training is over a two- to three-year period with courses leading to NVQs awarded jointly by City and Guilds and the Construction Industry Training Board.

Personal Qualities

As qualified craftspeople, carpenters and joiners must be able to work from technical drawings or notes without close supervision and produce neat accurate work. They must be manually skilled, possessing a steady hand and a head for heights. A good eye for form is necessary, plus a willingness to work outside in all weathers.

£ When qualified, the craftsman rate is about £175 per week.

i Construction Industry Training Board, Bircham Newton, King's Lynn, Norfolk PE31 6RH; 01485 577577

Institute of Carpenters, Central Office, 35 Hayworth Road, Sandiacre, Nottingham NG10 5LL; 0115 9490641
www.central-office.co.uk
A range of information leaflets are available from the Institute of Carpenters (address above)

CARPET FITTER

Carpet retailers, furniture stores and department stores all employ their own trained personnel who deliver and fit carpets and other floor coverings to customers' homes, shops, offices or hotels. Many fitters are also self-employed.

Qualifications and Training

GCSE English and maths or equivalents are usually required. Training is mainly given on the job, working with an experienced fitter, although in some firms there are possible opportunities for day-release courses leading to the examinations of the National Institute of Carpet Fitters.

Personal Qualities

Strength and fitness are important in order to handle heavy rolls of carpet. A good head for calculations and an eye for detail (such as matching patterns) are also essential. Generally, too, it is necessary to be able to drive.

£ About £180 a week; more in London.

i Local Jobcentres and Careers Offices
National Institute of Carpet Fitters, 4D St Mary's Place, The Lace Market, Nottingham NG1 1PH; 0115 958 3077
www.carpetinfo.co.uk

CARTOGRAPHY

(see also Ordnance Survey Work)

Cartography embraces not only all aspects of map-making, from the initial collection and editing of material (by cartographers) to the actual drawing and production of the finished product (by cartographic draughtsmen and assistants), but also the making of charts, globes and models of the earth. Most cartographic work is undertaken in Government departments such as the Ordnance Survey, the Ministry of Defence, the Meteorological Office and the Department of Environment, Transport and the Regions. Other vacancies sometimes occur in local authority planning departments, specialist publishing houses or with survey companies. Computers are reducing the need for manual draughtsmen, especially in repetitive work, and the increasing application of Geographical Information Systems (GIS) via a graphics workstation is significantly modifying the work of a professional cartographer.

There is substantial growth in the number of map/chart products becoming available on CD, many of which are designed for interactive use.

Qualifications and Training

Cartographers are increasingly being recruited from among graduates who have relevant undergraduate or postgraduate training (and usually include geography in their A level studies). There are few actual degree courses in cartography, GIS, topographic science or surveying and mapping science; admission is dependent on entry requirements of individual universities.

Personal Qualities

Neatness, precision, aesthetic appreciation and a fine attention to detail are important, as are mathematical awareness and an ability to analyse visual judgements on graphic efficiency.

£ For a graduate, from £13,000; mapping and charting technicians from £11,000, and assistants £8,500+.

i The British Cartographic Society, R W Anson, Oxford Centre for Cartography and Geographical Information Services, School of Planning, Oxford Brookes University, Headington, Oxford OX3 0BP; 01865 483346
www.cartography.org.uk

Ordnance Survey, Romsey Road, Southampton SO16 4GU; 023 8079 2000; fax 023 8079 2452
www.ordsvu.aou.uk

CATERING AND ACCOMMODATION MANAGEMENT

(see also Chef/Cook, Health Service, Hotel Work)

There is a wide variety of job opportunities in this category at all levels, from managers and supervisors to craft workers. Sometimes the dividing lines are not clear-cut, and it is quite usual for individuals to move up from one to another.

Management

Catering management can cover work in a roadside or motorway restaurant, a luxury restaurant, a hospital meals service, a snack bar, a take-away service, university and college restaurants, the armed forces, outdoor events or contract catering (providing meals and snacks to the management and staff of the contractor, for example, a bank or insurance company). The manager in charge is normally responsible for budgeting, menu planning, stock monitoring, seeing that good food is served as and when it is required (often round the clock), keeping customers satisfied and supervising staff.

Accommodation management is concerned with the domestic side of colleges and universities (where managers are sometimes known as bursars), hospitals, local authority day centres and residential homes (for the aged or disabled, for instance). The demanding duties of such a manager include responsibility for accommodation and catering (particularly in halls of residence, which may be used as conference centres during the vacation). The work can involve personal contact with the residents (in homes, for instance, where the population is fairly permanent) or be more in the nature of housekeeping (as in hospitals where the patients are constantly changing and are not the direct concern of the domestic staff).

Kitchen

In the kitchen there are opportunities at all levels, from the chef in charge of a select restaurant to the dish-washer in a snack bar. There are also opportunities for freelance work – catering for directors' dining rooms, private parties and business lunches, for instance. It is demanding work, often in 'unsocial hours', when most people are out enjoying themselves. Some cooking can be repetitious (such as take-away menus), some creatively satisfying.

Food Service Assistants
Waiters and waitresses, as well as serving, may cook special dishes at table or specialise in particular skills such as wine-waiting. As well as serving food and drink, they have to maintain contact with their customers; unfriendly servers may ruin the reputation of a restaurant; promotion is to head waiter/waitress.

Qualifications and Training

There are two main routes to qualification: attending a college or university as a full-time student, or joining a training programme operated by an employer or an organisation that works with employers to provide training, such as the Hotel and Catering Training Company (HCTC). In the latter case entrants learn on the job and attend college or a training centre on a short-course or day-release basis. Recruits on the work-based training programme will generally acquire NVQ awards.

Qualifications consist of NVQs levels 1 to 4, GNVQs levels 1 to 4, HNC/HND, HCIMA (Hotel and Catering International Management Association) and specialist degrees.

An increasing number of employers are offering Modern Apprenticeships. These provide a route to higher-level technical or supervisory skills, NVQ level 3, for 16- and 17-year-olds. They take two and a half to three years. There are four routes: accommodation services, chef, fast food, restaurant and pub.

The entry requirements for a college-based course vary from college to college.

Personal Qualities

Managers need to be confident and independent with a smart appearance and good speech. They have to command respect and trust as well as understand the various aspects of modern management techniques such as budgeting, profit making etc. Craft workers usually need physical fitness and stamina as well as high standards of personal hygiene. Skin complaints may disqualify entrants.

£ Average wages for hotel and restaurant staff are about £160 a week and for contract catering staff £150+. Salaries for hotel managers are about £16,000, and for restaurant managers and contract catering managers £15,000+.

i Hospitality Training Foundation, International House, High Street, London W5 5DB; 020 8579 2400

Hotel and Catering International Management Association (HCIMA), 191 Trinity Road, London SW17 7HN; 020 8672 4251
Springboard UK, 1 Denmark Street, London WC2H 8LP; 020 7497 8654
Careers in Catering and Hotel Management (Kogan Page)

Chartered Clinical Psychologist*, see *Clinical Psychologist

CHAUFFEUR

Chauffeurs are skilled car drivers who are employed either by one person or by companies or organisations where senior personnel need their own reliable transport on hand at all times. Private chauffeurs may live in accommodation provided and have various other duties. Apart from the actual driving, the job will also involve making sure the cars are well maintained and clean.

Qualifications and Training

Obviously the first requirement is to have a 'clean' driving licence, with no endorsements, and proven experience. Mechanical and/or geographical knowledge may be required, depending on the individual demands of the job. Some of the better-known car manufacturers run their own training schemes; Rolls-Royce, for instance, has its own driving school (enquiries to the head office at Crewe in Cheshire; 01270 255155).

Personal Qualities

Essential attributes are a calm, unflappable nature when under pressure (in heavy traffic and late for an appointment, for instance), patience (much time will be spent waiting for passengers), politeness and the discretion not to repeat confidential conversations which may well be overheard.

£ Salaries vary from £180 a week to £285. Accommodation may be provided.

i Local Jobcentres and Careers Offices
The Lady, 39–40 Bedford Street, London WC2E 9ER; 020 7379 4717 (job advertisements)

CHEF/COOK

In addition to creating, and supervising the preparation of all kinds of different dishes, a head chef/cook has to be trained in the management of a kitchen, being responsible for the staff and the organisation of their workload, planning the menus, budgeting, ordering and approving the necessary ingredients and maintaining high standards of efficiency and hygiene. Chefs are employed in hotels, restaurants, industrial organisations (such as offices or factories), institutions (such as hospitals, schools and universities or colleges) and in the armed forces. In large establishments the *chef de cuisine* is in overall charge while there may be a number of *chefs de partie* (in charge of their part of the kitchen) and a number of *commis chefs* (still learning the trade).

Qualifications and Training

Qualifications are the same as for Catering and Accommodation Management, *see* page 63.

Personal Qualities

Requirements include the ability to work under pressure in frequently hot and noisy conditions, and to enjoy practical as well as creative work. The higher chefs rise in their profession, the more they need to be able to take responsibility and the more management skills they require.

£ Salaries are similar to those indicated for Catering and Accommodation Management, *see* page 63. Experienced chefs may command very high salaries.

i Hospitality Training Foundation, International House, High Street, London W5 5DB; 020 8579 2400

Springboard UK, 1 Denmark Street, London WC2H 8LP; 020 7497 8654

Chemical Engineering*, see *Engineering

CHEMIST

Chemistry is the basis of a wide range of careers. The majority of trained chemists work in the manufacturing industries within organisations producing such materials as foodstuffs, plastics, pharmaceuticals, cosmetics, petroleum, detergents, fertilisers, and so on; large numbers teach in schools, colleges and universities, generally combining teaching with research work; there are also openings with local authorities, the NHS, the Civil Service and the nationalised industries, as well as in marketing and sales, information and patents and specialised publishing. Professional chemists are often assisted by laboratory technicians and assistants. Chemistry is essential in many other careers as a basic qualification – in medicine, for instance, or veterinary science.

Qualifications and Training

Most professional chemists have membership of the Royal Society of Chemistry, for which a degree or equivalent qualification is necessary. Entry requirements for degree courses generally include at least two A level or three H grade passes in science subjects, including chemistry and another distinct scientific or mathematical subject. A good GNVQ (Advanced) can provide an alternative method of entry. Edexcel (BTEC) and SQA offer GNVQ courses. Royal Society of Chemistry courses are offered, one year part-time, at three institutions. These, combined with HNC/HND, are equivalent to a pass degree. An Edexcel (BTEC) higher national diploma in chemistry may also be appropriate as it is approximately equivalent to a pass degree. Entry to such courses (which are either two-year full-time, three-year part-time or sandwich courses) normally requires one A level or two H grade passes, including chemistry, a GNVQ (Advanced) or an Edexcel (BTEC)/SQA award. Further study is necessary after gaining the higher diploma to reach full professional status, generally through part-time study leading to a degree.

Chemistry technicians usually need three GCSE or SCE Standard grade passes to gain entry to an Edexcel certificate in science course or SQA certificate in chemistry – these are generally part-time courses with day release. This can be followed by an Edexcel (BTEC)/SQA higher certificate in chemistry course, which may then lead to acceptance on a degree course. After gaining a degree, further study is generally required and individual employers normally run their own training schemes.

Personal Qualities

Chemists usually form part of a team, so an ability to work alongside others is helpful. The actual work varies enormously but generally a chemist also needs an enquiring mind and practical experimental ability and experience.

£ Varies according to type of employment. Newly qualified graduates can generally expect salaries of £13,000–£15,000+.

i The Royal Society of Chemistry, Burlington House, Piccadilly, London W1V 0BN; 020 7437 8656; www.rsc.org

Child Care,* see *Nanny, Nursery Nurse

Child Guidance,* see *Educational Psychologist, Psychologist, Psychotherapist, Social Work and Social Care – Children and Young People

CHIROPODIST

Chiropodists (also known as podiatrists) are concerned with the health of feet. They diagnose and treat ailments such as corns, bunions, malformed nails and sports injuries and also give foot health advice. They perform minor operations under local anaesthetic. They may work in the NHS in hospitals, clinics or health centres; or in private practice or large organisations. Many podiatrists follow postgraduate training to specialise in areas such as sports medicine, biomechanics and podiatric surgery.

Qualifications and Training

A recognised BSc degree in chiropody/podiatry or podiatric medicine is required for state registration, which is a compulsory requirement for employment in the Health Service. There are fourteen recognised chiropody/podiatry schools attached to universities and institutions throughout the UK (contact the Society of Chiropodists and Podiatrists for details). Normally, five GCSE passes are required, together with two A levels, but individual institutions may have their own requirements.

In private practice it is essential to belong to a reputable chiropodial association which operates a strict ethical code and offers professional liability insurance.

Personal Qualities

Chiropodists need good eyesight (with or without spectacles) and nimble hands as well as an ability to inspire confidence in the people they are treating. Organising ability is essential in private practice.

£ £14,845 when qualified. For those working in the NHS, London weighting is payable.

i Society of Chiropodists and Podiatrists, 53 Welbeck Street, London W1M 7HE; 020 7486 3381

Institute of Chiropodists and Podiatrists, 27 Wright Street, Southport PR9 0TL; 01704 546141
www.inst-chiropodist.org.uk

CHIROPRACTOR

Chiropractic is a health-care profession concerned with, but not limited to, the diagnosis, treatment and prevention of structural and functional disorders affecting the musculo-skeletal system. Common complaints which patients may present to chiropractors include low back and leg pain, headaches, and neck and arm pain, as well as sports injuries. Working in a primary contact profession, a qualified chiropractor may be approached directly, without a medical referral, by patients seeking help.

Chiropractors are trained to utilise a wide variety of diagnostic techniques including X-ray. Manual manipulation (adjustment) of spinal and extremity joints as well as soft-tissue structures is the most common treatment method employed. However, chiropractors are also trained to utilise a range of complementary treatment techniques such as physical therapy modalities, braces and supports, as well as offer advice on nutrition, rehabilitative exercises and modifications to activities of daily living.

With ever-increasing demand for chiropractic services, the prospects for graduates are bright both in the UK and Europe for the foreseeable future.

Qualifications and Training

Training is at the Anglo-European College of Chiropractic and leads to a BSc (Chiropractic) degree. Entry qualifications are five GCSEs to include English and physics and two A levels to include biology or zoology and chemistry. After successfully completing the course, applicants may apply to become members of the British Chiropractic Association.

Personal Qualities

Manual dexterity and practical skills as well as a sound theoretical knowledge of the body are necessary. An ability to communicate with patients and inspire confidence is important.

£ Salaries vary according to number of patients and how well established the practice is. Patients are usually charged per session.

i Anglo-European College of Chiropractic, Parkwood Road, Bournemouth, Dorset BH5 2DF; 01202 436200

British Chiropractic Association, Blagrave House, 17 Blagrave Street, Reading, Berkshire RG1 1QB; 0118 950 5950; fax 0118 958 8946

www.chiropractic-uk.co.uk

Choreography, **see** *Dancing*

THE CHURCH

Work within the church, in all denominations, is done by ordained ministers and priests and also by lay men and women (*see* below). Some denominations allow the ordination of women, but the Roman Catholic church does not; the Church of England ordains women as deacons and, following the vote of General Synod in November 1992, now ordains women priests. Most clergy work in their own parishes or individual churches, preaching, conducting baptisms, weddings and funerals, teaching the faith and generally caring for the spiritual welfare of their own community.

Nowadays, with the upsurge of ecumenical projects and changing social trends, a minister's horizons are much wider than they were in the past and a good deal of time may be spent outside the traditional confines of parish work. Other ordained ministers and priests work as full-time chaplains – in schools, universities and colleges, hospitals, prisons and in the armed forces. A number are also concerned with church administration or public relations (such as religious advisers to the media).

Religious Orders
Within the Anglican and Roman Catholic churches there are also opportunities – for both men and women – to work within a religious order. Such a community may either be a contemplative 'closed' order, where the emphasis is on prayer, or an 'active' order, working as teachers or nurses, running homes for orphans, the chronically sick, the aged, unmarried mothers or delinquents.

Lay Work
Full-time (and part-time) work is also done by the laity (men and women who are not ordained but who are confirmed followers of their particular faith and trained by the various denominations). They may work as preachers, parish workers, teachers or social workers. Laity are also needed for administrative work in central church offices, for running the various welfare agencies, dealing with finances, and so on.

Qualifications and Training

Prospective ministers normally require at least two A level or three H grade passes, and a degree is desirable. These requirements are by no means vital in every case or in every denomination and may be varied according to an individual's other attributes and suitability. Training does not normally begin before candidates have reached the age of 18. Length of courses varies between two and six years, again depending on the denomination. Entry to religious orders frequently demands qualifications similar to those of a prospective ordinand, although here too an individual's overall suitability is taken into account. Training for such orders is often longer than for the ministry or priesthood and it can take up to nine years or more to reach the stage of final vows.

Personal Qualities

Working for the church is not a job, but a way of life, and entering such work requires a deep and strong commitment to the chosen faith. It also requires sufficient maturity to cope with the intellectual, physical and emotional demands involved. The spouses of married clergy will need to share the commitment.

£ Varies according to denomination. Some ministers receive a basic stipend together with free accommodation. In some cases 'office' expenses such as postal and telephone charges or running expenses for a car are provided. In the Church of England, curates' salaries begin at £11,940 (the same salary is payable to licensed lay workers), and vicars in charge of a parish at £13,760.

i Those who feel drawn towards church work should consult their own minister or priest as a first step. Further information can also be obtained from the following:

The Vocations Officer, Advisory Board of Ministry, Church House, Great Smith Street, London SW1P 3NZ; 020 7222 9011 (for the Anglican Church)

Christians Abroad, 1 Stockwell Green, London SW9 9HP; 020 7737 7811 (offers free information and career counselling relating to work overseas with development agencies and mission organisations, and publishes *Opportunities Abroad*, which has a job list)

Agency for Jewish Education, Woburn House, Tavistock Square, London WC1H 0EZ; 020 7387 4300 (for the Jewish religion)

CINEMA MANAGEMENT

A cinema manager is responsible for the smooth running of a cinema, the box-office takings and the staff. Most cinemas are now controlled by major distribution companies, and the manager has little say about what films are shown, but there are also some independent cinemas. There may be special functions to organise such as live performances, late-night shows, and so on.

Cinema Projectionist

A projectionist is responsible for showing the correct films, in the correct sequence and for maintaining the necessary equipment. The work may often be repetitious and the hours 'unsocial' (mainly afternoons and evenings).

Cinema Attendant

Staff are also needed in cinemas to assist the public to their places, check and sell tickets, distribute refreshments and keep public rooms clean and tidy. This kind of work can be full- or part-time.

Qualifications and Training

Formal qualifications are not always specified but candidates for managerial positions need to show intelligence and aptitude (often working their way up from more junior positions). The main distributing companies have their own training programmes for cinema managers and projectionists and most of the training is done on the job.

Personal Qualities

A cinema manager needs to enjoy responsibility, to be able to handle a variety of demands and/or complaints with courtesy and forbearance, and to be a good leader in order to get the best teamwork from staff. A projectionist needs technical ability, organisation, and should not be bored by repetitious work. Attendants need to have a pleasant personality, as they will be dealing with the general public.

£ Salaries vary according to organisation and there is often a considerable supplement for Sunday working. Basic weekly salaries are in the region of £180 for a manager, £160 for a projectionist and £130 for other staff.

i Local Jobcentres and Careers Offices

CIVIL AVIATION

Pilot

Commercial pilots in the UK fly fixed-wing aircraft and helicopters. Before take-off the pilot must prepare a flight plan, study the weather, make sure that the craft is airworthy and that the cargo and fuel are safely loaded, and work out estimated times of arrival. Little time is spent actually flying the aeroplane manually. The pilot spends most of the time carefully monitoring sophisticated computer-controlled automatic flying, navigational and communications systems. He must keep in touch with air traffic control and be prepared to deal with sudden changes in weather and other conditions. Pilots work very irregular hours but their actual flying time is strictly controlled.

Most UK pilots are employed by one of the major carriers of passengers and goods, and when flying large aircraft they are part of a team of two or three pilots, and possibly a flight engineer.

Opportunities for pilots of small aircraft and helicopters are to be found in flying executive jets, or in the field of air taxiing (especially in the North Sea), conducting aerial surveys and also as test pilots or flying instructors.

Flight Engineer

Flight Engineers may be employed on long-haul, international flights as a link between maintenance engineers on the ground and the flying crew. They are rarely needed on modern aircraft. They make pre-flight inspections and are responsible for the efficient performance of the aircraft during the flight; they must be able to diagnose and deal with any systems failures, making possible repairs, reporting any defects to maintenance and later checking that they have been dealt with; they may also be responsible for refuelling.

Air Cabin Crew

Stewards and stewardesses look after the safety, comfort and welfare of passengers. Before a flight they check stocks of equipment, welcome passengers on board and go through safety routines. During the flight they will serve ready-cooked meals and drinks, sell duty-free goods and, on short-haul and domestic routes, they may also issue tickets. Flight reports are prepared by senior stewards or the cabin staff officer who also attends to first-class passengers and supervises junior staff.

Aircraft Maintenance Engineer

Aircraft Maintenance Engineers make sure that aircraft are airworthy. They maintain, service and overhaul the craft, their engines and equipment, working to very high standards set by the Civil Aviation Authority (CAA), and every part of every job is checked and certified. Engineers usually specialise in either mechanics or avionics and work on major overhaul or in 'turnarounds' – the work carried out after each flight. Apart from working with the airlines, other opportunities are found with firms that specialise in aircraft maintenance. There are also a few openings for professional engineers in works management, production, planning, and research and development.

Air Traffic Control

The safe and efficient movement of all aircraft through British air space and airports is the responsibility of the National Air Traffic Service (NATS) air traffic control officers and assistants. With the aid of sophisticated radio, radar and computer systems and with visual checks on visibility and weather conditions, made from the control tower, they ensure that aircraft are kept a safe distance apart, that pilots are well advised as to their position and prevailing conditions, give clearance to land, directions to loading bays, and so on.

Air traffic controllers may work for employers other than the NATS, such as local authorities or an aircraft manufacturer, but all must hold a CAA licence stipulating the service they are qualified to give, and where they can operate. Some of the more routine tasks, such as checking flight plans, updating weather information, logging aircraft movements and keeping runways clear, are carried out by the air traffic control assistants. Prospects for promotion to officer level are good but air traffic control staff are employed to work at any location within the country.

Air Traffic Engineer

Air Traffic Engineers are responsible for the efficient operation of the wide range of sophisticated telecommunications, electronic systems and specialist equipment needed in air traffic control centres, airports and other specialist centres. This involves the installation, calibration and maintenance of radar, air-to-ground communication systems, navigational and landing aids, computer data and processing equipment, visual display units, and so on. Opportunities may exist for engineers to look after day-to-day maintenance, and, at graduate level, for field management, installation and development work.

Qualifications and Training

Pilot

UK pilots are required to hold a professional pilot's licence issued by the CAA indicating, by a series of ratings, exactly what type of aircraft, and under what conditions, the pilot is qualified to fly. Applications for a professional pilot's licence and instrument rating can only be made by candidates who have successfully completed a college of air training course and have 200 hours of flying experience. Residential air training courses lasting approximately one year are available for aeroplanes at Air Services Training, Perth, the Oxford Air Training School, Cabair, Cranfield, and Prestwick and, for helicopter pilots, at Bristow Helicopters Ltd, Redhill and at the Oxford Air Training School. For full-time approved courses the student must have obtained at least five GCSEs including English language, maths and a science subject or the equivalent. Those who do not meet this minimum educational standard should seek advice on their acceptability from the flying training organisation at which the course is to be conducted. A good entry route is via a short service flying commission with either the RAF or RN as this is where many airlines recruit. Further training is completed by the airlines themselves with a combination of ground training and job experience. All pilots are expected to attend re-training and refresher courses throughout their career.

Flight Engineer

Flight engineers usually begin their career as maintenance engineering apprentices. Applications for a Flight Engineer's licence can only be made by candidates aged at least 21. Before being permitted to fly as a flight engineer under training, or being permitted to enter for the technical examinations or flight tests, the CAA demands proof from a prospective candidate of acceptable experience as an aircraft engineer, or as a professional pilot, or as an RAF air engineer. Forms for obtaining an assessment of acceptability of experience may be obtained from the Directorate of Flight Crew Licensing, Civil Aviation Authority, Safety Regulation Group, Aviation House, South Area, Gatwick Airport, Gatwick, West Sussex RH6 0YR; 01293 573563.

Air Cabin Crew

Airlines usually train their own cabin crews at special centres on courses lasting four to six weeks. Applicants should be over 18 and have a good level of general education to GCSE standard, preferably including English and maths, and have conversational fluency in at least one European language. Some experience of catering or nursing is also helpful.

Aircraft Maintenance Engineer

Entry to aircraft maintenance engineering is via craft, technician or student apprenticeships; entry qualifications depend upon the type of apprenticeship. The apprenticeships take the form of on-the-job training and part-time study at local colleges to prepare for aeronautical engineering qualifications offered by City and Guilds and Edexcel (BTEC)/SVQ or the CAA. Qualified aircraft engineers (including those from the armed forces) have to meet certain practical experience requirements before they can take CAA examinations to become licensed Aircraft Maintenance Engineers. There are some full-time courses in aeronautical engineering available, usually lasting two and a half years.

Air Traffic Control
Entrants for the NATS scheme must be eligible for work within the UK, have security clearance, be aged between 18 and 27 and pass a medical. The training lasts just under 18 months and includes practice at Bournemouth Airport. This is followed by an extensive period of practical training at a designated site.

Air Traffic Engineer
NATS runs a training scheme for graduate electrical/electronic engineers lasting a minimum of 15 months. The training is approved by the Institute of Electrical and Electronic Engineering and will lead after approximately three years to chartered engineering status.

Personal Qualities

Pilot
Pilots must be very well balanced, physically fit, have stamina, good eyesight and colour vision; they must be mentally and physically alert and ready to respond quickly to changing conditions. They must be unflappable, confident, self-assured leaders with considerable technical skill.

Flight Engineer
Flight engineers must be physically fit and have a sound technical understanding of aircraft maintenance, flying techniques and operations. The ability to work in a small team and get on well with people in a confined space is necessary.

Air Cabin Crew
Air cabin crew must be reassuring and approachable, smart, have lots of energy and stamina, confidence and the ability to act quickly, decisively and in a firm but polite and tactful manner.

Maintenance Engineer
Maintenance engineering requires a combination of practical interest, mechanical aptitude, accuracy and manual dexterity. Engineers must be willing to adapt and to re-train. Very high standards and a responsible attitude are also most important.

Air Traffic Control
Air traffic control officers must be able to read and interpret a great deal of different information instantly and act upon it. They must

be able to act quickly if conditions suddenly change, be healthy, reliable and well balanced emotionally; good eyesight and colour vision are also important.

Air Traffic Engineer
Colour vision, great care, accuracy and a basic understanding of electricity and magnetism and their practical applications are required of the air traffic engineer, who must work to very high standards and be reliable.

£ Salaries vary but the following is a guide: pilot £17,000– £26,000; cabin crew £7,000+; student air traffic controller £14,699, air traffic control officer £25,247.

i Civil Aviation Authority (CAA), 45–59 Kingsway, London WC2B 6TE; 020 7379 7311

Recruitment Services, National Air Traffic Services (NATS), T1213, CAA House, 45–59 Kingsway, London WC2B 6TE; 020 7832 6696

The Royal Aeronautical Society, 4 Hamilton Place, London W1V 0BQ; 020 7499 3515

Individual airlines

Civil Engineer*, see *Engineering

CIVIL SERVICE

Civil Servants work for the Government in a variety of departments and agencies that recruit individually. These include the Ministry of Defence, the Foreign and Commonwealth Office, the Departments of Health and Social Security, the Department of Environment, Transport and the Regions, the Inland Revenue, the Home Office (including the Prison Service), the Department of Trade and Industry, and the Ministry of Agriculture, Fisheries and Food. They also work in the new Executive Agencies set up to provide a more efficient and cost-effective service to the public and to other departments, for example, the Stationery Office, Companies House and the Driver and Vehicle Licensing Agency. Consequently, job opportunities are many and varied, but generally they fall into the following categories.

Eighty per cent of Civil Servants work outside London. Employees of the Government must be prepared to work anywhere in the UK and (sometimes) abroad.

Administrative Staff
This is the largest group and members work in all departments, carrying out the work of Government. At the top level it is responsible for policy and management. At a lower level, executive officers are responsible for carrying out the daily work. They are the junior management, often in charge of a section or acting as the personal assistant to a more senior Civil Servant. Graduates may enter the diplomatic service as Executive Officers or Administration Trainees. The Administrative Assistant (Clerical) level is responsible for routine office work, such as answering straightforward enquiries, sending out forms and filing, as well as for providing secretaries/typists; Administrative Officers have wider responsibilities, such as keeping records and figures and assisting the public.

Scientific Staff
They are employed in Government laboratories and research establishments, working in research, design and development. Most opportunities here are in physics and engineering, although there are also opportunities in maths and computing, chemical and life sciences. The majority of candidates are recruited at Scientific Officer grade (working on routine testing and analysis). Those with fewer qualifications can join as Assistant Scientific Officers.

Professionally Qualified Staff
Professionally qualified staff (particularly in the field of technology) are employed in great numbers since the Government needs its own architects, accountants, computer personnel, lawyers, librarians, statisticians, photographers, surveyors, draughtsmen, valuers and even veterinary surgeons in the various departments.

Qualifications and Training

Requirements vary from GCSE passes for junior posts to an honours degree for professional and higher administrative posts. For example, a good honours degree (or equivalent) is essential for fast-stream Administration Trainees, Scientific Officers and other professional posts. Candidates with Edexcel (BTEC) higher awards may be considered for some scientific jobs.

A level and H grade passes (or equivalent) are required for Executive Officers, Engineering Apprentices and grade 9 Officers in the diplomatic service.

Specified passes at GCSE or SCE Standard grade (or technical qualifications) are normally required for Administrative Officers, Assistant Scientific Officers and Technician Apprentices. NVQs at the appropriate level in a relevant subject may be acceptable for many posts. Much of the training is given on the job and is supplemented with attendance at formal courses (for example, in managerial or tax skills) when necessary. A large number of in-service training courses are also available (part-time, full-time and sandwich), to assist in gaining appropriate qualifications.

Personal Qualities

Qualities required vary considerably from department to department. Much of the Government's work is confidential, so loyalty and discretion are needed whatever the work.

£ Salaries compare favourably with those of outside staff. Some departments may pay a retention and recruitment allowance. One can gain promotion, and thus higher salaries, from all grades.

i Civil Service Commission; 020 7270 3000
www.cabinet-office.gov.uk/index/civilservice.htm
Civil Service (Recruitment), Units 2–4, Lescren Way, Avonmouth, Bristol BS11 8DG; 0117 982 1171

CLOTHING INDUSTRY

(see also Fashion)

The clothing industry is diverse and complex, with products ranging from off-the-peg garments that are turned out in hundreds and thousands, to exclusive *haute couture* designs from top fashion houses. There are job opportunities in large factories and in small workrooms, with large wholesaling firms and in small family businesses, and on production lines that turn out high-fashion clothes where designs change radically and frequently, or on more conservative lines such as underwear where the demand is fairly steady. The most important sections of the industry are men's and boys' outerwear, women's and girls' outerwear, children's clothing, bespoke tailoring (made to measure) and dressmaking. More specialised areas such as millinery and glove making are relatively small.

Skilled workers are generally in great demand in most areas; main craft jobs are pattern cutting and grading, lay making (positioning the pattern so as to make the best and most economical use of the cloth), cutting, marking or fixing (putting the different pieces of an individual garment together and marking the stitch lines), hand sewing and pressing. There are also plenty of opportunities for semi-skilled workers and operators, particularly machinists. Much of this work is repetitive – frequently, production lines are arranged so that each machinist sews only one part of a garment – but there may be opportunities to move up to more skilled work later (such as sample machining).

Technology is making itself felt in the clothing industry and more advanced sewing machines, computer-controlled pattern laying and die cutting of bulk quantities are only a few of the more recent developments. The industry in the future will need more skilled mechanics to maintain and care for the increasingly sophisticated machines. More and higher-skilled operatives will also be required. The clothing industry also employs people in its commercial sections – marketing and sales, for instance, or purchasing and supply – where there are often very close links with the major textile and fibre companies.

Qualifications and Training

Formal educational qualifications are not always needed to train for the craft skills. These are traditionally learnt by courses leading to City and Guilds examinations. Trainee tailors and cutters normally serve an apprenticeship of four and a half years. Machinists are trained on the job by the employing company.

For more senior or technical jobs, GCSEs are needed. The London College of Fashion and Clothing Technology runs a four-year full-time course for would-be managers (entry requires candidates to be over 18 with a minimum of five GCSEs and two A levels). There is a three-year full-time course (requiring five GCSEs, to include maths and English) in tailoring as well as two-year courses in clothing and tailoring and one-year courses in clothing production and garment making. No formal academic qualifications are needed for the garment-making course. The Mabel Fletcher Technical College, Liverpool, offers a three-year full-time diploma course in tailoring.

Personal Qualities

These vary according to the particular sector of the industry concerned. It is generally advantageous to have deft hands and high standards of neatness and precision. In factories, a willingness to be part of a team is needed, while in bespoke tailoring a candidate should have a pleasant manner and be able to put potential customers at their ease.

£ Depends upon individual employer, but generally low.

i CAPITB Trust, 80 Richardshaw Lane, Pudsey, Leeds LS28 6BN; 0113 239 3355

COACH

Football and cricket are the main sports in which there are opportunities for coaches and these are for ex-professionals only. Sports centres, clubs, schools and swimming baths also provide opportunities for coaches on a part-time basis.

Some local authorities employ coaches to offer facilities for local schools at one or more centres in the authority. The sports offered are likely to be: badminton, basketball, climbing (on indoor walls), ice skating, swimming, squash, tennis, trampolining and weight training. A coach employed in these circumstances must be able to coach in all or nearly all of the above.

Increasingly, there is a need for coaches in the summer months to work in outdoor pursuits centres.

Qualifications and Training

Coaches must gain recognised coaching qualifications, which are awarded by the governing bodies of the various sports and acquired either at evening class or weekend school. Swimming coaches must also hold a national lifeguard award.

Personal Qualities

Coaches need the ability to communicate, as well as perseverance, patience and tact. The ability to inspire children or adults of very different abilities, often in less than ideal situations, is also needed.

£ Salaries vary greatly. Coaches paid by the hour by local authorities receive £10.15–£11.30 an hour.

i Sport England, 16 Upper Woburn Place, London WC1H 0QP; 020 7273 1500
The Scottish Sports Council, Caledonia House, South Gyle, Edinburgh EH12 9DQ; 0131 317 7200
The Sports Council for Wales, Sophia Gardens, Cardiff CF1 9SW; 029 2039 7571

Coach Driver, **see** *Bus Companies, Road Transport*

COASTGUARD

When vessels and small craft are in trouble or missing off the coast, the coastguard is called in to organise and coordinate the necessary search and rescue measures. The UK area of responsibility is divided into six regions, each headed by a regional controller who is based at a Maritime Rescue Coordination Centre. These centres have officers who keep a constant watch on international distress frequencies and are trained to handle radio, telephone and telex messages, which are received automatically. At other stations, regular officers are helped by auxiliaries. New technology is making it possible for the coastguard to provide a greatly enhanced service.

Qualifications and Training

Most coastguard officers are ex-seamen who have done previous marine work in services such as the Royal Navy or the Merchant Navy. They must have a strong maritime background, with at least six years' sea-going experience, a knowledge of communications or navigation and three GCSEs to include maths and English. There is an eight-week training course at the Coastguard Training School in Highcliffe (Dorset) for new entrants, who subsequently train on the job, complete a task book, then attend a further short course and take a proficiency test.

Personal Qualities

Good eyesight and hearing are essential and candidates are expected to pass a strict medical. Candidates must be prepared to adapt to shift work and to serve anywhere in the UK.

£ £12,000 for a probationer, rising to £13,000 once qualified.

i The Maritime and Coastguard Agency, Personnel Section, Spring Place, 105 Commercial Road, Southampton SO15 1EG; 023 8032 9461
www.mcagency.org.uk

COLOUR SCIENCE AND TECHNOLOGY

Colour technologists are concerned with producing dyes and pigments that have a wide range of applications, including those in the textile, paint, rubber, plastics, paper, leather and foodstuffs industries. They must ensure that exact colours can be produced at an economic price and in the right quantities whenever they are needed. They are often involved in research and development projects. Technologists are also employed in sales, management, buying, development and research, quality control, customer liaison and technical services departments (depending on the industry involved and the expertise needed).

Textile technologists may work in the design, manufacture and operation of textile machinery, and in the design, production, coloration, finishing and manufacture of fibres, yarns and fabrics of all types.

Qualifications and Training

Two, preferably three, A levels or three H grades, one of which must be chemistry or a subject including chemistry, or a relevant Edexcel (BTEC)/SVQ award or an ND or NC in sciences are required for entry to a degree course in colour chemistry or textile chemistry. Minimum entry requirements for part-time technician courses leading to the Edexcel (BTEC)/SVQ certificate and higher certificate in textile coloration (textile dyeing) are GCSE or SCE Standard grade passes in maths, an appropriate science and English.

For textile technologists, the basic professional qualification is the Associateship and Chartered Textile Technologist (CText ATI) of the Textile Institute, awarded on the fulfilment of the academic and industrial/professional experience requirements. The professional qualification for a specialist in colour technology is the Associateship and Chartered Colourist of the Society of Dyers and

Colourists (CcolASDC) or the Licentiateship of the Society of Dyers and Colourists (LSDC).

Personal Qualities

Good colour vision is essential, as is scientific or technical ability and the ability to work as one of a team.

£ £11,500–£12,000+ with a degree; £8,000+ for a textile technologist.

i The Society of Dyers and Colourists, PO Box 244, 82 Grattan Road, Bradford, West Yorkshire BD1 2JB; 01274 725138 www.sdc.org.uk

COMPANY SECRETARY

The Company Secretary as an officer of the company plays a major part in the organisation's governance. Duties include ensuring the company complies with relevant legal and regulatory matters, administration of meetings, advising the board of directors on company law and procedures and maintaining company records. Other duties can include pensions administration, personnel matters, shareholder issues, property management and finance.

Qualifications and Training

The law recognises the importance of the Company Secretary role, mandatory for every company, by requiring the Company Secretary of a public company to have specific knowledge and experience. Only the Institute of Chartered Secretaries and Administrators (ICSA) qualification specifically addresses the requirements of the role.

The ICSA Qualifying Scheme comprises 17 examinations over three programmes: Foundation, Pre-Professional and Professional. The Professional Programme is considered equivalent to a postgraduate award. Exemptions are available for holders of relevant academic and professional qualifications. Holders of recognised degrees and postgraduate qualifications are eligible for direct access on to the Professional Programme.

Upon completion of the ICSA Qualifying Scheme, candidates become Graduates of the Institute (Grad ICSA). To become a Member, an ICSA Graduate has to demonstrate between three and six years' relevant work experience and have two sponsors of professional status to confirm their fitness to practise. There are two grades of Membership: Associate and Fellow.

Personal Qualities

The Company Secretary must possess integrity and sound judgement, with the ability to act with authority for the good of the company. High-level organisational skills and a flair for administration are also important, along with strong communication skills and an understanding of figures and IT.

£ Those with little previous experience can expect a starting salary of between £15,000 and £20,000. A salary above £50,000 is not uncommon for an experienced fully qualified Company Secretary. Salaries will vary depending on the size and location of the company.

i Student Services Office, The Institute of Chartered Secretaries and Administrators (ICSA), 16 Park Crescent, London W1N 4AH; 020 7580 4741; fax 020 7323 1132
www.icsa.org.uk/icsa/

COMPUTING

Computers have now taken their place in virtually every aspect of modern life and the demand for trained personnel is likely to be high for some time to come. The uses of computers are almost limitless; there are applications in industry (on production lines), in commerce (for preparing salaries, invoices and all kinds of routine paperwork), in retailing (for stock control), in scientific research (for analysing and comparing results), in travel (for making and confirming bookings and flight reservations) and in banking (for storing information about accounts). These are just a fraction of the tasks a computer may be asked to perform. Computer personnel may be divided into several specialised categories.

Computer Operator/Network Support

Today, networked PCs are generally operated by their users, for example, market analysts, accounts clerks, nurses, archivists or toolsetters. The computer operator of a mainframe system is responsible for the actual running of the computer, loading the magnetic disks or tapes that carry the programs and the data, monitoring the running of programs, record keeping and storage. Computer operators are now being replaced by systems support staff, who install, maintain and update networked systems of PCs and workstations, and stand-alone PCs, and are responsible for hardware and software.

Computer Programmer
A computer programmer composes the instructions and puts them into the special computer language, to enable the computer to carry out the tasks in the way the systems analyst has designed.

Data Processing
Data-preparation operators organise the routine input of data into programs, often via keyboards and screens. Much of the work is now done by users, especially in commercial installations.

DTP Operator
Desktop publishing operators should have excellent software package and design skills. A background in art is very useful because of the visual and graphic aspects of the job.

IT Support
A good working knowledge and interest of computers is essential. Workers in IT support also need to keep abreast of constant changes and developments.

Software Engineer
Software engineers design, test and maintain large-scale software, frequently utilising 'library routines', written by programmers. They work in teams, which include systems analysts, programmers and systems engineers. Much of the work is with people, and team skills are developed.

Systems Analyst/Designer
This work involves analysing a business requirement and designing a system which the computer can use to solve it. They have to work out what type of computer is necessary, how the information available should be fed into it and how the results should be presented, bearing in mind the amount and type of data the computer will be given, what the customer proposes to do with the results and the likely direction of expansion and future development.

Training
Modern sophisticated software packages run more efficiently if used by trained personnel. Trainers are employed by software vendors, by training companies and by user companies for their own staff. They need to be familiar with the packages at all levels, and have people and teaching skills, and may also have the opportunity to develop training materials.

Web site Designer
A Web site Designer focuses on the graphic and visual aspects of a Web site. They need to have a basic working knowledge of HMTL, an understanding of how Web sites work and awareness of how audiences respond to visuals.

Web site Programmer
Web site programmers build Web sites. They need a good working knowledge of HTML and an awareness of new Internet technologies. Knowledge of JAVA is highly desirable in the employment market.

In addition to the above categories, there are also openings in sales and marketing of computers, and in service engineering. Computer (maintenance) engineers/service engineers install, maintain and repair computers.

Qualifications and Training

No rigid academic qualifications are demanded, as employers tend to set their own entry requirements. There are, however, a large number of relevant courses and these do have set requirements. Potential systems analysts are generally expected to hold degrees and/or programming and/or business qualifications (entry for such courses requires A levels, often in mathematical subjects). Programmers are usually expected to have A level/H grade or HNC/HND passes as well as GCSEs or equivalent in English and maths. Some firms recruit graduates as trainee programmers.

Computer operators need at least three GCSE/SCE Standard grades including maths and English; one in computer studies can be an added asset. Data processors do not always require formal qualifications, although experience in typing is advisable. Secretarial word-processing courses may require GCSEs. Trainee service engineers need maths and physics qualifications (usually at least GCSE level/Standard grade passes).

Training opportunities are wide and varied. Many companies run their own training programmes as well as sending their trainees on relevant outside courses. Most candidates are asked to take an aptitude test before embarking on their training, to assess their numeracy, logic, accuracy and thinking speed. Various full- and part-time courses are available leading to Edexcel (BTEC) and City and Guilds qualifications. NVQs are available at levels 1 to 4, in Systems Development and Service Provision. Awarding bodies include Edexcel (BTEC), RSA, City and Guilds and, in Scotland, SQA.

Personal Qualities

Clear communications abilities and team working should come high on the list, together with the ability both to give out and receive information.

£ Typical minimum salaries are as follows: data-preparation VDU operator £9,000+; data-preparation supervisor £12,000+; computer operator £21,039; senior operator £21,039+; junior programmer/graduate trainee £12,000+; programmer £22,959+; senior programmer £18,500+; systems analyst £28,265+; senior systems analyst £21,000+.

i Association of Computer Professionals, 204 Barnett Wood Lane, Ashtead, Surrey KT21 2DB; 01372 273442

The British Computer Society, 1 Sanford Street, Swindon, Wiltshire SN1 1HJ; 01793 417417
www.bcs.org.uk

Institution of Analysts and Programmers, Charles House, 36 Culmington Road, London W13 9NH; 020 8567 2118

Local further education colleges

CONFERENCE ORGANISER

A number of large companies and industrial concerns have their own department with staff responsible for making and coordinating the necessary arrangements for regular sales conferences, staff conferences, product launches and special events. Some institutions, associations and charities also employ staff specialising in the organisation of meetings and events. In several firms, the organising work is combined with other promotional or administrative duties. Other firms employ professional conference organisers.

Conference organisers select and book the most suitable venue, organise the invitations and accommodation (if necessary) of the various participants, the relevant paperwork, the catering and reception facilities, any specialist equipment necessary (such as video, microphones, projectors, closed-circuit television, and so on), media coverage (if applicable), and a host of minor details. Some firms of professional organisers have a small staff and also employ temporary freelancers as and when necessary.

Conference centres and hotels specialising in conference facilities have their own staff who are responsible for arrangements for conferences already booked and for advertising and encouraging further bookings.

Qualifications and Training

There are currently no formal educational requirements, but occupational standards and NVQs are being established. Useful experience could include sales and marketing, knowledge of hotel and venue operations, and language skills, as well as secretarial duties. Computer literacy is important.

Personal Qualities

A flair for organisation and forward planning is needed, as are tact, discretion and the ability to talk to all kinds of people and anticipate their various demands. In addition, some conference organisers should be prepared to work abroad.

£ £14,000–£16,000 is the salary a large firm might offer. Salaries for freelancers vary according to the type and amount of work undertaken.

i Association for Conferences and Events, ACE International, Riverside House, High Street, Huntingdon, Cambridgeshire PE18 6SG; 01480 457595
www.martex.co.uk/ace

How to Organise Effective Conferences and Meetings (Kogan Page)

CONSERVATION (ENVIRONMENTAL)

Conservation is the term used for the careful preservation and protection of a natural resource: the land itself, plants and animals. Government departments are actively and extensively involved in conservation.

The Countryside Agency is the statutory body working for people and places in rural England. It was established on 1 April 1999 following the merger of the Rural Development Commission and the Countryside Commission. It aims to conserve and enhance the countryside, to promote social equity and economic opportunity for the people who live there, and to help everyone, wherever they live, to enjoy this national asset. This is achieved by leading via research and advice, influencing others, especially central and local government, and by demonstrating ways forward through practical projects.

English Nature is the statutory adviser to Government on nature conservation in England and promotes the conservation of England's wildlife and natural features. Its work includes the selection, establishment and management of national nature reserves and marine nature reserves, the identification and provision of advice and information about nature conservation, and the support and conduct of research relevant to these functions.

The *Countryside Council for Wales* is the Government's statutory adviser on wildlife, countryside and maritime conservation matters in Wales. It is the executive authority for the conservation of habitats and wildlife. Through partners it promotes the protection of landscape, opportunities for enjoyment and the support of those who live and work in and manage the countryside.

The *Department of Environment, Transport and the Regions* supervises and advises upon land reclamation and coastline protection schemes carried out by local authorities. It is also involved with national parks projects and the restoration of derelict country sites.

The *National Environment Research Council* involves itself in a broad range of activities concerned with conservation (mainly involving scientists), including geological surveys, studies of the ocean, terrestrial ecology and the British Antarctic Survey, which studies atmospheric, earth and life sciences.

Scottish Natural Heritage fulfils a similar role for Scotland as the Countryside Council does for Wales.

In addition to these statutory bodies, there are a number of non-Government bodies, including the following.

The *National Trust* is the largest single private landowner in the country. It is concerned with the conservation of places of natural beauty and historic buildings. It employs land agents and various specialist staff to care for such sites and to supervise the visiting public.

The *Royal Society for the Protection of Birds* has its own protected reserves and employs nature wardens, researchers and surveyors in reserve management, although such posts are relatively few.

In addition, conservation is carried out by a large number of voluntary societies, such as the *Councils for the Protection of Rural England, Wales* and *Scotland*, the *Commons Open Spaces Trust* and the *Footpaths Preservation Society and Wildlife Trust*. Such organisations have few full-time posts and these are mainly confined to administrative staff.

Qualifications and Training

Qualifications vary, as there are many different jobs. Conservation officers and science specialists need relevant degrees or equivalent; much of the training is done on the job but the advent of NVQs in Landscapes and Ecosystems provides an important set of standards and defines levels of competence for most people working in the environmental conservation field. Administrative officers need at least five GCSEs or equivalent, one of which must be English language; reserve wardens do not always need formal qualifications although A level biology is an advantage. Much of the training is done on the job. Competition for posts in conservation is strong.

Personal Qualities

Conservationists must show dedication in their chosen field and be prepared to work as one of a team.

£ Salaries vary but are in the region of Scientific Officer £11,500–£19,000, Administrative Assistant £5,000–£10,000, Administrative Officer £5,500–£11,500, Estate Worker £150 a week.

i The Countryside Agency, John Dower House, Crescent Place, Cheltenham GL50 3RA; 01242 531381

Countryside Council for Wales, Plas Penrhos, Ffordd Penrhos, Bangor, Gwynedd LL57 2LQ; 01248 370444

English Nature, Northminster House, Peterborough PE1 1UA; 01733 455000 (brochures and leaflets available)

National Trust, 36 Queen Anne's Gate, London SW1H 9AS; 020 7222 9251
Natural Environment Research Council, Polaris House, North Star Avenue, Swindon SN2 1EU; 01793 411500
The Royal Society for the Protection of Birds, The Lodge, Sandy, Bedfordshire SG19 2DL; 01767 680551
Scottish Natural Heritage, 12 Hope Terrace, Edinburgh EH9 2AS; 0131 447 4784
Careers in Environmental Conservation (Kogan Page)

CONSERVATION (HISTORICAL)

Conservation is the ethical preservation of works of art and historic objects such as paintings and sculpture, historic buildings, furniture, textiles (such as costumes and tapestries), manuscripts, clocks and china. Some museums and art galleries employ specialist conservators who are responsible for conserving, repairing and protecting the exhibits in their charge, using the latest scientific techniques. Such work generally calls for scientific training and historical knowledge. There are also a number of conservators working in the private sector. Increasingly, museums and art galleries are sending out more of their objects to private conservators rather than taking on more in-house staff.

Qualifications and Training

Requirements for conservators are becoming more academically based but do vary depending on the organisation involved. The training courses for conservators, whether employed by museums or in private practice, are mainly at degree or postgraduate level although the more craft-based subjects, such as clock or ceramics restoration, are available as college diplomas.

Personal Qualities

Those working in this area need scientific ability, good problem-solving skills, a strong sense of ethics, meticulous attention to detail and patience.

i UK Institute for Conservation of Historic and Artistic Works, 109 The Chandlery, 50 Westminster Bridge, London SE1 7QY; 020 7721 8721
www.ukic.org.uk

Historic Scotland, Scottish Conservation Bureau, Longmore House, Salisbury Place, Edinburgh EH9 1SH; 0131 668 8668 www.historic-scotland.gov.uk

Cultural Heritage National Training Organisation (CHNTO) 1st Floor, Glyde House, Glydegate, Bradford BD5 0UP; 01274 391056; fax 01274 394890

Museum and Galleries Commission, 16 Queen Anne's Gate, London, SW1H 9AA

Constituency Agent, see *Politics*

COURIER (MESSENGER)

Couriers deliver and collect parcels, generally in larger towns and cities. Mostly, the delivery or collection is in the same town, sometimes in a different one and, occasionally, another country. Most couriers travel using a motorcycle, which they may be required to buy. Couriers carrying packages abroad travel by air.

Qualifications and Training

No formal educational qualifications are necessary. Motorcycle couriers must be 17 and hold a clean motorcycle licence.

Personal Qualities

Couriers are generally required when speed is important or when the package cannot be entrusted to the post. Reliability is most important as is the ability to arrive without undue delays. Common sense and initiative are also useful.

£ Some couriers are self-employed, with the firm paying a certain amount per mile, and the messenger being responsible for petrol, insurance and other overheads. Others are employees and receive vouchers for petrol which they cash at a nominated garage. Starting salaries vary, but an employed courier can earn £180+ a week and a self-employed person much more.

Some air couriers are employed on a one-off basis and receive a free or reduced-cost flight in lieu of salary and baggage allowance.

i Local Jobcentres and Careers Offices

COURIER (TRAVEL)

Couriers are employed by major tour companies as official guides for parties of tourists travelling with them. The courier is responsible for the welfare of the tourists and must attend to any worries or complaints. In addition, they are responsible for all the paperwork necessary when the party stays overnight in a hotel or crosses a frontier post. Much of their work is seasonal and generally only senior staff are kept on a permanent basis.

Qualifications and Training

A good general education including GCSE passes in English, geography and maths is usually required by the travel trade. Qualifications in relevant languages and experience of living and working abroad are an obvious advantage; a courier on a particular tour may need to be conversant with local customs and fluent in the relevant languages. Most training takes place on the job and there are NVQs available. The Institute of Travel and Tourism has professional examinations (three to four GCSEs required), but these are not intended for trainees, but for experienced staff wishing to take more senior positions in the travel industry.

Personal Qualities

Couriers must have infinite patience, tact and a pleasant personality. They need to be able to get on with a wide variety of people of all nationalities and from all walks of life, without becoming flustered or panic-stricken in a crisis.

£ Couriers may expect to earn £130+ a week with full accommodation. There are also opportunities to earn more money by organising extra trips for the tourists.

i Institute of Travel and Tourism, 113 Victoria Street, St Albans, Hertfordshire AL1 3TJ; 01727 854395

Major tour operators

Careers Using Languages (Kogan Page)

Careers in the Travel Industry (Kogan Page)

COURT STAFF

Court Reporter

Court reporters attend court sittings and take down a complete report of all the evidence, the summing-up or judgment and, on occasions, the speeches of counsel in the various cases. Formerly, the proceedings were taken down in shorthand; now a stenograph, a typewriter-like machine, is used, which enables the reporter to achieve 200 words per minute. In addition, computers may be used to prepare transcripts with all the advantages of on-screen editing and speed of preparation. The work sometimes involves travelling to a number of different courts.

Justices' Clerk

A Justices' Clerk is either a Solicitor or a Barrister. Their job is to advise and assist lay magistrates by providing them with guidance on the law and the procedure relevant in any particular case. The Clerk will often sit in court while cases are being heard and remind the bench of their powers and give general advice.

Justices' Clerks' Assistant

Administrative Assistants and Administrative Officers assist Justices' Clerks in the administration of the magistrates' courts. Their work involves the preparing of summonses and warrants, the issuing of licences and fine notices and seeing that correct court procedures are followed.

In Scotland, the administration of the court comes under the province of the Scottish Court Administration, which is part of the Civil Service. This includes staff who do a similar job to Justices' Clerks' Assistants.

Qualifications and Training

No specific academic qualifications are demanded for court reporters, although GCSE and A level passes can be an advantage. Applicants do need to have proven ability in shorthand or steno-typing (usually over 150 words per minute), good typing speeds, and a thorough knowledge of grammar and punctuation. Legal experience can also be an asset. Training is undertaken by a number of specialist firms who supply shorthand writers to the courts. On successful completion of the training, trainees are awarded a certificate issued by the Institute of Shorthand Writers or the Association of Professional Shorthand Writers.

Justices' Clerks must be Solicitors or Barristers with five years' experience. Administrative Assistants need two GCSE passes (grade C or above), one of which must be English. Administrative Officers need five GCSE passes (grade C or above), one of which must be English.

Scottish Court Service applicants need several Standard grades and preferably H grades. Training lasts for two to three years, during which time trainees work and undertake courses run by the Court Service.

Personal Qualities

Anyone concerned with the courts must be discreet, honest and trustworthy, as most of the work is confidential. Reporters must show a high degree of accuracy.

£ A newly qualified court reporter earns over £11,000, trainees about £8,000; Justices' Clerk £20,000; Administrative Assistant from £5,000 and Administrative Officer from £8,000. Additional payments are made to those working in London.

i British Institute of Verbatim Reporters, 61 Carey Street, London WC2A 2JG; (for court reporters; send an sae)

Individual Courts of Law

Northern Ireland Court Service, Windsor House, Bedford Street, Belfast BT2 7LT; 028 9032 8594

The Law Society of Scotland, 26 Drumsheugh Gardens, Edinburgh EH3 7YR; 0131 226 7411

Careers in the Law (Kogan Page)

CROUPIER

Croupiers work at the gaming tables of gaming clubs and casinos. They are in charge of accepting the bets, allocating chips, spinning the roulette wheel or dealing the cards, and giving out the winnings, or gathering in what customers have lost.

Qualifications and Training

No formal educational qualifications are demanded but a good head for figures is vital, and GCSE level maths is an advantage. A good appearance and pleasant personality are assets. A clean record is essential – no one with a criminal record can be granted a gaming licence by the Government Gaming Board, and without such a licence it is impossible to be legally employed as a croupier in Britain. Most of the major gaming clubs have their own training schools where candidates are taught how to dress, how to behave and how to treat the customers as well as the rules of the various games, the special skills for counting chips, memorising and calculating the bets, and so on.

Personal Qualities

Nimble fingers and an agile brain are essential, as are a pride in one's appearance and an unflappable nature. The job involves working with people so good communication skills and an ability to defuse potentially awkward situations are also needed (though these are, to a certain extent, taught). A croupier must also be scrupulously honest, and willing to work shifts and anti-social hours.

£ Salaries vary but a trained croupier in London or abroad could expect to earn £400+ a week. A starting salary elsewhere in Britain would be over £10,000, depending on area.

i British Casino Association, 29 Castle Street, Reading, Berkshire RG1 7SL; 0118 958 9191; fax 0118 959 0592 (list of members and training notes)

Local Jobcentres and Careers Offices

Curator, **see** *Museum and Art Gallery Work*

CUSTOMS AND EXCISE

HM Customs and Excise is responsible for collecting about 40 per cent of central Government taxation and protects society against illegal importations of drugs and other prohibited goods.

Most new entrants to the Department begin their career in a local VAT office. There they give advice to local businesses and are responsible for ensuring that the correct amount of tax is paid. Executive officers are likely to spend four days out of five visiting companies to find out what they do and to audit their records.

The Department is also responsible for collecting excise duties; for example, on petrol, spirits, cigarettes, and betting and gaming. Again, the Department's role is to ensure that businesses understand their responsibilities.

Probably the most familiar role is the control of imported and exported goods at ports and airports throughout the UK. As well as checking passengers' baggage, commercial importations of cargo are examined.

The work is interesting and varied, with opportunities to get out of the office. With offices all over the UK, there are often opportunities to work near home.

Qualifications and Training

There are three main entry levels into Customs and Excise. On the bottom rung of the ladder is the Administrative Assistant. To join at this level you require two GCSEs at C grade or above including English language. Administrative Officers require five GCSEs at C grade or above including English language. Alternatively, with two A levels and three GCSEs including English language, it is possible to join at junior management level as an Executive Officer.

Full training is given as necessary. This may involve a combination of classroom training, self-learning packages and on-the-job training.

Personal Qualities

An ability to get on with people, and tact, sensitivity and firmness are all useful qualities. Candidates also need to be able to use their initiative and common sense.

£ Varies depending on age and location but an indication is: Administrative Assistant £7,300–£7,900; Administrative Officer £10,755–£11,250; and Executive Officer £12,675–£14,000. Rates are higher in London.

i HM Customs and Excise, New King's Beam House, 22 Upper Ground, London SE1 9PJ; 020 7620 1313
www.hmce.gov.uk

D

DANCING

Dance is enjoyed in many forms, whether as a leisure activity or as career. It can be divided into the two main categories of theatre dance (ballet, modern and contemporary dance, jazz, tap, and so on) and social dance (ballroom, folk dance and disco). However, there are no hard and fast divisions between the different forms.

The profession of dancing consists of two main areas: performing and teaching. Choreography, notation, dance animation and dance therapy are related areas of work.

Performing

Many of those who wish to perform have had early training in ballet and/or other forms of theatre dance. Opportunities in ballet and contemporary companies are limited and many dancers find their first employment in companies abroad. Dancers also work in pantomimes, shows and musicals, and on cruise ships, for example. Professional performers find it useful to be members of the British Actors' Equity Association.

Teaching

Teachers of dance can specialise in one area of dance teaching or teach in a variety of areas. The demand for teachers is high especially as dance is now seen as a form of recreation. Teachers may work in commercial dance studios and professional dance schools in the UK, and some find work abroad.

Dance Notator

Notators are employed by dance companies to record their repertoire and assist choreographers and rehearsal staff in the revival of choreographic works. Most notators are graduates of vocational dance schools or ex-professional dancers as the work involves close and informed observation of the choreography, the ability to demonstrate the movement accurately and the ability to work effectively with professional dancers.

Dance Animateur
Dance animateurs work in the community or education in order to encourage participation and involvement and to raise the profile of dance activity locally. Their precise role is dependent on the funding organisation, and on the needs of the local community or environment in which they work.

Dance Therapy
Dance movement therapy uses movement and dance as a medium through which the individual can engage creatively in a process of growth and personal integration. Dance movement therapists work with individuals and groups in health, education and social service settings. Their clients include people who are emotionally disturbed or have learning difficulties, and those who want to use this therapy for personal growth.

Qualifications and Training

Ideally, ballet students should attend a recognised residential establishment such as the Royal Ballet School from the age of 11 to 18. Means-tested financial assistance is available to those UK students who come to the school under the Music and Ballet Scheme of the DfEE. Dancers who want to become teachers must obtain the relevant qualifications, for which full-time or part-time courses are available. These generally have an entry requirement of four to five GCSEs at grade C and above. The Royal Academy of Dancing offers certificates, diplomas and degrees in classical ballet teaching. The courses are available on a part-time and full-time basis.

Personal Qualities

Dancers need to be hard-working, self-disciplined both physically and mentally, dedicated and determined. They must be imaginative, able to express themselves artistically and have a good sense of timing and an ear for music.

£ Starting salaries vary according to the organisation or company.

i The Benesh Institute, Royal Academy of Dancing, 36 Battersea Square, London SW11 3RA; 020 7223 0091 www.benesh.org.uk

Royal Ballet School (Upper), 155 Talgarth Road, London, W14 9DE; 020 8237 7100

Royal Academy of Dancing, 36 Battersea Square, London SW11 3RA; 020 7223 0091; fax 020 7924 3129 www.rad.org.uk

Council for Dance Education and Training (CDET), Studio 8, The Glasshouse, 49A Goldhawk Road, London W12 8QP; 020 8746 0076; fax 020 8746 1937 (directory of Regional Teachers available for £3.50)

Dance UK, 23 Crisp Road, London W6 9RL; 020 8741 1932

Association of Dance Movement Therapy UK, c/o The Quaker Meeting Rooms, Wedmore Vale, Bedminster, Bristol BS3 5JA

Data Processing*, see *Computing

DENTISTRY

Dentist

Dentists aim to prevent gum disease and tooth decay and to identify and treat such diseases. This involves filling, crowning and extracting first teeth, scaling and cleaning teeth and gums. They design and fit dentures and plates and take corrective measures for teeth growing abnormally. They are also involved with the rectification of fractured jaws, and so on, and with surgery of the mouth. Opportunities exist both in the UK and abroad. In general dental practice, dentists work on contract to the NHS, but growing numbers work in private clinics. Some work in hospitals, in community services, school services or armed forces. There are also opportunities for dentists to work in university dental teaching and research.

Dental Hygienist

Dental hygienists clean, polish and scale teeth and, in some cases, prepare patients for oral operations. Through lectures and practical experience they also endeavour to educate children and adults on the importance of proper dental care. Dental hygienists work to the written prescription of a dentist.

Dental Nurse
The dental nurse, formerly known as a surgery assistant, looks after all aspects of the surgery, from clerical tasks such as updating patients' records, looking after reception and keeping the books, to care of the dentist's instruments, the preparation of fillings and processing X-rays.

Dental Technician
Dental technicians design and fabricate a wide variety of different materials and equipment to make crowns, dentures, metal plates, bridges, orthodontic braces and other appliances as prescribed by a dentist.

Dental Therapist
Dental therapists work in local authority clinics and hospitals assisting dentists by carrying out simpler forms of treatment such as fillings and the extraction of first teeth. They also give guidance on general dental care. Dental therapists must always work to the written prescription of a dentist.

Qualifications and Training

Dentist
To qualify, a dentist must have a degree in dental surgery. All dentists must be registered to the Dentists' Register, which is maintained by the General Dental Council. From the age of 17, students may enter one of the 13 UK dental schools. Competition for places is stiff and the A level grades required in physics, chemistry and biology will be high; these will vary, however, and some schools have pre-dental courses for students who have not attained the appropriate A levels. The pre-dental year is for those who have gained high-grade A levels, but have not covered the relevant science subjects. It is not appropriate for those who do not get the required grades.

The undergraduate course lasts at least five years. It incorporates a sound academic education combined with theoretical and practical training in all aspects of dental practice.

In the armed forces, dental cadetships leading to a commission are open to candidates who have completed part of their training at a dental school.

Dental Hygienist

At least five GCSE passes are required for entry to the course, which leads to the diploma in dental hygiene; preferred subjects are biology and English language. Students must be over 18, although the average age is 21. The full-time course lasts two years and may be taken at most dental hospitals. Previous dental surgery experience is required, and some hospitals insist on candidates already having a dental surgery assistant qualification.

Dental Nurse

Currently there are no set qualifications to become a dental nurse in general dental practice, although this may change in the future. Many dentists like to train their own assistants, but they will probably expect applicants to be educated to GCSE standard. Students may enter for the national certificate of the examining board for dental nurses. Preparation for this exam can be obtained either at evening or day-release classes or via full-time attendance on a course lasting between one and two years. A certificate is awarded on passing the exam and completing 24 months' practical experience. Courses are offered by colleges of further education and dental hospitals. Courses offered by dental hospitals usually require four GCSE passes, including English and biology.

Dental Technician

The usual entry requirements for courses are five GCSEs or equivalents (English, maths, physics and chemistry). The Edexcel (BTEC) diploma in dental technology is a full-time three-year course. This is also available part-time.

Dental Therapist

To become a dental therapist it is necessary to take a 27-month full-time course. The minimum course entry requirement is five GCSE passes or equivalents; these should include English and biology. Applicants should also hold the national certificate for dental nurses, which requires at least two years' practical experience. As competition for places is fierce, actual requirements are likely to be higher than this.

Personal Qualities

Manual and visual dexterity combined with medical knowledge and clinical skills are essential. Candidates should be equable, sympathetic and have an agreeable nature and an ability to communicate.

The ability to work in a team, and good administrative and managerial skills are also important.

£ Typical minimum salaries are: dental hygienist £11,334+; dental nurses £4,940, rising to £8,606 after eight years' experience; dental technicians £4,681–£7,801, rising to £10,401+ when qualified; dental therapists £11,718+ on qualification. General dental practitioners earn the fees that they receive from patients or the NHS. There is no longer a target income set by Government, but average earnings for 1996-7 were in the range of £46,950–£61,753 (source: Inland Revenue).

Most new graduates start in a salaried position as Vocational Dental Practitioners and receive £22,464 (source: HMSO, 1998/9). Hospital and university dentists have a graded career structure, which goes from £16,710 as House Officer to £61,605 as Consultant. Dentists in the Community Dental Service receive £22,464 as VDP, rising to £48,825 as Senior Dental Officer.

i British Association of Dental Nurses, 11 Pharos Street, Fleetwood, Lancashire FY7 6BG; 01253 778631 (enclose an sae)

British Association of Dental Therapists, Dental Auxiliary School, Heath Park, Cardiff

The British Dental Association, 64 Wimpole Street, London W1M 8AL; 020 7935 0875
www.bda-dentistry.org.uk

British Dental Hygienists' Association, 13 The Ridge, Yatton, Bristol BS19 4DQ; 01934 876389

The Dental Technicians' Education and Training Advisory Board (DTETAB), 5 Oxford Court, St James Road, Brackley, Northamptonshire NN13 7XY; 01280 702600

General Dental Council, 37 Wimpole Street, London W1M 8DQ; 020 7486 2171

For courses and training: The Tutor Dental Nurse, The Dental Auxiliary School, 36 New Road, Whitechapel, London E1 2AX; 020 7377 7634

Designer, see *Artist, Fashion, Industrial Designer, Interior Designer, Jewellery Trade, Publishing, Theatre*

DETECTIVE/PRIVATE INVESTIGATOR

A private detective can either be self-employed, and work alone, or as part of an agency. The investigation profession has a diverse workload and is therefore difficult to categorise. A small cross-section of the subjects that an investigator may be instructed to assist with are as follows: tracing missing persons, debtors, witnesses and taking statements; video and photographic surveillance for matrimonial or insurance company fraud; process serving (the correct delivery of legal documents); pre sue and means enquiries; verification of credit worthiness; road traffic and industrial accident investigations involving sketch plans and photographs; land registry searches; land and property repossession; and test purchases.

Qualifications and Training

No formal qualifications are necessary but a good standard of education will be an advantage in the preparation of reports and the taking of statements. Training seminars are run by the Association of British Investigators. A sound knowledge of computers, experience in credit control, or a service industry, with direct contact with the public are useful. NVQs level 3 and 4 are available in Investigation Techniques.

A private detective needs personal indemnity and public liability insurance, and should also register with the Office of Fair Trading and the Data Protection Registrar. It is also advisable to obtain membership of a recognised association.

Personal Qualities

Honesty, integrity, and discretion are vital. Patience, perseverance, self motivation, ability to work on own initiative, adaptability and a good outgoing personality are all useful qualities.

£ This is regional and depends upon experience. An agency can charge approximately £20 per hour but will pay lower rates to staff. The self-employed may be able to charge similar rates. (Check with local legal aid board for acceptable hourly rate.)

i Association of British Investigators, ABI House, 10 Bonner Hill Road, Kingston-upon-Thames, Surrey KT1 3EP (the General Secretary can assist with finding a local agency that may offer further information)

Local Jobcentres and Careers Offices
Libraries hold directories of investigators

DIETITIAN

A dietitian is an authority on diet and on the application of the principles of nutrition. There are a great many opportunities and interesting posts for dietitians, particularly in the NHS. Dietitians working in hospitals collaborate with medical staff, other health-care professionals and catering staff in planning the correct balance of foods for all the patients, depending on their general state of health and medical requirements. Dietitians are also employed by local health authorities to work with general practitioners, in health centres and clinics dealing with infant welfare and ante-natal treatment. Some dietitians may now be employed directly by fund-holding GPs. They are also called upon to educate other health-care professionals in nutrition. Other opportunities for dietitians exist in education, research, the food industry and the media. Increasingly, dietitians work in a freelance capacity.

Qualifications and Training

GCSEs in maths and English are required, and two or three A levels, preferably chemistry and another science subject, are required for entry to a dietetic degree course. Edexcel (BTEC) qualifications may be acceptable and mature students may also apply. Dietitians are all university graduates.

It is possible to take a degree in dietetics or nutrition and dietetics. Graduates with a degree with an acceptable level of human physiology and biochemistry may take a postgraduate diploma course in dietetics. Leeds Metropolitan University, University of Ulster, Coleraine, University of Wales Institute, Cardiff, and Glasgow Caledonian University offer two-year full-time courses.

Personal Qualities

A dietitian's special skill is to translate scientific and medical decisions relating to food and health into terms which everyone can understand. An interest in food, coupled with an understanding of how different cultural, social and economic factors can determine a person's dietary requirements, are needed in the dietitian. Dietitians must therefore be interested in people, not just the scientific aspects of their problems, and have a non-judgmental approach.

£ £15,405; senior dietitians earn £19,640–£23,130 and managers up to £32,000.

i British Dietetic Association, 5th Floor, Elizabeth House, 22 Suffolk Street, Queensway, Birmingham B1 1LS; 0121 616 4900; fax 0121 616 4901 (send an sae)
www.bda.uk.com

Diplomat, **see** *Civil Service*

DISC JOCKEY

Disc jockeys provide music at a range of venues such as clubs, private parties and radio stations. The music is provided using vinyls and CDs. DJs also 'mix' music – this means continuous changes in music without necessarily completing a track. DJs work with MCs (microphone controllers) who entertain the audience while the DJ concentrates on playing the music.

Qualifications and Training

A strong interest and enjoyment of different music styles is a good basis to build from. Some DJs specialise in specific music genres such as soul, funk, hip hop and pop. Most DJs are self-taught and usually begin their career by volunteering their services at clubs, radio stations or within their social circle. It is useful to send a tape demonstrating the aspiring DJ's skills when asking for work.

Personal Qualities

DJs must have a lively personality and a sense of fun, and be able to be creative. They need to have a good knowledge of and genuine interest in music, and be able to interact effectively with an audience.

£ This varies enormously, depending on the hours worked and the venue. Successful DJs are offered lucrative financial deals.

i Local and national radio stations
Clubs and social venues

DISTRICT NURSE

(see also Nurse)

District nurses are employed by NHS Community Trusts. They work closely with GPs, health visitors, practice nurses and other community nurses, providing skilled nursing care for patients and their families in their own homes, in surgeries and in other health and community centres. The district nurse is the leader of the district nursing team, which includes staff nurses, district enrolled nurses and care assistants.

Qualifications and Training

Applicants must be registered general/adult nurses, usually with post-registration experience. Since October 1998, all qualifications have been replaced by the new Specialist Practitioner (District Nursing) qualification, for which courses are available at degree level at institutions of higher education.

Personal Qualities

The district nurse must have good leadership skills, the ability to understand the needs of individuals and families in the community, and the confidence to work independently and to relate well to other members of the primary health care team. As well as the ability to work efficiently and manage their own workload, district nurses need good communication skills and, often, a sense of humour.

£ Dependent upon previous experience, but from £18,156–£21,007; district nurses employed in the London zone or outer London zone receive London weighting.

i NHS Careers, PO Box 376, Bristol BS99 3EY
Careers in Nursing and Related Professions (Kogan Page)

DIVER

Until the mid-1970s, professional divers were mainly employed in ports, harbours and docks by water authorities, and in support of 'wet' civil engineering work. The growth in offshore oil and gas exploration greatly increased the opportunities open to qualified divers. There has recently been a decline in demand in the North

Sea, and now the majority of the work is based in under-developed countries, and in the Far and Middle East. The growth of diving as a popular sport has created a large number of positions for full-time instructors worldwide. Fairly large numbers of divers are employed by the police force and the Royal Navy while a few find employment in salvage work.

Qualifications and Training

Diving is an occupation for the few. It is potentially hazardous and efficient training is absolutely essential to ensure maximum safety. HSE-recognised assessment centres and approved diving schools provide full-time courses of instruction. These are expensive, at around £5,000 for the offshore divers course; courses for inshore work are shorter and less expensive. Applicants must be at least 18 years of age. Clubs and diving schools offer amateur qualifications, which should be recognised by the world federation, the Confédération Mondiale d'Activités Subaquatiques (CMAS). The Royal Navy and the police force give training for their own personnel. In the case of the latter, pupils must have a minimum of two years' experience as a constable. All divers who do paid work must attend and pass the courses approved by the Health and Safety Executive (HSE): scuba, surface supplied, wet belt and closed-bell diving. In addition, other courses are required, including welding, cutting, first aid, medic and underwater tools.

Personal Qualities

Divers must be sound swimmers and physically fit; all professional divers have to pass a full commercial diving medical, which complies with HSE Diving Operations at Work regulations. They must be able to tolerate hard exercise, extreme conditions and recognise and work within their own personal limits. They must be very responsible and willing and able to work as part of a team. Initiative and the ability to sell their own skills to a potential employer are essential.

£ Some openings in water authorities, fish fares, fish capture and civil engineering offer around £15,000. Potential rewards for deep-sea and oil-rig divers are much greater. A recent increase in shallow closed-bell diving has created a limited number of jobs at £50-60,000 per year; the age of offshore senior staff is a concern and there is a demand for younger divers. Sport diving instructors do their work largely for travel and enjoyment reasons, and pay is very low.

i Health and Safety Executive, Row Court, 1 Southwark Bridge, London SE1 9HS; 020 7717 6000
Fort Bovis and Underwater Centre, Plymouth, Devon PL9 OAB
Society for Underwater Technology, 80 Coleman Street, London EC2R 5BJ; 020 7382 2601; fax 020 7382 2684
The Underwater Centre, Fort William, Inverness-shire, Highland PH33 6LZ; 01397 703768
Local police forces
Local Royal Navy Careers Offices
See also ROV Pilot Technician

Doctor of Medicine,* see *Medicine

DOG GROOMER

Dog grooming is a growing industry, with more and more dog owners taking advantage of the services provided by grooming salons. There are over 2,000 grooming salons in the UK, the majority of which are individual premises. Increasing numbers are part of other establishments, including pet shops, garden centres, boarding and breeding kennels. Some mobile groomers visit animals in their own home.

Each breed has different requirements and there are many types of coat, which all require specialist skills and techniques. The work involves bathing, shampooing, drying, clipping, trimming and brushing a variety of long- and short-coated dogs. Specialist procedures include nail clipping, teeth cleaning, ear care and treatments for parasites.

Qualifications and Training

There are three main routes into training: a fee-paying course at a private grooming training centre; learning on the job; or, for 16- and 17-year-olds, a training place as part of a youth training programme. Candidates with at least 18 months' practical dog-grooming experience may enrol for the City and Guilds Dog Grooming Certificate 775. This two-part exam, with a written paper and a practical element, tests candidates' skills on three different types of dog. The 775 indicates to future employers that the groomer has had correct training, and gives customers confidence that the groomer is competent.

The Advanced Grooming Diploma tests the expertise and skill required of the experienced groomer working in a commercial environment. A good working knowledge of the Kennel Club Breed Standards, styles and trimming techniques are required in order to pass all components. The exam consists of a written paper and seven practical modules, which can be taken over a period of time until all seven are complete, working at a timescale to suit the individual.

Personal Qualities

A love of animals is essential, as is a good deal of patience, and a firm but gentle way of handling. Good customer care plays a large part, and a pleasant courteous manner, combined with a neat and tidy appearance, is essential. Dog groomers should be manually dextrous with good hand-eye coordination and an eye for detail. Artistic flair is an advantage.

£ This varies from area to area, and hours and rates of pay are negotiable.

i British Dog Groomers Association, Bedford Business Centre, 170 Mile Road, Bedford MK42 9TW; 01234 273933; fax 01234 273550

Our Dogs, 5 Oxford Road, Station Approach, Manchester M60 1SX; 0161 237 1273; fax 0161 236 5534 (job advertisements, grooming events and certain breed features relevant to grooming)
www.ourdogs.k9.co.uk

Local Jobcentres and Careers Offices

DOMESTIC SERVICE

Although far fewer people are engaged in domestic service today than in the past, there are still some job openings. Posts include butler, cook, housekeeper, maid and, occasionally, footman and valet.

Butlers' duties involve announcing guests, serving drinks and supervising other staff; cooks are responsible for preparing food; housekeepers for the general running of a household, often in the absence of the owner; while maids wait at table, clean and/or look after the lady of the house's clothes.

Some jobs such as buttling can be done on a temporary basis, and agencies exist to provide domestic staff for special occasions.

Qualifications and Training

Formal educational qualifications are not necessary, although a City and Guilds or other catering qualification may be a bonus. Experience and good recommendations are important.

Personal Qualities

Discretion, tact and the ability to put someone else first are important.

£ Salaries vary depending on whether full board and lodging are provided, hours worked and individual employers.

i Local Jobcentres and Careers Offices
The Lady, 39–40 Bedford Street, Strand, London WC2E 9EN; 020 7379 4717 (job advertisements)

DRAMA THERAPIST

The main focus of drama therapy involves working and playing using action methods to facilitate creativity, imagination, learning, insight and growth. It is used in many different settings, including mental health care centres, training centres, education, prison and probation, child care and private practice.

Qualifications and Training

To train as a drama therapist a person usually needs to have a relevant first degree, either in drama, theatre or performing arts, or a nursing qualification. Six UK institutions currently offer postgraduate training courses in drama therapy: University of Hertfordshire, College of Art and Design, St Albans; University College of Ripon and York, St John, York; South Devon College of Arts and Technology, Torquay; Sesame/Central School of Speech and Drama, London; Institute of Dramatherapy at Roehampton, London; and City College Manchester.

Personal Qualities

This is demanding work, which requires awareness, insight, integrity and compassion.

£ Salaries vary according to whether the work is full- or part-time and the type of setting. Many drama therapists work on a freelance basis, or practise drama therapy while employed in some other capacity, perhaps as a teacher, social worker, nurse, occupational therapist, psychiatrist or manager.

i British Association for Drama Therapists, 41 Broomhouse Lane, London SW6 3DP; 020 7731 0160

DRAUGHTSMAN

(see also Architectural Technician, Technical Illustrator)

A draughtsman produces clear, detailed scale drawings of a design concept with the object of showing a craftsman exactly what needs to be done. Draughtsmen, or technicians, as they are often called, are employed in a variety of industries: architecture, building services, cartography, construction engineering, electrical and electronic engineering and surveying.

Qualifications and Training

It is possible to train as a craft apprentice in any field except architecture. GCSEs are not required, but candidates should be able to show mathematical, artistic and mechanical aptitudes, and good use of English. For entry to areas of work other than as a craft apprentice, requirements vary. Some firms will ask for GCSEs and some require two A levels. Training is on the job and by day- and block-release and leads to a City and Guilds qualification or an Edexcel (BTEC) certificate or diploma.

Personal Qualities

Draughtsmen must be accurate and neat in their work and pay great attention to detail.

£ Trainee £8,000–£9,000; fully qualified £15,000+.

i Local Jobcentres and Careers Offices

DRESSER

(see also Broadcasting, Theatre)

Dressers may find employment in theatre, television, films and fashion houses. They prepare and maintain costumes and help the performers and models to dress, especially where quick changes are needed.

Qualifications and Training

No formal qualifications are necessary. Experience, especially in the theatre, is helpful as is sewing ability.

Personal Qualities

Calmness and speed, a soothing and sympathetic nature, discretion and tact are all helpful.

£ Dependent on age, experience and employer, but generally relatively low.

i *The Stage* newspaper, 47 Bermondsey Street, London SE1 3XT; 020 7403 1818 (job advertisements)

DRESSMAKER

(see also Theatre)

Opportunities for dressmakers occur in *couture* houses which make specially designed costumes for a particular collection or customer, in wholesale fashion houses making mass-produced garments, and in theatres both making and adapting costumes. Dressmakers may also be employed by large stores to carry out alterations, or they may be self-employed making clothes either from home or from a workshop. Teachers of dressmaking are employed in schools, colleges and by adult education centres.

Qualifications and Training

No formal qualifications are necessary; but a City and Guilds qualification may be obtained by full-time study at a technical college or by entering a workroom on leaving school and studying on a day-release basis.

Personal Qualities

Dressmakers need to combine artistic and practical skills with an ability to follow instructions and to recognise problems as they arise and make the necessary adaptations. They may have to deal with temperamental designers and their customers.

£ Dependent on experience and practical ability and specialisations, but about £105–£155 a week when qualified.

i Local Jobcentres and Careers Offices

DRIVING EXAMINER

The Driving Examiner must ensure that candidates are competent to drive without endangering other road users, and demonstrating due consideration for other drivers and pedestrians. The Examiner directs learner drivers over an approved route and asks them to carry out various exercises. While doing this, the Examiner must take notes without distracting the candidate's concentration and must make a fair assessment of the learner's ability.

Qualifications and Training

Driving Examiners are required to complete a strict selection process, followed by four weeks' training. They must have detailed knowledge of *The Highway Code* and road and traffic safety problems, some mechanical understanding, and have held positions of responsibility and dealt with the public. Driving Examiners must be over 25 years of age and have had extensive experience of a variety of different vehicle types. Vacancies are advertised both locally and nationally by the Driving Standards Agency. Selection is dependent upon passing a special driving test and interview. For those who are successful, there are continuous checks by a supervising examiner to ensure the maintenance of a high standard.

Personal Qualities

Examiners should be fair, sympathetic, friendly, clearly spoken and have a calm, unflappable nature. The ability to work to a strict timetable is important.

£ Varies according to length of contract and experience.

i Driving Standards Agency, Stanley House, Talbot Street, Nottingham NG1 5GU; 0115 901 2805
www.driving-test.co.uk
Local Jobcentres and Careers Offices

DRIVING INSTRUCTOR

Driving Instructors teach clients how to drive in preparation for all categories of the Driving Standards Agency's theory and practical driving tests. Instructors can also provide post-test training for the Pass Plus scheme as well as prepare clients for advanced driving tests, such as the DIAmond Advanced Motorists test.

The industry is now very much structured to self-employment, with Instructors either having their own business or existing as an independent operation within a franchise agreement.

Qualifications and Training

In order to be allowed by law to accept payment for teaching people to drive, car Driving Instructors must either be registered or licensed by the Registrar of Approved Driving Instructors (ADIs) at the Driving Standards Agency. This requires them to have passed the stringent three-part qualifying test within the space of two years. The ADI exam consists of: a written test, a practical driving test and a practical test of the ability to instruct. Training is available from any of the establishments listed in the Official Register of Driving Instructor Training (ORDIT) which is included in the AD114 starter pack (*see* below). ORDIT establishments are regularly required to satisfy the inspection criteria under the voluntary scheme of minimum required standards set up and agreed by the Driver Training Industry and the Driving Standards Agency.

Personal Qualities

Driving Instructors must have a calm and friendly nature, be very alert and quick to react, and should be clearly spoken and able to express themselves well. Patience, confidence and tact are also important characteristics, as is the willingness to abide by a professional Code of Practice.

£ Typical earnings, after business or franchise fees, will vary widely, depending on tuition hours worked and operating costs. Annual gross income can vary between £8,000 and £20,000.

i Driving Instructors' Association, Safety House, Beddington Farm Road, Croydon CR0 4XZ; 020 8665 5151; fax 020 8665 5565 (*So You Want To Be A Driving Instructor?* starter pack, including information on ORDIT Approved Training Establishments, £3.99, payable to DIA)

Registrar of Approved Driving Instructors, Driving Standards Agency, Stanley House, 56 Talbot Street, Nottingham NG1 5GU; 0115 901 2500; fax 0115 901 2940

Your Road to Becoming an Approved Driving Instructor, AD114 starter pack, including application forms, for £3.00, payable to Driving Standards Agency, from DSA

Local driving schools, Jobcentres and Careers Offices

The Driving Instructor's Handbook (Kogan Page)

The Driving Instructor's Manual (DIA Publishing)

Dry Cleaning Work,* see *Laundry and Dry Cleaning Work

E

Ecologist, see *Conservation (Environmental)*

ECONOMIST

Economists study the use and organisation of the world's resources, and the way in which they are distributed. The field of investigation is very wide, but may include the study of such topics as the reasons for balance of payments crises, the effects of different forms of taxation, international trade or business economics. Economics is not a precise science; it is only possible to forecast degrees of probability of a particular economic model having certain results. Economists are employed in Government, nationalised industries, large industrial and commercial companies, teaching and research, banking and stockbroking, journalism, international organisations and independent consultancies. Their primary task is to give advice on the probable consequences of a course of action; for example, they might advise a company on the effects of a rise in the price of its products. Economists are concerned too with collecting data, preparing reports, and, to an increasing extent, with building complex mathematical models.

Qualifications and Training

A good honours degree in economics, or in one of the specialised branches of the subject, is needed. In addition, many economists take a postgraduate qualification. Some degree courses are mathematically biased, and for these an A level pass in maths is essential. For most other courses, GCSEs in maths or English are required. A levels in arts subjects, such as history and modern languages, are useful.

Personal Qualities

An analytical mind, numeracy and the ability to express oneself clearly, verbally and in writing, are required.

£ £14,000+.

i Institute of Economic Affairs, 2 Lord North Street, London SW1P 3LA; 020 7799 3745

EDUCATION WELFARE OFFICER

(see also Social Work and Social Care – Children and Young People)

The Education Welfare Officer is a social worker, employed by local authorities to liaise between schools and families, and to deal with problems affecting children's behaviour at school. One of the main roles is to ensure regular school attendance, and to deal with persistent cases of truancy. They also work in child guidance clinics.

There are relatively few posts for Education Welfare Officers in Scotland, where the responsibility for school welfare is shared between social work and education departments.

Qualifications and Training

The main professional qualification is the Diploma in Social Work (DipSW), which can be studied part-time while working, or full-time at a college. Entry requirements are five GCSEs including two at A level or five SCEs including three at H grade. Mature entrants may be accepted without these qualifications.

Personal Qualities

Maturity, emotional stability, tact and patience are necessary.

£ £13,581–£19,818.

i Institute of Welfare, Newlands House, 137–139 Hagley Road, Birmingham B16 8UA; 0121 454 8883
homepage.virgin.net/i.w.o/

ELECTRICIAN

Electricians are needed in a number of different areas, and a variety of jobs come under the title of 'electrician'.

Installation
The installation industry has the biggest electrical training scheme in the country. In the main, it comprises thousands of private firms of electrical contractors; some installation apprenticeships are also offered by electricity boards and local councils. The electrical installation industry works on new construction and refurbishment sites and also, on contract, on repair and maintenance work.

Factory Maintenance
Most factories employ maintenance electricians.

Servicing
Service engineers usually concentrate on a particular range of equipment and travel from house to house, or firm to firm. They repair domestic equipment such as televisions, office equipment or electrical equipment in factories.

Manufacturing
Electricians are involved in inspection and testing.

Auto Industry
Auto electricians check, repair and replace the electrical/electronic circuiting and components in all types of motor vehicle.

Theatre Industry
Theatre electricians are responsible for the lighting of theatres: rigging and lights, operating them during performances and dealing with any problems.

Qualifications and Training

At craft level, GCSEs in maths, science and English are helpful. Training is normally by Modern Apprenticeship and lasts three to four years. NVQs are available in Electrical Installation Engineering and Electricity Generation, Supply and Distribution. Technician engineers need four GCSEs or equivalents including maths, a science subject and English. Training takes four years and usually leads to an Edexcel (BTEC)/SVQ certificate.

Installation apprenticeships include City and Guilds qualifications and a comprehensive practical Achievement Measurement Test is also taken. Success in all elements leads to NVQ level 3.

Personal Qualities

Technical aptitude is essential, and service electricians must have the ability to deal with the public. The work can be strenuous and it may be necessary to work from heights. Colour blindness prevents entry to the industry.

£ Low to start with, but upwards of £250 a week when qualified.

i JT Ltd, Stafford House, 120/122 High Street, Orpington, Kent BR6 0JS; 01689 884100; fax 01689 891658
www.jtlimited.co.uk

ENGINEERING

The British engineering industry is a major wealth producer, and almost every other industry depends upon engineering in some way. The Engineering Council gives a simple definition of engineering, saying that it involves 'the application of science and maths to the solving of practical problems and the making of useful things'. The variety of specialisation is described below.

Aeronautical Engineering

Aeronautical engineering is one of the most technically advanced areas of engineering. It is both exciting and rewarding, involving leading-edge technology, variety, skill and innovation. This diversity means that career opportunities can be found across the entire global aerospace spectrum, from research, design, manufacture and maintenance, through to operation and support. Opportunities can be found with many leading aerospace employers such as British Aerospace, Rolls-Royce, GEC-Marconi, Lucas Aerospace, GKN Westland, the Defence & Evaluation Research Agency and the Civil Aviation Authority. Some airline operators and some small and medium employers which supply to the aerospace industry also offer good employment prospects.

Agricultural Engineering
The main fields in which agricultural engineers are involved are: design and production of agricultural machinery; planning, design and construction of farm buildings and associated equipment; field engineering – irrigation, drainage and land resource planning; and service engineering, involving sale, servicing, repairing and installation of farm machinery. They are also involved in forestry engineering, amenity and ecological engineering, and precision farming using satellite positioning systems.

Air Conditioning*, see *Building Services Engineering

Automobile Engineering
When engaged in vehicle manufacture, engineers tend to be qualified at higher technician graduate levels. In motor vehicle servicing, the work involved spans the craft, engineering technician and higher technician grades, with some engineers using their technical base to develop into motor vehicle engineering management. Currently, NVQs in Vehicle Mechanical and Electronic Systems Maintenance and Repair are on offer at levels 2 and 3. Registration through a professional body rests exclusively with the Institute of Road Transport Engineers.

Biochemical Engineering
Involves the application of engineering principles to industrial processing. Biochemical engineers are involved in the research, design, construction and operation of plant used for the processing of biochemicals such as those used in effluent treatment, fermentation and the production of drugs.

Biomedical Engineering
Involves the application of engineering techniques and principles to medicine and biology. Most biomedical engineers are employed in hospitals or by companies manufacturing medical equipment.

Building Services Engineering
Building services engineers are concerned with heating and ventilation, refrigeration, lighting, air conditioning, electrical services, internal water supply, waste disposal, fire protection, lifts, and acoustic and communication systems. The work involves the planning and design of engineering systems, and supervision of

contracts, working in collaboration with architects, surveyors, structural engineers and builders.

Chemical Engineering
Chemical engineers are concerned with large-scale processes, not always in the chemical industry. The term 'process engineering' is often used to describe their work, as they are more interested in the physical factors involved in a process than in the chemical reaction itself. Chemical engineers are employed in the oil, chemical, pharmaceutical, food, brewing and process industries.

Civil Engineering
The profession of civil engineering plays an important part in everyday life. Civil engineers devise, plan and manage development in vital areas – the design and construction of state-of-the-art roads, dams, harbours, railroad systems, bridges and airports. Civil engineers also play an important part in the provision of electricity and water supplies, and in managing traffic and transport. Every project is unique and involves the expertise of a team of people who plan, design, build and maintain these essential assets.

Civil engineering provides a challenging career for men and women, with employment offered by consulting engineers, contractors, local authorities and the armed forces.

Control Engineering
A multi-disciplinary field involving electrical and electronic engineering, maths, computer science, instrument and mechanical engineering. Specialisation in control engineering often follows the study of another branch of engineering.

Drainage Engineering,* see *Building Services Engineering, Civil Engineering, Water Engineering

Electrical and Electronic Engineering
The technology of electrical engineering deals with heavy current, while electronic engineering deals with light current. Applications of heavy current include electrical machinery of all kinds, generating stations and distribution systems. Light current is used for such products as transistors, microprocessors and telecommunications equipment. The two fields are often interdependent and training is closely related. Electronics is a rapidly developing field, and offers

excellent opportunities, as do the allied disciplines of computer and software engineering.

NVQs will be available at levels 1 to 5. The Institution of Electrical Engineers (IEE) is involved with the development of level 5 (equivalent to Chartered Engineer) and the Institution of Electronics and Electrical Incorporated Engineers with levels 4 and 3.

Energy Engineering

This branch of engineering is concerned with the use, production, distribution, conversion and conservation of energy, with due regard to the environment. Energy engineers are employed across the whole spectrum of industry, as energy management and control are essential elements in containing costs, reducing pollution and addressing environmental concerns. The majority of openings are in major fuel industries (including renewables), consultancy and research.

Environmental Engineering, see *Building Services Engineering*

Fire Engineering

This involves the application of engineering principles to the assessment, prevention and inhibition of fire risk within buildings, manufacturing plant and industrial processes. The various stages include the use of mathematical principles in the assessment of fire risk, the application of scientific principles to fire safety practices and the use of management techniques to the inhibition and prevention of the onset and spread of fire.

Fire engineers are employed in the fire services, architectural and building design, project management, insurance assessment, industrial processing, the aircraft industry, environmental health and any area of safety where the possibility of fire or combustion represents a hazard.

Flight Engineer, see *Civil Aviation*

Gas Engineering

Gas engineering involves specialisation in the use, transmission and distribution of gas (natural or manufactured), or in the production of gas, or in related fields such as exploration.

Heating and Ventilation Engineering,* see *Building Services Engineering

Highway Engineering,* see *Transport Engineering

Instrument Engineering
Instrument engineers are concerned with the measurement of pressure, temperature, and so on, designing, installing and maintaining instrument systems. *See also* Control Engineering.

Manufacturing Systems Engineering
This new branch of engineering deals with the skills required to operate new manufacturing systems: computerised production, computer-controlled assembly, robotic systems and flexible manufacturing systems.

Marine Engineering
This discipline is related to offshore engineering under the general title of 'maritime engineering', which involves engineering systems and equipment in a maritime environment. Both marine and offshore engineers are involved in design, research, consultancy, survey, manufacture, installation and maintenance activities, the former with vessels of all sizes and types, the latter with offshore platforms, sub-sea installations and under-sea vehicles. Employment opportunities exist within firms offering design and research activities, engine- and shipbuilding firms, classification societies, Government bodies, the Merchant Navy and the Royal Navy.

Mechanical Engineering
Mechanical engineering is the biggest branch of the engineering industry. It involves the skills of designing, developing, producing, installing and operating machinery and mechanical products of many types. The field is enormous in scope, and most engineers specialise in a particular area. Other branches of engineering, such as electrical and civil engineering, overlap with mechanical engineering to a certain extent.

Mechanical engineers are employed in almost every sector of industry. Some of the largest areas of employment are machine tools, railway engineering, aerospace and the automobile industry. NVQs will be available, levels 1 to 5, in the future. The Institution of Mechanical Engineers (IMechE) is involved with the development of level 4 (equivalent to Incorporated Engineer) and level 5 (Chartered Engineer).

Mining Engineering
In Britain, most mining engineers are employed by companies in mining areas, working for consultants who monitor mining activity and subsidence. They need some knowledge of related disciplines such as mechanical, electrical and civil engineering, and to understand geology and surveying in relation to mining. The majority of openings in metal mining are overseas.

Municipal Engineering
Municipal engineering is the application of civil engineering to the public service. Municipal engineers are employed by local authorities or other public bodies. They work on a wide range of projects concerned with public works, and in such fields as traffic engineering, environment, land reclamation, marine works (harbours and jetties), and building and infrastructure maintenance.

Nuclear Engineering
Nuclear engineering involves the applications of nuclear energy and associated research and development. The work of designing and constructing nuclear reactors and the management of nuclear power stations through waste management and storage and decommissioning of plant, is carried out by nuclear engineers.

Offshore Engineering
Offshore engineers are concerned with the construction and operation of drilling platforms and wellheads, and other engineering problems related to the exploitation of offshore oil and gas.

Petroleum Engineering
Petroleum engineers are concerned with exploration and drilling for oil. They obtain and interpret information – for example, the quantities and quality of oil discovered.

Production Engineering
Production engineers develop and improve manufacturing techniques. They are responsible for designing production systems to ensure that products can be manufactured to the specified design, in the right quantities, at the right price and by the required date. Their work overlaps with production management.

Recording Engineering
Recording engineering is a specialised branch of electronic/radio engineering. Recording engineers are mainly employed by broadcasting authorities and recording studios, and vacancies are limited. *See also* Broadcasting.

Refrigeration Engineering,* see *Building Services Engineering

Structural Engineering
Structural engineers are concerned with the design and maintenance of the framework and fabric of large structures such as bridges, motorways and office blocks.

Transport Engineering
Transport (or traffic) engineers are concerned with planning the best use of roads and other traffic facilities, and work mainly with road traffic. Transportation planners, who are not necessarily engineers, are concerned with the provision of all types of transport.

Water Engineering
Water engineers mostly work for water boards and river authorities, ensuring the supply of fresh water, and dealing with the reclamation and disposal of water which has been used.

Qualifications and Training

Professional qualifications are important throughout the industry as they are an independent review by peers to confirm both technical and managerial competence and the professional experience of individuals. In civil engineering, the Institution of Civil Engineers sets standards for awarding its own professional qualifications. There are three types of professional qualification: Technician Member (TMICE), Associate Member (AMICE) and Member (MICE). Individuals achieving these qualifications are eligible for registration with the Engineering Council (a national body responsible for the Register of Engineers across all disciplines), as Engineering Technicians (EngTech), Incorporated Engineers (IEng) or Chartered Engineers (CEng).

There are five main grades of employment in the engineering industry, as follows.

1 Graduate and Chartered Engineers

Graduate and Chartered Engineers analyse and solve engineering problems. Their work is rarely routine, and they must constantly keep up with technological advances and developments. Their main activities are research, design and development, manufacture, production planning and control, commissioning equipment and technical sales. Two or three A levels, including maths and a science (generally chemistry or physics), and four GCSE/SCE passes (or equivalent) are the usual entry requirements. An Edexcel (BTEC) certificate or diploma in appropriate subjects is also acceptable. Entry is normally by means of an accredited degree course (full time or sandwich). In addition to an accredited degree, a period of industrial training is necessary together with a period of working experience at a suitable level of responsibility, before qualification as a chartered engineer.

It is still possible to qualify as a Chartered Engineer without taking a degree, by taking the professional examinations of the Engineering Council. Chartered Civil Engineers, however, must have an accredited degree in either civil or general engineering, and must also complete the Professional Qualification Scheme of the Institution of Civil Engineers. This involves a period of approved practical training and examinations.

2 Incorporated Engineers

The work of an Incorporated Engineer overlaps with that of an Engineering Technician (*see* below), but is at a more senior level, working in the areas of design, manufacturing, commerce and quality control. An Incorporated Engineer might, for example, lead a team of Technicians. The range of technical knowledge required is broader than that of a Technician. Education is by means of a Edexcel (BTEC) higher award course. Five years' training and experience in the industry is needed before registering with the Engineering Council as an Incorporated Engineer. It is possible to proceed to an Edexcel (BTEC) higher award after taking an Edexcel (BTEC) national certificate or diploma, in which case GCSE passes may not be required.

3 Engineering Technicians

Engineering Technicians usually have less responsibility than Incorporated Engineers, but their work is broadly similar. Many employers require four GCSE/SCE passes (or equivalent), including maths, science and English. Training is by means of an apprenticeship scheme, with release for a part-time or full-time course leading to an Edexcel (BTEC) national certificate or a GNVQ Advanced qualification.

4 Craft Workers
Craft Workers specialise in a particular practical skill, such as tool making or welding. They must be able to interpret engineering drawings, and to work with a minimum of supervision. Entry is normally at 16 or 17, to an apprenticeship lasting three to four years. GCSE/SCE passes in maths, science and English are an advantage, although not absolutely essential. On-the-job training, together with day or block release, leads to NVQs awarded by the City and Guilds and the Engineering Industry Training Board. With very good exam results, transfer to Technician courses is possible.

5 Operators
Operators are employed in a wide range of jobs, and make up about a third of the engineering industry's labour force. Their work is often simple and routine, but in some cases they may require some skill or skills similar to those of craft workers.

No specific academic requirements are needed, but aptitude in English and arithmetic and knowledge of metalwork or technical drawing are useful. Operators may work towards NVQs at an appropriate level.

Aeronautical Engineering
There are four main routes to registration as an Incorporated Engineer in aeronautical engineering: the Standard Route, Registration for Licence Holders, the Mature Candidate Route and the Mature Servicemen's Route. Details are available from The Royal Aeronautical Society (address below).

Personal Qualities

Graduate and Chartered Engineers need academic ability, an imaginative and problem-solving approach and social and communication skills. Incorporated Engineers and Engineering Technicians should have reasoning ability, numeracy and the ability to communicate. Craft Workers, as well as manual dexterity, need basic mathematical ability, patience and self-discipline. Operators should show reliability, patience and the ability to work with others.

£ Newly qualified graduate engineers start at £14,000+.

i The Chartered Institution of Building Services Engineers, Delta House, 222 Balham High Road, London SW12 9BS; 020 8675 5211

The Engineering Council, 10 Maltravers Street, London WC2R 3ER; 020 7240 7891

The Institute of Energy, 18 Devonshire Street, London W1N 2AU; 020 7580 7124

The Institute of Marine Engineers, The Memorial Building, 76 Mark Lane, London EC3R 7JN; 020 7481 8493 www.imare.org.uk

The Institute of Measurement and Control, 87 Gower Street, London WC1E 6AA; 020 7387 4949

The Institute of Road Transport Engineers, 22 Greencoat Place, London SW1P 1PR; 020 7630 1111

The Institution of Agricultural Engineers, West End Road, Silsoe, Bedford MK45 4DU; 01525 861096 www.iagre.demon.co.uk

The Institution of Chemical Engineers, 165–171 Railway Terrace, Rugby CV21 3HQ; 01788 578214 Www.icheme.org.uk

The Institution of Civil Engineers (Careers Department), 1 Great George Street, Westminster, London SWIP 3AA; 020 7665 2106; fax 020 7233 0515; e-mail *careers@ice.org.uk* www.ice.org.uk

The Institution of Electrical Engineers (Educational Activities), Michael Faraday House, Six Hills Way, Stevenage, Herts SG1 2AY; 01438 313311

The Institution of Electronics and Electrical Incorporated Engineers, Savoy Hill House, Savoy Hill, London WC2R 0BS; 020 7836 3357

The Institution of Fire Engineers, 148 New Walk, Leicester LE1 7QB; 0116 2553654

The Institution of Gas Engineers, 21 Portland Place, London W1N 3AF; 020 7636 6603

The Institution of Highway Incorporated Engineers, 20 Queensbury Place, London SW7 2DR; 020 7823 9093 www.ihie.org.uk

The Institution of Mechanical Engineers, 1 Birdcage Walk, London SW1H 9JJ; 020 7222 7899

The Institution of Mechanical Incorporated Engineers, 3 Birdcage Walk, London SW1H 9JH; 020 7799 1808

The Institution of Mining and Metallurgy Engineers, Danum House, South Parade, Doncaster DN1 2DY; 01302 320486 www.imm.org.uk

The Institution of Nuclear Engineers, 1 Penerley Road, London SE6 2LQ; 020 8698 1500; e-mail *inuce@lineone.net*

The Institution of Structural Engineers, 11 Upper Belgrave Street, London SW1X 8BH; 020 7235 4535

The Royal Aeronautical Society, 4 Hamilton Place, London W1V 0BQ; 020 7499 3515

The Royal Institution of Naval Architects, 10 Upper Belgrave Street, London SW1X 8BQ; 020 7235 4622

THE ENVIRONMENT AGENCY

The Environment Agency and British Waterways are the main employers in the area of environmental issues. Local authorities, trusts and private companies are also concerned with waterways. The work is concerned with the organisation, maintenance and running of Britain's canals, rivers, lakes and reservoirs for recreational and commercial purposes.

British Waterways manages and cares for over 2,000 miles of canals and rivers and employs a wide range of professional and skilled staff in a variety of jobs at a number of locations. It employs staff in a wide range of disciplines including engineering, finance, marketing, conservation, ecology and water management, as well as support staff. Posts are advertised either in the national media or appropriate professional journals or locally, depending on the post.

Qualifications and Training

British Waterways employs both qualified staff and staff for posts offering training, but does not run any formal training courses. Entry requirements vary from no formal academic or vocational qualifications to a degree and professional qualifications.

Personal Qualities

The specific needs of a post mean that the qualities required will vary but a commitment to working in a team is essential. For many posts, a preference for working outdoors is desirable.

£ Salaries vary according to each post and the qualifications and experience of the applicant.

i British Waterways, Willow Grange, Church Road, Watford WD1 3QA; 01923 226422
www.britishwaterways.co.uk
The Environment Agency, Coverdale House, Aviator Court, Clifton Moor, York YO3 4UZ; 01904 692296

ENVIRONMENTAL HEALTH OFFICER

Environmental Health Officers are enforcers, educators and advisers. They are employed in both the public and private sectors, and their aim is to protect the public from environmental health risks. Their responsibilities include pollution control and environmental protection, the inspection of food and food premises, health and safety in workplaces and in the leisure industry, and the control of housing standards, particularly in the private rented sector. Much of their time is spent out of the office, dealing with the public and visiting premises of all types.

Qualifications and Training

Training in England, Wales and Northern Ireland involves a four-year sandwich course leading to a degree in environmental health, or a two-year postgraduate sandwich course, for those with a good honours degree in a natural science. The course must be accredited by the Chartered Institution of Environmental Health (CIEH). Degree entry qualifications are a matter for the college concerned.

In Scotland, candidates for the professional qualification (Diploma in Environmental Health, awarded by REHIS) must hold an honours degree in environmental health. Applicants for the four-year degree course offered by the University of Strathclyde must have four H grade passes (B level) in maths, chemistry, biology or physics and one other subject. Before being awarded the diploma, candidates must have undergone a minimum of 48 weeks' training with a local authority.

Personal Qualities

These should include social responsibility, tact, integrity, an enquiring mind and good communication skills.

£ Trainee grade £10,000+, qualified officers £16,000–£18,000.

i The Chartered Institution of Environmental Health, 15 Hatfields, London SE1 8DJ; 020 7928 6006
The Royal Environmental Health Institute of Scotland, 3 Manor Place, Edinburgh EH3 7DH; 0131 225 6999

ESTATE AGENT

Estate agents are responsible for the sale, letting and management of any kind of property – factories, shops, offices and farms as well as houses. They also, in many cases, deal with valuation and auctioneering, and often they are qualified surveyors. Large firms may employ specialists to deal with surveying, auctioneering and valuing, and sales staff as property negotiators. Smaller firms may consist of just one or two agents, carrying out some or all of the various functions.

Qualifications and Training

The principal professional bodies are the National Association of Estate Agents (NAEA), The Royal Institution of Chartered Surveyors (RICS) and the Incorporated Society of Valuers and Auctioneers (ISVA). Minimum entry requirements for the RICS are three GCSEs and two A levels, and for the ISVA, five GCSEs to include English and maths. Full- or part-time training courses are available, and practical experience is required before qualification. NVQs in Residential Estate Agency and Lettings and Management are available through the NAEA's National Assessment Centre. The NAEA also offers examination-based, nationally recognised qualifications.

Professional qualifications are an asset, but not essential: anyone can set up in business as an estate agent unless he has been forbidden to do so by the Director of Fair Trading, or is bankrupt, and established firms take on unqualified staff for property negotiation.

Personal Qualities

For most people the purchase or sale of a house is the biggest financial transaction they will ever make, and there are bound to be attendant worries and problems. Estate agents must be able to deal with their clients' problems sympathetically, but in a businesslike way. They should be numerate and able to express themselves well, verbally and in writing.

£ £5,000 upwards for a school leaver with A levels, graduates £11,000+. Firms of estate agents charge a commission for selling or letting a property; the rate for a sale is usually 1½ to 2 per cent of the selling price.

i ISVA (Incorporated Society of Valuers and Auctioneers), 3 Cadogan Gate, London SW1X 0AS; 020 7235 2282

The National Association of Estate Agents, Arbon House, 21 Jury Street, Warwick CV34 4EH; 01926 496800 www.naea.co.uk

The Royal Institution of Chartered Surveyors, Surveyor Court, Westwood Way, Coventry, West Midlands CV4 8JE; 024 7669 4757

Estate Manager*, see *Land Agent

EVENTS OFFICER

Events officers generally work for a place visited by the public such as a national park or a stately home. They may also be appointed on a temporary basis to cover a festival lasting one or two weeks only.

Events officers are responsible for organising long-standing events such as a series of waymarked walks, and also extra activities such as a music festival or summer holiday entertainment for children. If appropriate, the events officer will be in contact with the local education department to encourage school visits.

Events officers working for a large concern will coordinate their work with other members of staff such as the information officer and press officer.

Qualifications and Training

Events officers do not necessarily need formal qualifications but a background in marketing and experience at promoting events and campaigns is useful. A knowledge of simple financial planning is looked for and, often, experience in preparing material for print. The ability to drive is essential.

Personal Qualities

Events officers should be energetic, sociable and adaptable, able to talk to a variety of people, have the ability to think up new ideas and have organisational skills.

£ £12,500–£13,500.

i Jobs advertised in the Monday edition of *The Guardian*

EXHIBITION ORGANISER

Exhibition organisers usually work for specialist companies. They plan and coordinate exhibitions, negotiating with all those concerned – managers of the exhibition, exhibitors, stand suppliers, and designers and caterers. With overseas exhibitions, Government departments are often involved.

Qualifications and Training

Training is usually on the job and graduates or those with HNDs in business or marketing are preferred. CAM or Institute of Marketing qualifications are a useful asset. NVQs are to be introduced. Leeds Metropolitan University has recently begun to offer a BA/BA (Hons) course in events management.

Personal Qualities

Applicants should be good at dealing with people and at administration with the ability to keep a large amount of information at their fingertips. Physical and mental stamina is essential.

£ £12,000–£16,000.

i Association of Exhibition Organisers, 113 High Street, Berkhamsted, Herts HP4 2DJ; 01442 873331; fax 01442 875551 www.aeo.org.uk

Leeds Metropolitan University; 0113 283 2600

F

FACTORY WORKER

Factories employ people in three different areas: production, research and development and administration. In production, depending on the product being made and the processes involved, varying proportions of skilled, semi-skilled and unskilled workers may be employed.

Skilled craftsmen operate sophisticated machines such as lathes and precision grinders; they may be welders, sheet metal workers, tool makers or fitters responsible for the assembly of precision engines and machines. Tool setters may 'set' assembly lines ready for operation by semi-skilled workers who feed in materials and semi-finished components and who ensure that the production process runs as smoothly as possible.

Unskilled labourers are mainly employed to fetch, carry and clean. There are many other jobs related to the production process such as store keeping, purchasing, tool-room maintenance and repair, transportation and quality control. Prospects for promotion are often good in factories and Government legislation ensures that conditions of working and engagement are fair.

In research and development, opportunities exist for scientists, engineers, technicians, designers and draughtsmen, and for general office workers; financial, marketing and sales staff are employed in administration. The functions carried out in these two areas are similar to those performed in other job areas and individual entries should be referred to for further details.

Qualifications and Training

To work in a factory as an unskilled or semi-skilled worker no formal qualifications are required. Training is given on the job and may vary in length from one hour to weeks or months, depending on the type of work.

Those wishing to follow a career as a skilled craftsman must follow a three- to four-year apprenticeship scheme starting at the age of 16 or 17; a minimum qualification of two or three GCSE grades D to E passes (or equivalent) in maths and science will probably be required, and other useful subjects are technical and engineering drawing, metalwork, woodwork and English. Apprenticeships, when available, take the form of training at work with day release to attend colleges and study for City and Guilds or other craft certificates.

Personal Qualities

Craftsmen must have a sound understanding of machinery, manual dexterity, a good eye for shape, sound eyesight, patience and concentration. Semi-skilled workers, especially on production lines, must be able to cope with repetitive work and to work quickly. All factory workers must be safety-conscious and able to tolerate dirt and noise.

£ Dependent upon industry. £70+ a week at 16 rising to over £200 is average, and this may be helped by incentives, bonus schemes and shift allowances.

i Local Jobcentres and Careers Offices

FARMING

In recent years, economic conditions and increasing mechanisation have resulted in larger farms and a tendency towards greater specialisation. Mixed farms are now in a minority and most farmers choose to specialise in one or two areas of production. The most common of these are milk, cereals, poultry, sheep, pigs or beef. In order to make a farm profitable, the modern farmer needs a thorough working knowledge of the type of farming to be undertaken, an understanding of general agricultural science, years of practical experience and an aptitude for farming and farm management.

Opportunities are few, since it is now very expensive to buy land and equip even the smallest farm. While most of today's farmers start with smallholdings, land prices have now made the chances of a beginner becoming a tenant farmer almost impossible.

Farm Manager

Farm managers are employed by the landowner, and are responsible in the same way as farmers for all aspects of the day-to-day working of the farm. They must plan ahead, organise the staff and work schedules, decide which crops to plant or which animals to rear and keep a check on buildings and machinery. In addition, they must deal with the office work and accounts.

Farm Worker

Specialisation and large-scale farming have led to a fall in demand for the farm worker who can turn his hand to anything. There is now a need for highly skilled personnel and new entrants should aim at becoming skilled in a special area such as animal husbandry, mechanics or food, flower or fruit production.

Qualifications and Training

There are a number of possible qualifications related to farming, including a degree in agriculture or agricultural science, or a national diploma in general agriculture. Farm workers may work towards the Preliminary Certificate in Agriculture offered by the National Council for Vocational Qualifications. Various NVQ awards are available at different levels, such as Crop and Livestock Production, levels 1, 2 and 3.

£ A farm manager's salary may start at £12,000+ rising, with experience, to £16,000–£20,000. Rent-free accommodation and a vehicle may be provided, and the manager may also be part of a profit-sharing scheme. Farm workers receive from about £80 per week at 16 to £145 at 20, with additional payments for specific skills or NVQ awards.

i Careers Education and Training Advice Centre, Warwickshire County Council, 22 Northgate Street, Warwick CV34 4SK; 01926 410410

FASHION

(see also Clothing Industry)

Clothing is one of the UK's largest manufacturing industries and employs over 175,000 individuals. The fashion industry covers all aspects of clothing and accessories for men, women and children and falls into three main sectors: *haute couture* houses, where original model garments are made for individual customers; wholesale *couture*, where trends set by the *haute couture* houses are closely followed, and limited numbers of model garments in stock sizes are made for retail; and wholesale manufacture, which occupies the largest sector of the fashion industry. Here, the latest trends are adapted to styles that are attractive to the main market, and mass produced at acceptable prices.

Designer

Designers do more than produce stylish sketches. Their work will, depending on the size and organisation of the particular establishment, include a wide variety of tasks. The work of the *haute couture* designer is both highly creative and intricate. Unfortunately, there is little scope for young designers or assistants as many houses are designer owned; they are nevertheless an excellent training ground for future designers willing to work as sketchers, stylists, fitters, hands, and so on. In wholesale *couture*, designers produce original garments, but they generally follow the instructions of an employer as far as style and cost are concerned.

The wholesale manufacture designer must be able to predict future trends, combine this with the firm's own 'brand image', match it to available fabrics and produce a garment which can be produced economically and will appeal to its particular section of the market. When sketches have been drawn, it is necessary to produce working drawings and translate the drawings into flat patterns, so that sample garments can be made to show to retail buyers (*see* Buyer) and estimates can be made about the garment costs in fabric and manufacturing time.

Pattern Cutter/Grader

Pattern cutters make the patterns that enable a designer's sketch to be made into a garment. Pattern graders work from a pattern representing a basic size and create the patterns needed for a range of sizes. Jobs vary from company to company. The two ways of making patterns are by flat pattern cutting, when the cutter works from the designer's sketches or working drawings and makes a pattern for each part of a garment, or by modelling on to a stand, when the cutter works from the designer's drawings and drapes and pins fabric on to a dummy and fits it in accordance with the drawings. Computers are increasingly used to help in designing garments, creating patterns and for pattern grading.

Cutter/Spreader
The cutter or spreader checks that the cloth is smooth and free of wrinkles and flaws, and that patterns or other features will match when it is sewn together. The laying-up process is done manually by two people or by machine. Once it is ready, the fabric can be cut using a number of methods. Hand cutting is done using shears, an electric knife or a vertical band knife. Die-cutting is done by machine. Computer-controlled cutting is also being introduced and these machines are capable of cutting up to 250 inches per minute, depending on the depth of the lay. Laser cutting is when computer images are used to operate the laser cutter with great accuracy.

Qualifications and Training

Pattern Cutter/Grader
A Modern Apprenticeship in product development leading to at least an NVQ level 3 is one route of entry. Most employers are looking for GCSEs at grade C and above for entry on to a Modern Apprenticeship programme. A range of courses validated by City and Guilds and Edexcel (BTEC) are also an excellent entry point for the clothing industry. Degrees in clothing studies are also offered at a number of universities.

Cutter/Spreader
Training is largely given on the job. Some employers offer the HEADstart training programme with the Kingscourt training organization (details from local Careers Offices). This leads to an NVQ in Manufacturing Sewn Products at level 2.

Personal Qualities

Pattern cutters/graders should have an interest in fashion and an appreciation of what their designers are aiming for. Numerical ability is essential for measurement and calculation. Some technical drawing skills and an aptitude for working on computers are also useful.

Spreaders/cutters need to be physically fit. They must have good eyesight and perfect colour vision. Some numerical ability is required.

£ For a pattern cutter/grader, earnings vary tremendously, from £6,000–£20,000, depending largely on qualifications and experience. Experienced cutters/spreaders are paid according to their skill and the level of responsibility in their job.

i CAPTIB Trust, 80 Richardson Lane, Pudsey, Leeds LS28 6BN; 0113 227 3345 ('Qualifications for Industry') www.careers-in-clothing.co.uk

Textile Institute, 10 Blackfriars Street, Manchester, M3 5DR; 0161 834 8457 (professional membership organisation; list of UK universities offering textile courses, ring for cost)

FILM PRODUCTION

(see also Broadcasting)

Opportunities to work in film production arise in television, film companies and advertising. Most people who work in this area are self-employed freelancers. Film production involves both studio and location work. Jobs within film production are much sought after, vacancies are few and competition is consequently fierce. Individuals who are serious about working in this area will need to develop personal marketing skills in addition to their creative craft skills.

Animation

Animation involves the design, creation and operation of animated production and effects. It may be traditional 'cell' animation, computer imagery or, increasingly, a combination of both forms.

Announcers

Announcers work to detailed and carefully timed scripts, communicating information to the viewer from a soundproof 'behind the scenes' office. They sometimes write or adapt their own material, and need to be able to work on their own.

Archivists/Librarians

Archivists and librarians collect, collate, preserve and make available collections of recorded visual, sound, written and other materials for use by various productions. Archives are valuable business resources and some archivists are now involved in selling and marketing materials to likely purchasers.

Art and Design

The art and design function is to create a visual effect to meet the needs of the production, creating manual or computer-generated graphics.

Costume/Wardrobe

The wardrobe department interprets the production requirements in terms of costumes and accessories to ensure historical accuracy and an accurate portrayal of the style and ethos of the period.

Direction

The Director is responsible for achieving the creative, visual and auditory effect of a production and, equally importantly, motivating a team.

Engineering

Engineers provide a design, maintenance and installation service to the production site and equipment. Research specialists are usually employed by the equipment manufacturers or design consultancies.

Film, Video and Audio Tape Editing

Raw tape or film is shaped to interpret the requirements of the Director, either by physical cutting (film) or by selecting sequences and re-recording on to a master tape using sophisticated computer equipment.

IT Specialists

IT specialists support many aspects of broadcasting, film and video, either within the companies or as consultants, providing and maintaining relevant systems and software.

Journalists

Generate and report on local, national or international stories, and research relevant background information. BI-media (radio and TV) contracts are increasing. Some journalists present their own work.

Laboratory

Lab technicians develop and process film, duplicate and check video tapes, ensuring high technical quality.

Lighting
Lighting specialists ensure that the stage or set is correctly lit to meet the needs of the production.

Make-up and Hairdressing
Make-up and hairdressing professionals interpret the requirements of the production and research to ensure accurate representation of the historical or design concept. They maintain a continuity of approach throughout the production in studio or on location.

Management
Directs and coordinates the different elements of the industry to ensure their efficient function – ranging from commissioning a production to negotiating international rights. Specialists work in a full range of business areas.

Marketing and Sales
Marketing and sales staff work in an international marketplace to raise revenue for broadcasters or film makers. Airtime is sold, sponsorship and co-production rights are negotiated and spin-off products, such as books, toys, videos, are developed.

Producers
Producers perform a variety of management and operational roles to bring together the many elements of a production either, in studio or on location. Often responsible both for the initial concept and raising the essential finance, they are the team leaders.

Production Assistants
Production Assistants provide high-quality administrative and secretarial support to the Producer and Director at every stage of production, coordinating all activities and preparing schedules and scripts.

Production Management
Production Managers organise all essential support facilities for the team, from accommodation and transport to on-set catering. They will also roster crews and arrange payments.

Production Operatives
Perform the operational duties of the production such as vision mixing and autocue operations.

Recording Still and Moving Images (Camerawork)
Workers in this area operate and assist with still, film and video cameras to record images as directed, using different techniques.

Researchers
Support the producer, helping to turn ideas into reality – providing and following up ideas, contacting and interviewing people, acquiring relevant factual material, and writing briefings for presenters.

Runners/Gofers
The traditional entry-level job for the industry. Bright, highly motivated – often highly qualified – people act as general assistants, taking messages, making deliveries, being indispensable...and learning the basics of the commercial business.

Setcraft/Props
People working in this area construct the scenery, sets and backdrops to meet the production brief reflecting both historical accuracy and required design and style. They also maintain sets during a production, and operate any mechanical features as directed. Props (hired or made) are used to dress the set.

Sound
Sound craftspeople interpret requirements of a production in terms of sound collection. During post-production they may be involved in recording, editing and dubbing, using a range of sophisticated equipment.

Special Effects
Special effects designers create and operate effects for a production, within technical limitations and budget, and operate the necessary machines.

Support Staff
Many people working in film, video, television and radio fulfil essential support roles, including administration, catering, driving, cleaning.

Transmission
Technicians and engineers work to exhibit the production in a high-quality form, which can involve projecting images or

operating transmission equipment linking electronic signals from the studios to a transmitter.

Writers
Writers work to produce or edit scripts for a variety of radio, TV, video or film productions.

Qualifications and Training

BECTU (Broadcasting Entertainment, Cinematograph and Theatre Union) is working with Skillset, the national training organisation, in developing related vocational qualifications to create clearer progression from college and university courses into the industry. The National Film and Television School runs a three-year course in film making, taking about 25 students each year, none of whom is a complete beginner. Most are graduates and all will have shown some previous ability in either writing, direction, production or photography. Other institutions offering previously accredited courses are the London International Film School, the University of Westminster, the West Surrey College of Art and Design, Bristol University's Film and Television Department, the London College of Printing and Distributive Trades, and Bournemouth and Poole College of Art and Design. New-entrant training is offered by FT2; competition for places is fierce. A database of courses in maintained by the BFI and Skillset.

Camera operators train differently in different sectors of the industry. Skillset has established NVQ levels 2-4 within the industry. Modern Apprenticeships and National Traineeships are also available in certain categories. A good general level of education is required and some operators start off as film loaders or clapper-board operators. One way into continuity work is via shorthand typing; a general education to GCSE standard is required and a foreign language would be helpful.

Personal Qualities

In film work it is important to combine artistic ability with technical expertise, to pay attention to detail, to have patience, good powers of concentration and an interest in colour and design. An even-tempered, logical and visually imaginative approach is necessary. It is important to keep in touch with what is happening in the industry, and to be able to create a network of friends and contacts. Absolute reliability is essential, especially at the start of a career.

£ Salaries are too varied to give an appropriate indication. Many people negotiate their own salary, and skill-shortage areas, such as set crafts, can be very well paid.

i Broadcasting Entertainment, Cinematograph and Theatre Union (BECTU), 111 Wardour Street, London W1V 4AY; 020 7437 8506

British Film Institute, 21 Stephen Street, London W1P 2LN; 020 7255 1444
www.bfi.org.uk

The Moving Image Society, M6–14 Victoria House, Vernon Place, London WC1B 4DF; 020 7242 8400
www.bksts.com

FT2 (Film and Television Freelance Training), Fourth Floor, Warwick House, 9 Warwick Street, London W1R 5RA; 020 7734 5141

Skillset, National Training Organisation for Broadcast, Film, Video and Multimedia, 2nd Floor, 91–101 Oxford Street, London W1R 1RA; 020 7534 5300; fax 020 7534 5333
www.skillset.org.uk

Careers in Film and Video (Kogan Page)

Great Careers in Film, Video and Photography (Kogan Page)

FIRE SERVICE

Firefighters attend fires and numerous other emergencies, often requiring new techniques, to save life and property. They give a 24-hour service; typical emergencies other than fires include tanker spillages, car, train and aeroplane crashes, flooding and building collapse, and explosions where people and animals may have to be rescued. Some firefighters specialise in particular areas such as training or communications, and the Fire Service also provides advice on fire protection and prevention by inspecting existing properties and studying proposals for new buildings. In addition they must enforce legal regulations to reduce risks of injury by fire such as the provision of secure escape routes.

The Fire Service is administered by local authorities in the UK. The Ministry of Defence, Army, Royal Air Force, Royal Navy and the British Airports Authority all have their own brigades.

Qualifications and Training

Firefighters should have a good general level of secondary education. Qualifications in English, maths and science are useful but not essential. The minimum age is 18, although it is possible to join the service as a junior at 16. There are strict requirements for entrants concerning physical fitness, hearing and physique. Initially, training takes place in a training school and is followed by regular courses of instruction for special situations and the use of specialist equipment.

Personal Qualities

Members of the Fire Service must be practical, courageous, able to use their own initiative, prepared to work shifts and work as part of a team. Some scientific understanding is helpful when dealing with dangerous chemicals.

£ £15,522 rising to £19,725 after five years' service. Leading firefighters earn £21,600–£21,993 and Sub-Officers £21,660–£23,364. Various allowances increase these basic wage figures, and London firefighters are paid London weighting.

i BAA Plc, Jubilee House, Furlong Way, North Terminal, Gatwick Airport, Gatwick, West Sussex RH6 0JN; 01293 595323

Home Office, Fire Policy Unit, Horseferry House, Dean Ryle Street, London SW1P 2AW; 020 7217 8752 www.homeoffice.gov.uk/fssu

The Secretary, The Emergency Fire Services Lead Body, Room 662, Horseferry House, Dean Ryle Street, London SW1P 2AW

The Scottish Office Home and Health Department, Fire Service and Emergency Planning Division, St Andrew's House, Edinburgh EH1 3DG; 0131 244 2170

Local Chief Fire Officer/Firemaster, Fire Brigade Headquarters (address in local phone book)

Ministry of Defence (contact the nearest Ministry of Defence establishment with a fire service)

FISHERMAN

Fishermen perform many tasks: they cast out and haul in the nets when they are full; gut, clean and stow away the catch; mend nets;

maintain the tackle; and wash down the decks. Fishermen may work on deep-sea trawlers in the North Sea or on 'factory' stern vessels which prepare and deep-freeze the catches of cod, haddock, plaice, halibut and sole at sea. They may fish as far away as Newfoundland and stay at sea for weeks at a time. While fishing is actually taking place, all hands must work for stretches of up to 18 hours. On the older ships all work is done on the decks but the more modern factory ships process the catch below decks. Catering staff, engineers and radio operators are also employed on these large vessels.

Fishermen on drifters carry out similar tasks but these boats follow fish around the coast and land a catch every day. Small seine-net boats with a crew of only four stay at sea for two weeks. Inshore fishing boats are usually family concerns using a variety of different methods to catch white fish, herring, cod, haddock, whiting, shrimps, lobster and crab.

Although the fishing industry is in decline, there may be opportunities at the five main ports of Grimsby, Hull, Lowestoft, Fleetwood and Aberdeen.

Qualifications and Training

No formal education qualifications are necessary for a career in fishing, although an understanding of maths would be helpful and the local nautical college at Hull requires 100 days to have been spent at sea before entry on to its pre-seagoing course. Other courses are available at Fleetwood, Grimsby, Lowestoft and Aberdeen. Further training is gained in employment and further qualifications can be obtained leading to promotion from deck hand to third hand, second hand and then skipper.

Personal Qualities

Physical fitness, stamina and courage are essential for fishermen, who may have to withstand terrible Arctic conditions and long periods of very hard work. They must also be good sailors, able to turn their hand to any task, react quickly to emergencies, and be able to work in a team.

£ Inshore fishermen all take a share of the catch; if there's no catch, there's no money. However, for someone starting, wages average out at about £100 a week or just over, more for deep-sea work.

i Jobcentres and Careers Offices in port towns
The Institute of Fisheries Management (IFM), 22 Rushworth Avenue, West Bridgford, Nottingham NG2 7LF; 0115 982 2317
www.ifm.org.uk

FISH FARMER

In Britain, some 500 fish farms produce quality fish for consumption and sport. This is a growing activity; although most farms are owner-run, opportunities exist for farm managers and workers. Opportunities exist for scientists to test new methods for improving conditions, stocks and disease control, and for bailiffs, who look after the general welfare of the fish from hatchery to harvesting. In the future, as food manufacturers move into fish farming, there is likely to be a need for marketing staff.

Qualifications and Training

NVQs are offered in Fish Husbandry, level 2. Certificates, diploma and degree courses in fish farming and agriculture are offered by universities and specialist colleges. A Diploma in Fisheries Management is offered by the Institute of Fisheries Management to students who have first taken their correspondence course and passed the certificate. The IFM also runs a correspondence course leading to a Certificate in Fish Farming. The diploma has been credit-rated with the Open University Validation Service, which means that the credits gained can be used towards an OU degree.

No formal qualifications are required to become a bailiff, although correspondence courses are available from the IFM. Graduate and postgraduate biologists are employed on the scientific side and specialist courses are available, as are courses dealing with the more sporting aspect of fish farming.

Personal Qualities

Physical fitness, a willingness to work outside, in remote areas and in all conditions, and an ability to think ahead and act independently are necessary.

£ £10,000+ for technicians, £11,000+ for bailiffs, £14,000–£15,000+ for scientists, and £15,000–£20,000 for managers.

i British Trout Association, 8 Lambton Place, London W11 4PH; 020 7221 6065 (send sae for list of courses)

The Institute of Fisheries Management (IFM), 22 Rushworth Avenue, West Bridgford, Nottingham NG2 7LF; 0115 982 2317; fax 0115 945 5722
www.ifm.org.uk

The Environment Agency, Coverdale House, Aviator Court, Clifton Moor, York YO3 4UZ; 01904 692296

Flight Engineer,* see *Civil Aviation

FLORIST

The florist's job involves visiting flower markets early in the morning to buy flowers, plants and other stock. As well as selling cut flowers and plants, they make up plant and flower displays such as table decorations, bouquets, sprays and wreaths. Some florists also work outside the shop, providing office displays, making arrangements for banquets, functions and receptions, and decorating hotels and public buildings.

Qualifications and Training

The industry has a well-established qualifications structure, giving recognition to those who achieve floristry skills, and professional standing to those who achieve the industry's highest accolade – the National Diploma of the Society of Floristry. NVQs in Floristry are established at levels 2 and 3. These qualifications are offered by the National Examinations Board for Agriculture and Horticulture and Allied Industries (NEBAHAI), which also offers a business qualification and a national certificate in floristry for more senior florists.

Edexcel (BTEC) qualifications are also offered by some colleges, from the first certificate in floristry, through to the ND and the HND in floristry. The Society of Floristry offers two professional qualifications – the Intermediate Certificate (ICSF) and the National Diploma (NDSF).

Personal Qualities

Imagination and creative flair, colour sense, organisational ability, an ability to work to deadlines, a friendly manner, patience and dexterity. Good health and stamina are essential because the work can be physically demanding.

£ Florists generally work a 40-hour week, including Saturdays. Rates of pay vary according to size and location of the business, and according to the individual's own skills and qualifications, experience and seniority. Rates of pay are on a similar scale to other retail work. Part-time work may be available.

i LANTRA, Lantra House, NAC, Kenilworth, Warwickshire CV8 2LG; 01203 696996; fax 01203 696732

The Secretary, The Society of Floristry, 6 Carroll Avenue, Ferndown, Dorset BH22 8BP; 0870 241 0432; fax 01202 855520

FOOD SCIENCE AND TECHNOLOGY

Food scientists study the properties and behaviour of foods from raw materials through processing to the final product, using a variety of scientific disciplines, notably chemistry and biology, but also physics and nutrition. Food technologists use food science and other technological know-how to turn raw materials into finished products for the consumer in an industry which is becoming increasingly sophisticated.

The majority of those qualifying in food science or technology will readily find employment in a variety of positions in the food industry, which covers not only the manufacture of food but its ingredients, food packaging and the manufacture of food-processing machinery. Positions exist in production, quality assurance or in product or process development. The growth of 'own label' products has led to additional opportunities in the food retailing sector where technologists are responsible for developing new products, identifying suppliers, and ensuring the quality of the product from manufacture, through distribution to the store and, ultimately, to the consumer's table. Those keen to secure a career in research will find opportunities in Government service, in research associations, as well as commercial organisations and the universities. There are additional opportunities in environmental health, education, consultancy, public health laboratories and in technical publishing and journalism.

Qualifications and Training

Food science and technology qualifications may be gained via NVQs (levels 1–4), GNVQs (levels 1–3), Edexcel (BTEC) national certificates and diplomas, HNC, HND and degree courses. There is also the opportunity to train while in a job. Qualifications at all levels can be taken as full-time and sandwich courses. There are also a few part-time courses. For minimum entry requirements, contact colleges directly.

Membership of the Institute of Food Science and Technology depends upon satisfying both academic qualifications (minimum HND) and having several years' experience at a responsible level for higher grades.

Personal Qualities

Food scientists and technologists require a sound theoretical knowledge and scientific ability, a practical approach and an ability to communicate with people, and a willingness to work as one of a team.

£ Technologists with A levels or equivalent would earn £10,000+; graduates or HND holders £13,000+ depending on qualifications, employer and location.

i The Food and Drink National Training Organisation, 6 Catherine Street, London WC2B 5JJ; 020 7836 2460 www.foodanddrinknto.org.uk

Institute of Food Science and Technology, 5 Cambridge Court, 210 Shepherds Bush Road, London W6 7NJ; 020 7603 6316 www.ifst.org

FORENSIC SCIENTIST

The Forensic Science Service, administered by the Home Office, employs scientists both for research and operational forensic science. Their backgrounds are mostly as chemists and biologists, and as forensic scientists they examine and try to identify, by means of analytical chemistry, molecular biology and microscopic analysis, samples of such materials as clothing, hair, blood, glass, paint and handwriting, in order to provide evidence to expose criminals, the location of a crime, the weapons used, and so on.

Qualifications and Training

Scientific Officers must have a degree or equivalent. The progression is then to Higher Scientific Officer (for which a degree and postgraduate laboratory experience are necessary) and to Senior

Science Officer, which requires four years' postgraduate laboratory experience. NVQs will become available in document examination, scenes of crime examination and the recovery of evidential material.

Personal Qualities

Forensic scientists should adopt a logical, practical and methodical approach, pay great attention to detail, and be willing to try every possible permutation. A naturally inquisitive, unsqueamish nature and a concern for accuracy are also important.

£ A Scientific Officer in the Civil Service earns from approximately £11,500.

i The Forensic Science Service, Headquarters, Priory House, Gooch Street North, Birmingham B5 6QQ; 0121 607 6800

The Forensic Science Society, Clarke House, 18a Mount Parade, Harrogate HG1 1BX; 01423 506068

Local police forces

A Career in Forensic Science (The Forensic Science Society)

FORESTRY

The main business of the forestry industry in Britain is to grow trees to provide timber, but this has never been its sole purpose. As well as being involved in timber production, foresters are acutely conscious of the visual impact of forestry on the environment, and of its effect on wildlife.

Forest Officer

Forest officers have a variety of roles to perform depending on the level they reach in their career. In the lower grades they are technical supervisors with responsibility for planning and controlling operations. As a career progresses, an individual will be asked to perform a variety of management functions and be expected to plan, control and implement policies and operations. There are opportunities to undertake more specialised work and most officers will find themselves in regular contact with the general public and professional people.

Forest Worker
The forest worker's role is mainly manual or operating machines in the forest with a wide range of work including planting, fencing, draining, weeding and timber harvesting.

Qualifications and Training

Forest officers' qualifications range from an Edexcel (BTEC) diploma in forestry to an honours degree in forestry and membership of the professional body, the Institute of Chartered Foresters (MICFor). Forest workers must now have nationally recognised chainsaw and pesticide application qualifications, such as those provided by NPTC.

Personal Qualities

Forestry work requires a good standard of physical fitness, a willingness to work outside, all year round, in all weathers and in remote areas. Foresters and managers should be able to organise others and be prepared to do varying amounts of office work.

£ Trainee forest workers earn about £100 a week at 16, rising to £180 for a forest craftsman. Forest officers start at about £14,000.

i Forestry and Arboricultural Safety and Training Committee (FASTCo), The Forestry Commission, Personnel Management Branch, 231 Corstorphine Road, Edinburgh EH12 7AT; 0131 314 6247

Institute of Chartered Foresters, 7a St Colme Street, Edinburgh EH3 6AA; 0131 225 2705

The Royal Forestry Society of England, Wales and Northern Ireland, 102 High Street, Tring, Hertfordshire HP23 4AF; 01442 822028
www.rfs.org.uk

The Royal Scottish Forestry Society, Hagg-on-Esk, Canonbie, Dumfriesshire DG14 0XE; 01387 371518; fax 01387 371418

Careers Working Outdoors (Kogan Page)

FOUNDRY WORK

(see also Engineering)

Foundry work is craft-based. The industry provides metal-cast components for a wide range of industries, such as propellers, turbines, crankshafts, all types of machinery, and domestic items such as fireplaces.

Craftsmen are employed in foundry work as pattern, mould and model makers and to maintain the equipment. Technical engineering staff are concerned with estimating, inspection and laboratory work. There are many opportunities for operatives in foundry work as die casters, dressers, finishers, moulders, coremakers and in metal melting. There are also limited openings for foundry technologists, metallurgists, chemists and engineers and, as the industry becomes more sophisticated, the demand for specialist skills will increase in research and development. Graduate managers are also in greater demand for both production and administrative posts.

Qualifications and Training

To become a Corporate Member of the Institute of British Foundrymen it is necessary to have a degree in metallurgy or engineering. HND and HNC qualifications are also acceptable when backed by appropriate endorsements or a metallurgical engineering qualification.

For the craftsman, a three-year craft apprenticeship scheme results in the Foundry Institute Training Committee Craft Certificate; training is at a special centre, at work and with day release to attend college.

Entrants to the industry with three GCSE passes (or equivalent) in maths, a science and English can take NC or ND courses which cover the basics of cast-metal technology. Successful students and school leavers who have followed A level courses can then progress to HNC and HND courses in foundry technology, which combine theoretical and technological study with supervisory techniques. City and Guilds also offers courses intended to complement industrial training, and NVQs are available in various areas of engineering.

Personal Qualities

Workers in the foundry industry must be fit and strong as the work is heavy. They should have good eyesight and be skilful in the employment of tools. They must be willing to work in noisy conditions and possibly to work shifts.

£ Production workers £80+ a week at 16, £200+ when trained.

i Local Jobcentres and Careers Offices

FREIGHT FORWARDING

(see also Logistics)

Moving goods internationally can be very complicated and it is usual to employ the services of a freight forwarding firm, which will arrange for the most efficient means of transport and will also ensure that all documentation, legal and insurance requirements are met and customs duties paid, and so on. Freight forwarders may be individuals or firms; they may specialise in a particular method of transportation, certain goods or countries. They may arrange for a number of different shipments to be grouped together for more economical transport. Some very large organisations have their own freight forwarding department or a subsidiary company.

Freight forwarders are usually located near ports or airports and in the provincial centres. They employ people to deal with a wide range of clerical and administrative tasks such as sales, personnel, timetabling, accounting and computer work. The most likely entry route to freight forwarding is as a clerk and then to progress through supervisory to managerial positions. There are opportunities also to work abroad.

Qualifications and Training

Some large organisations recruit graduates, usually with degrees in transport subjects or business studies with a transport bias, as trainees, but generally there are opportunities for people at all levels. For freight forwarding, training is mainly through practical experience and part-time study. A minimum of one A level is recommended for enrolment to the part-time and correspondence courses of the Institute of Freight Forwarders. Edexcel (BTEC) national certificate courses are available at colleges of further education, and there is a Network option in freight forwarding. An NVQ at levels 2, 3 and 4 in international trade and services is in place and a Modern Apprenticeship framework is being developed.

For promotion prospects, A levels and languages are an advantage. Five GCSEs including maths and English are required for the Chartered Institute of Transport's (CIT) qualifying examination course or the CIT certificate in transport (road freight).

Personal Qualities

People working in freight forwarding need a good working knowledge of commercial geography; they may be required to work unsocial hours and will find that scheduling requires a logical, detailed and accurate approach.

£ Minimum clerical salaries are in the region of £6,000–£7,000; management trainees start at £10,000+.

i British International Freight Association, Institute of Freight Forwarders, Redfern House, Browells Lane, Feltham, Middlesex TW13 7EP; 020 8844 2266

The Institute of Logistics and Transport, 80 Portland Place, London W1N 4DP; 020 7467 9400; fax 020 7467 9440 www.iolt.org.uk

The Freight Transport Association, Hermes House, St John's Road, Tunbridge Wells, Kent TN4 9UZ; 01892 526171

Institute of Transport Administration, 32 Palmerston Road, Southampton SO14 1LL; 023 8063 1380

A Career in Freight Forwarding (British International Freight Association)

FUNERAL DIRECTOR

Funeral directors collect bodies from hospital or the residence of the deceased and prepare them for burial or cremation; this may include embalming. Most funeral premises include private viewing rooms for family visitations. On behalf of the family, at their request, and after ascertaining their wishes, the funeral director usually makes all the funeral arrangements such as the date, time and place of the service and interment or cremation. The funeral director places the relevant notice of death and acknowledgement of thanks for sympathy in newspapers, pays all the fees, arranges flowers, transports the coffin and mourners to and from church, and will act as a collection point for flowers, or donations in lieu, if desired.

Funeral directors may be employed by large firms such as co-operative societies, or by small family-run concerns. In remote rural areas, the local carpenter or other craftsman may also work as a funeral director.

Qualifications and Training

Those wishing to obtain their Diploma in Funeral Directing must register with the National Association of Funeral Directors (NAFD) and will also have student membership of the British Institute of Funeral Directors (BIFD). Full details of the diploma course are forwarded to each student. Every student must follow the foundation module – there are no exceptions.

A satisfactory standard must be reached in the foundation module before proceeding to the diploma. A student will be required to have 24 months' experience and have arranged 25 funerals before the diploma is awarded.

NVQs levels 2 and 3 in Funeral Services are available for those employed within the profession.

Personal Qualities

Tact and sympathy and a reassuring, helpful nature are essential to funeral directors when they are advising the bereaved. They also need to combine administrative ability with technical expertise in the varied preparations of funeral arrangements. On-call and out-of-hours work is an integral part of the job and an ability to adapt to irregular hours is essential.

£ Salaries vary greatly depending on size of firm, many of which are family concerns.

i British Institute of Embalmers, Anubis House, 21c Station Road, Knowle, Solihull, West Midlands B93 0HL; 01564 778991

National Association of Funeral Directors, 618 Warwick Road, Solihull, West Midlands B91 1AA; 0121 711 1343

FURNITURE AND FURNISHING

(see also Upholsterer)

Furniture is rarely hand-made any more and is no longer constructed solely from timber, but from a variety of materials and with the help of a wide range of machines. However, a craft-based industry, using skilled workmen at all stages of the production process, still exists. The sawyer stacks wood for seasoning, and cuts it into suitable lengths for the machinist who shapes it into furniture parts. These may be made more attractive by the application of a veneer and are then assembled by the cabinet maker and finally stained and polished either by hand or with sprays. Skilled frame makers provide frames to be filled, sprung and covered by upholsterers; much of this work is done by hand and is similar in many ways to that done in the clothing and textile industries.

There are opportunities in this industry for people to work on a freelance or self-employed basis, or for one of the many manufacturing units which may specialise in particular items, or materials, or in certain types of furniture such as school, office or domestic furniture. In the design of furniture, carpets, fabrics, curtaining and wall coverings, opportunities exist to work freelance, in studios and in the retail trade. There are also a number of openings for teachers; craft design and technology teachers are in short supply.

Qualifications and Training

Craft training is generally gained through a three- to four-year apprenticeship with part-time study on a day- or block-release basis to obtain the City and Guilds certificate or Edexcel (BTEC) certificate and diploma. The City and Guilds first-year course covers all aspects of the furniture trade with specialisation in the second and subsequent years. A general education to GCSE level standard is required for these courses; woodwork, maths and English, although not essential, are an advantage. NVQs at level 2 are available in various aspects of furniture production.

For those wishing to follow a career in design, training usually begins at 16 with education to GCSE level standard being followed by attendance on a two-year foundation course covering all aspects of art and design. This is reduced to one year for older students with five GCSEs and one A level or equivalents.

Full-time and sandwich degree courses lasting three and four years respectively and leading to BA (Hons) in art and design are available at various universities and colleges of higher education. For entry, applicants should be 18 and have either five GCSEs and two A levels or equivalents, or have successfully completed a foundation course and have five GCSEs and one A level or equivalents.

Personal Qualities

Furniture craftsmen must be neat, accurate and able to follow drawings exactly. They must be interested in practical work which requires great precision, have care and patience, and strength sufficient to lift heavy furniture. Good eyesight is an advantage. Designers are required to work as part of a team to a busy schedule and present their work well; a sound knowledge of how furniture is made is most valuable.

£ Apprentices at 16 earn £70+ a week, and when qualified from £170. Individual craftsmen working for themselves set their own rates. Designers start at £7,500–£8,000+ upwards.

i The Countryside Agency, John Dower House, Crescent Place, Cheltenham GL50 3RA; 01242 521381

Rural Development Commission, 141 Castle Street, Salisbury, Wiltshire SP1 3TP; 01722 336255

G

GAMEKEEPER

Gamekeepers work on large country estates for private landlords, management firms and for private syndicates who wish to organise a shoot. They rear the game birds and fish, and protect them from poachers and predators. They must ensure that the proper environment for the game is maintained and, on shooting days, organise the beaters.

Qualifications and Training

No formal qualifications are necessary, although a keeper should be able to use a gun, handle a dog and be able to drive. Training is usually on the job, but there is a one-year full-time course available at Hampshire Agricultural College. There is an NVQ award available in Gamekeeping, levels 1 and 2. A number of other agricultural colleges run courses on keeping and allied subjects.

Personal Qualities

Gamekeepers should love the outdoor life, be self-reliant and independent.

£ Based on agricultural wages, generally with a house provided.

i The Game Conservancy Trust, Fordingbridge, Hampshire SP6 1EF; 01425 652381

GARAGE WORK

This involves selling and buying cars, supplying car parts, selling petrol, repairing and maintaining cars and other vehicles and the overall management of the garage.

Qualifications and Training

No specific educational qualifications are necessary for people working on a petrol forecourt as training is given on the job, but an aptitude in dealing with cash transactions and good numeracy skills are generally required. Mechanics generally need to have at least three GCSEs (grade C or above) preferably in maths, science or a craft subject. Training via Modern Apprenticeship usually leads to NVQ level 3. Preferred qualifications for salespeople and parts people are four GCSEs (grade C or above). A range of NVQs are available as qualifications in these areas. Managers are recruited with varying qualifications and some have a degree. Membership of the industry's professional institute is encouraged.

Personal Qualities

Mechanics must have a high degree of responsibility, be strong and get on well with people. Salespeople need to be friendly, polite and have a good sense of humour. Parts people need to be well organised with good administrative skills. Managers need to have all the above qualities and also the ability to inspire confidence and gain respect.

£ Varies across the country and is dependent on experience and level of responsibility.

i Retail Motor Industry Training (ReMIT), 201 Great Portland Street, London, W1N 6AB; 020 7580 9122
www.remit.co.uk

GARDENER

(see also Horticulturist, Landscape Architect, Market Gardening)

Gardening involves not only planting and caring for flowers, trees and shrubs, but also the routine jobs of cleaning out beds, sweeping leaves and, in the winter, shovelling snow.

Gardeners may be employed by local authorities to care for parks, school and hospital grounds, work for a garden centre, landscape contractor, or be self-employed. If self-employed, they may run their own business or work for a variety of people.

Landscape Gardening
This involves either renovating an old garden for a client or creating an entirely new one. Landscape gardeners, using their own ideas and the customer's design, make a plan of the 'new' garden. Such items as drainage systems, rockeries, garden paths and plants are all shown.

Qualifications and Training

It is desirable but not always necessary to have formal qualifications to become a gardener. Training is given on the job, often as part of an apprenticeship. However, day-release courses are available leading to NVQ levels 1, 2 and 3, and Royal Horticultural Society qualifications. Education and training courses are available at many colleges throughout the country with varying entry qualifications up to GCE A level.

Personal Qualities

Gardeners should enjoy working outdoors in all weathers and be patient and caring. The ability to drive may be useful.

£ £120–£160 a week when trained.

i Local Jobcentres and Careers Offices
Institute of Horticulture, 14-15 Belgrave Square, London SW1X 8PS; 020 7245 6943 (tel/fax)
www.horticulture.demon.co.uk
Royal Horticultural Society, 80 Vincent Square, London SW1P 2PE; 020 7834 4333
Careers Working Outdoors (Kogan Page)
'Come into Horticulture' and 'Education and Training Courses in Horticulture' (both available free from the Institute of Horticulture)

GAS FITTER

The work involves fitting and repairing appliances such as cookers, boilers, water heaters, the installation, maintenance and replacement of gas appliances, and inspecting for the source of reported leaks. Most fitters are employed by the area gas boards.

Qualifications and Training

No formal qualifications are necessary but a good general education with some knowledge of maths and physics is advantageous. Training is by a four-year apprenticeship; apprentices learn on the job and are given time off to attend courses leading to a City and Guilds qualification.

Personal Qualities

As much of the work takes place in private houses, fitters must be friendly, polite and honest. It is necessary to be able to drive.

£ About £75 a week at 16; £175+ when qualified.

i Area gas boards

Construction Industry Training Board, Bircham Newton, King's Lynn, Norfolk PE31 6RH; 01485 577577

GENEALOGIST

Genealogists trace lines of descent from ancestor to ancestor and also study pedigrees. Their work is useful to the legal profession in cases of intestacy or disputed will claims and, sometimes, to doctors when trying to establish the origins of a disease. However, the vast majority of genealogists work for private clients who are interested in tracing their family trees. There are some firms of genealogists, and other individuals who work from home.

Qualifications and Training

Genealogists must have knowledge of history, Latin and legal terminology. The Institute of Heraldic and Genealogical Studies provides full-time, part-time and correspondence courses leading to professional qualifications. There are also short courses on ancestry available for beginners provided by the Institute, certain local authorities and the Society of Genealogists.

Personal Qualities

Curiosity, historical integrity and attention to detail are all useful attributes.

£ Salaries vary depending on whether full- or part-time work is undertaken, for a firm or on one's own behalf. The hourly rate is around £12.

i The Association of Genealogists and Record Agents, 29 Badgers Close, Horsham, West Sussex RH12 5RU

The Institute of Heraldic and Genealogical Studies, 79–82 Northgate, Canterbury, Kent CT1 1BA; 01227 768664; fax 01227 765617; e-mail *education@ihgs.ac.uk* www.ihgs.ac.uk

The Society of Genealogists, 14 Charterhouse Buildings, Goswell Road, London EC1M 7BA; 020 7251 8799

General Practitioner, **see** *Medicine*

GEOLOGIST

Geoscience is fundamental, as all energy resources and raw materials come from the Earth. Keeping these resources available and safe relies upon the expertise of the geoscientist. There are many different disciplines within geoscience.

Geologists study the earth's crust, the materials which comprise it, their origin, formation and composition. The work involves the examination of rocks and mineral deposits; some deposits (for example, coal) are assessed for their value. Specimens of rock, soil, water, fossils and minerals are collected for laboratory analysis and preservation for future reference. Geology not only includes field work but much laboratory work, testing and analysing, often using computers. Findings are then compiled into reports. Geologists work mainly for oil, mining, quarrying or engineering firms and Government establishments, and are becoming increasingly involved in environmental issues.

Closely allied to the work of the geologist is that of the geophysicist (*see* Oil/Gas Rig Work), geochemist and hydrogeologist, who use field and laboratory-based techniques to better understand the earth's physical and chemical properties and its underground water supplies. Hence, most of their work is related to the resources and the environment.

Qualifications and Training

The common route for entry into a professional geoscience career is a first degree (BSc/BA) in one of the geosciences. Such a degree also forms the basic qualification for membership of the Geological Society, and for becoming a Chartered Geologist.

Personal Qualities

Geologists must be fit, as they are often required to work in difficult climatic conditions or even underground. They must be able to work both as team members and as team organisers when required. Relevant foreign languages are useful.

£ £12,000+ to £16,000+; higher abroad.

i The British Geological Survey, Nicker Hill, Keyworth, Nottingham NG12 5GG

Natural History Museum Earth Galleries, Exhibition Road, London SW7 2DE; 020 7589 4090

The Geological Society, Burlington House, Piccadilly, London W1V 9AG; 020 7434 9944 www.geolsoc.org.uk

Geophysicist, **see** ***Oil/Gas Rig Work***

GLAZIER

Glaziers fit glass into window frames for domestic use and also for commercial buildings, some of which require the use of enormous sheets. They work for private contractors, local authorities and independently, in private homes and on building sites.

Qualifications and Training

No formal educational requirements are necessary. Training is on the job by three-year apprenticeship. It is usual for time off to be allowed to attend classes leading to NVQs, levels 1 and 2, awarded jointly by the City and Guilds and the Construction Industry Training Board.

Personal Qualities

Useful attributes are strength, a liking for being outdoors, a steady hand, neatness and agility.

£ Recommended rates are: £73.90 at 16; £103.46 at 17; £147.81 at 18; and, when qualified, the craftsman rate is £178.62.

i Construction Industry Training Board, Bircham Newton, King's Lynn, Norfolk PE31 6RH; 01485 577 577

GROOM

Grooms look after all aspects of the horse's welfare. Their duties include grooming and strapping, mucking out, feeding, cleaning tack, saddling up, exercising and leading both mounted and dismounted, elementary veterinary care and sick nursing, preparation for and travelling with horses by road, sea and air, and care of the horse when at grass. Grooms work in racing stables, hunting establishments, private stables, studs and breeding concerns, riding schools and occasionally (seasonally) with polo ponies and at trekking centres.

Qualifications and Training

No formal qualifications are necessary but it is recommended that grooms take the British Horse Society examinations stages 1, 2 and 3, in Horse Knowledge and Care, which comprise the Grooms Certificate. Alternative options are NVQs in Horse Care, levels 1, 2 and 3.

Training is usually on the job and should be sufficient to prepare students for exams. There are also courses of varying lengths to prepare students for particular exams; however, the fees are often high. Further Education Funding Council assistance may be available for the achievement of British Horse Society qualifications providing that the person is not eligible for any other type of funding. Details may be obtained from a local further education college.

Personal Qualities

A love of horses is essential, plus patience and the willingness to work long hours and perform many routine tasks. A heavy goods vehicle driving licence may be an advantage.

£ Stable staff at 20 years of age earn around £135–£140 a week. In some cases, food and accommodation may be free, and in others they may be deducted from the wage. The hours may be long.

i The British Horse Society, Stoneleigh Park, Kenilworth, Warwickshire CV8 2LR; 01926 707700

GROUNDSMEN/WOMEN

Groundsmen and women prepare, maintain and care for the various types of sports surfaces, both natural and synthetic turf – cricket and football pitches, bowling greens, athletic tracks, tennis courts, racecourses, polo grounds and amenity areas. Nowadays, they have to be familiar with the developments in science and technology both in machinery and materials used in the maintenance of grounds. Employment can be found in both the private and public sectors with local authorities, sports clubs and schools.

Qualifications and Training

Training can take place either on the job, or through colleges on residential or day release courses. The Institute of Groundsmanship (IOG) also organises courses and has its own examination structure. There are a number of routes to gain qualifications including NVQs, HNCs and HNDs.

Personal Qualities

A groundsman/woman is a resourceful person who prefers working outdoors regardless of the weather. An enjoyment of the physical challenge plus an interest in sport are an advantage.

£ This ranges from about £6,000 at 16, £9,000 at 18, to £23,000 for a head groundsman, and agreed salaries for grounds managers.

i Institute of Groundmanship, 19–23 Church Street, The Agora, Wolverton, Milton Keynes MK12 5LG; 01908 312511; e-mail *iog@iog.org*
www.iog.org.uk

H

HAIRDRESSER

Hairdressers offer a variety of services involving hair such as cutting, styling, perming and colouring. Salons, or individual stylists may specialise in male or female hairdressing, or a niche market such as specialist colouring, Afro-Caribbean or ethnic hairstyles. They work in salons, hotels, airports, cruise liners, hospitals and prisons. Some hairdressers work as freelancers.

Qualifications and Training

There is no legal requirement for formal training to become a hairdresser, but it is strongly recommended. NVQs in Hairdressing are awarded jointly at levels 1, 2 and 3 by City and Guilds and the Hairdressing Training Board in England and Wales, and SVQs by the Hairdressing Training Board in Scotland. An NVQ at level 4, to focus on the management issues in hairdressing, is also being negotiated. Training is available at further education colleges and at private training organisations. Courses are run in a range of flexible delivery modes, including day release, part-time, short intensive courses and full-time courses.

Personal Qualities

Hairdressers should have a genuine interest in people, a natural friendliness, the ability to stay calm under pressure, creative ability and an eye for detail. A presentable personal appearance is also essential.

£ Initial earnings vary. When qualified, hairdressers' earnings reflect their skills and artistic talent.

i Hairdressing Council, 12 David Street, 45 High Street, South Norwood, London SE25 6HJ; 020 8771 6205

Hairdressing Training Board, 2nd Floor, Fraser House, Nether Hall Road, Doncaster, South Yorkshire DN1 2PH; 01302 380000

National Hairdressers Federation, 11 Goldington Road, Bedford, MK40 3JY; 01234 360332

Careers in Hairdressing and Beauty (Kogan Page)

Health Care Assistant* see *Nursing Auxiliary

HEALTH SERVICE

There are many non-medical jobs within the health service, employing a wide range of skills, but services are increasingly being provided by private contractors, especially for laundry and cleaning.

Management

Management is concerned with efficiency and cost effectiveness at all levels of the health service. General management within a hospital, where the managers will be in contact with professional staff, patients and the public, will involve forward planning, finance, personnel management, purchasing and supply, building maintenance, and the organisation of laundry, catering and cleaning. At district and regional health authority levels the responsibilities are for ascertaining the health needs of the local population and for an overall monitoring role.

Catering

In hospitals, ordinary meals are provided for both patients and staff, as well as special diets. The Catering Officer supervises the kitchen, plans menus in consultation with the dietitian, and is in control of ordering the food as well as its preparation.

Domestic Services

This covers all grades, from basic domestic cleaner level, through domestic supervisors and housekeepers. This section is responsible for cleaning groups of beds and areas within the hospital, under the charge of the Domestic Superintendent. It includes district and area domestic managers, who coordinate the hospital domestic services.

Laundry
This department deals with the supply of sterilised sheets, towels, blankets and overalls; the number of items handled weekly within one hospital may run into millions.

Medical Records (Patient Services)
Clerks arrange appointments, patients' registration, maintain waiting lists and filing systems, keep patients' records and maintain statistical data. The Medical Records Officer may work within the hospital, in charge of the clerks and medical secretaries, or may work at regional or district authority level.

Ancillary Staff
Includes porters, who move supplies and people around the hospital, general building maintenance staff, and ambulance services.

Qualifications and Training

Staff are recruited and trained by the hospitals and health authorities. Some health care staff may work towards NVQs levels 1 and 2. The Institute of Health Services Management accredits courses leading to professional management qualifications. Entry to courses is not restricted to those in management but is open to a wide range of staff, from clerks to doctors. Entry qualifications vary and are set by individual colleges.

There is also a General Management Training Scheme run by the NHS Training Division which is open to graduates and lasts for 22 months. Those already employed in the health service and over 21 and with two A levels may also apply.

Personal Qualities

Working for the health service requires a real and sympathetic concern for people, and management calls for a sense of responsibility as well as a capacity for organisation.

£ Approximate salaries are: clerical grades £5,500+ at 16, £6,000+ at 17, £7,000+ at 18 upwards; administrative grades £10,000–£12,500+.

i The Institute of Health Services Management, 39 Chalton Street, London NW1 1JD; 020 7388 2626

NHS Training Division, St Bartholomew Court, 18 Christmas Street, Bristol BS1 5BT
Local Jobcentres and Careers Offices

HEALTH VISITOR

Health visitors promote health and contribute to the prevention of mental, physical and social ill health in the community. This involves educating people in ways of healthy living and also making positive changes in the environment. Education may be achieved by teaching individuals or families in their own homes, in health centres, clinics or in informal groups, or through campaigns for the promotion of good health practices through local or national mass media.

The health visitor may work with people who are registered with a GP or who live within a defined geographical area. The work includes collaboration with a wide range of voluntary and statutory organisations.

Qualifications and Training

Applicants must be registered general or adult nurses with post-registration experience. One-year health visitor courses are provided at institutions of higher education.

All approved programmes now lead to the award of Specialist Practitioner (Public Health Visiting/Health Visiting). These programmes are at a minimum of first degree level.

Personal Qualities

Health visitors must have a desire to help people. They should be friendly and able to respond tactfully. An ability to communicate with all types of people and to speak in public is useful.

£ Approximately £18,156–£21,007.

i Community Practitioners and Health Visitors Association, 40 Bermondsey Street, London SE1 3UD; 020 7717 4000

HOME ECONOMIST

Home economics covers a variety of subjects connected with the home and family life. They include nutrition and health, the preparation of food, equipment used in the home, home management, budgeting; and may extend further into textiles, consumer affairs, family problems and community work. A trained home economist may be able to work abroad. There are several levels of training, from certificate courses to a full degree course.

Demonstrator
Home economists may demonstrate products for manufacturers in shops or exhibitions, organise exhibitions themselves and train demonstrators, or give talks to institutions or in the home on products or services, or give advice on home management.

Industry
Many home economists are employed in the food industry in marketing and/or the research and development of new products to supply retailers. Their counterparts in retailing are the home economists who, as buyers/selectors, choose the products to be stocked. Home economists are similarly employed in the domestic appliance manufacturing industry and with those retailers.

Local Authorities
Home economists are used by local authorities in the social services, housing departments, consumer services and health promotion units.

The Media
There are opportunities on magazines, newspapers, in broadcasting, advertising and in public relations.

Teaching
A knowledge of science, particularly chemistry, is advisable for teaching, which necessitates a degree course. There are openings for teachers in colleges and universities, as well as in schools. Food and textiles are taught under technology.

Qualifications and Training

Standard entry requirements for degree courses are a minimum of two A levels or three H grades, preferably including home economics, and three other GCSEs/S grades (A to C/1–3) or equivalent qualifications such as Edexcel (BTEC) ND/GNVQ Advanced/NVQ level 2 for GCSE. (No specific A levels, but maths, English language and a science are usually required at GCSE level.) Three GCSEs to include a subject showing the use of English are needed for the Edexcel (BTEC) national diploma for students of 17 and over; this is a two-year course. NVQs offer five levels of attainment from level 1, for those at the start of their career, to level 5, at senior management level.

Personal Qualities

Home economists care about people and their quality of life, and need therefore to have an interest in the quality, performance and safety of goods and services related to the people who use these products. Much of the work involves communicating with the general public on the one hand and specialists on the other, so home economists must be confident and have the ability to express themselves in both oral and written work. Good self-management and good interpersonal skills are needed.

£ From £13,500 for those with a degree or diploma, maybe a little more in London.

i Institute of Home Economics, 21 Portland Place, London W1N 3AF; 020 7436 5677

National Association of Teachers of Home Economics and Technology, Hamilton House, Mabledon Place, London WC1H 9BJ; 020 7387 1441

HOMOEOPATH

Homoeopathy is a method of treating the whole person to create a healthy individual. There are three main principles of homoeopathy. First, treating like with like – what produces the symptoms of a disease may also cure it; the patient is treated by a small amount of the substance causing the symptoms and the natural defences are stimulated. Second, the lower the dose the better the result. Third, the remedy should be unique to the particular patient at a particular time. Homoeopathic remedies may be used to treat almost any reversible illness in adults, children or animals.

Many newly qualified homoeopaths set up in partnership in a clinic with other homoeopaths and some now work with GPs in fundholding practices. Homoeopathic patients may come privately or be referred by GPs.

Medical homoeopaths (doctors who have trained in homoeopathy) work as GPs, private practitioners or in one of the NHS homoeopathic hospitals.

Qualifications and Training

Medical doctors who have been qualified for a minimum of two and a half years may take a postgraduate course at one of the five teaching centres accredited by the Faculty of Homoeopathy.

Non-medically qualified candidates have a choice of institutions, of which the following are two examples: the British School of Homoeopathy (four-year part-time training course; two A levels required, but this may be waived for students over 25); and the London College of Classical Homoeopathy (a four-year full-time/part-time course; candidates under 21 should offer five GCSEs or three A levels; those over 21 should have a GCSE in human biology).

Personal Qualities

Homoeopaths must have an interest in people, an ability to consider and interpret information and be good listeners and communicators.

£ Varies greatly, depending on hours worked and number of patients.

i Faculty of Homoeopathy, 15 Clerkenwell Close, London EC1R 0AA; 020 7566 7810

London College of Classical Homoeopathy, Morley College, 61 Westminster Bridge Road, London SE1 7HT; 020 7928 6199

London School of Classical Homoeopathy, 94 Green Dragon Lane, Winchmore Hill, London N21 2NJ; 020 8360 8757

Society of Homoeopaths, 2 Artizan Road, Northampton NN1 4HU; 01604 621400

Working in Complementary and Alternative Medicine (Kogan Page) (contains details of courses)

HORTICULTURIST

(see also Gardener, Market Gardening)

Commercial Horticulture
Commercial horticulturists grow crops, such as vegetables on open land, and tomatoes, lettuce and cucumbers in glasshouses. Both orchard and soft fruits account for over one-fifth of the value of all horticultural production. Commercial horticulture also covers the growing of flowers and ornamental plants, including chrysanthemums, roses and carnations under glass and, for the gardening market, nurseries, landscaping and seedsmen.

Amenity Horticulture
Landscape architects, parks directors, landscape gardeners and groundsmen maintain public and private gardens and parks, sport and recreational facilities, industrial and residential areas, and the landscaping and planting of roadsides. Employers may be local authority public parks and recreation departments, commercial landscaping or contract garden maintenance firms, or owners of major gardens.

Arboriculturists, who care for and maintain trees, are mainly employed by local authorities, although there are some opportunities in private firms. The term 'tree surgeon' is often used for a commercial arboriculturist.

Research
Horticultural scientists work on pests and diseases and general research to produce better and healthier plants, in industrial and government organisations and in universities and colleges. There is a wide range of prospects for graduates.

Advisory Work
The adviser provides a link between research workers and the grower, to pass on the result of experimental work. The commercial and consultancy firms and producer organisations provide opportunities for advisers. A degree plus practical experience are necessary.

Teaching
Opportunities for teaching in horticulture occur in universities, colleges and schools. A degree or diploma is required.

Qualifications and Training

There are openings in horticulture for all standards of education. No GCSEs are required for part-time or full-time initial training courses, although beginners should be competent in biology, chemistry and maths. Applicants may work towards NVQs, levels 1 to 4. The Royal Horticultural Society offers the prestigious qualification of Master of Horticulture; entry qualifications are five GCSEs or equivalent to include maths and science. All candidates must have spent at least five years in horticultural employment or education.

Those with five GCSEs, including science and maths plus one A level pass in a science subject, or SCE passes with two at H grade and one year's experience can study for the higher national diploma, specialising in commercial or amenity horticulture.

Two GCE A levels or three SCE H grades, including chemistry and biology, plus maths and chemistry at GCSE level, are necessary to study for a degree in horticulture at university, or as a postgraduate course.

Personal Qualities

As machinery is now used a great deal in horticulture, it is essential to be able to work with it, as well as being interested in growing plants. For commercial horticulture, business acumen is essential, and artistic ability is important in the field of landscape gardening.

£ Unqualified staff when trained, £120–£160 per week; qualified technical staff from £11,000, and graduates after two years' training £15,000 upwards.

i Institute of Horticulture, 14–15 Belgrave Square, London SW1X 8PS; 020 7245 6943
www.horticulture.demon.co.uk
'Come into Horticulture' and 'Education and Training Courses in Horticulture' (available free from the Institute of Horticulture)

HOTEL WORK

(see also Catering and Accommodation Management)

Cooking

Depending on the type and size of hotel, cooking may involve traditional British and International cookery, large-scale kitchen production or the re-heating of pre-cooked meals. It may entail working under pressure in a hot and noisy kitchen, but leads to good career opportunities as a chef.

Food and Drink Service
Staff serving food, beverage and alcoholic drinks may have to work on early or late shifts and carry out weekend duties, but there will be compensating time off.

Housekeeping
Room staff, cleaners and other support staff keep the hotel clean and comfortable. The Head Housekeeper is in charge of this side of hotel life.

Management
Large hotels have a General Manager, Food and Beverage Manager, Personnel and Training Manager and House Manager, and there may also be heads of departments or sections. There are specialised opportunities in the fields of finance, administration, food and beverage operations, accommodation services, sales and marketing product development, public relations, personnel and training.

Reception
Receptionists receive guests and handle reservations, and also perform bookkeeping duties, so it is important to be good at figures, and be able to handle cash and use computers. Languages are an advantage. Working hours are arranged to deal with early and late arrivals and departures, and may entail shift and weekend work.

Qualifications and Training

Qualifications are the same as for Catering and Accommodation Management (*see* page 63).

Personal Qualities

Depending on which aspect of hotel work is undertaken, candidates need an understanding of food and drink, good social skills and an ability to establish relationships with staff and colleagues, and with customers and guests. Those serving food and drinks will benefit from a pleasant personality, alertness and a good memory for customers. Some may need a good head for figures and a grasp of statistics.

£ Salaries vary according to the field of work and degree of responsibility. Many employees live in hotel accommodation and have food provided. Salaries are similar to those given for Catering and Accommodation Management (*see* page 63).

i Hospitality Training Foundation, International House, High Street, London W5 5DB; 020 8579 2400

Hotel and Catering International Management Association (HCIMA), 191 Trinity Road, London SW17 7HN; 020 8672 4251

Springboard UK, 1 Denmark Street, London WC2H 8LP; 020 7497 8654

Careers in Catering and Hotel Administration (Kogan Page)

HOUSING OFFICER

Housing Officers work mainly for local authorities and housing associations but there are also opportunities in voluntary and private housing concerns. The work covers a broad range of areas that will vary by organisation and sector. In catering for the demand for rented accommodation, the Housing Officer will manage and maintain properties, which includes dealing with rent arrears, reporting repairs, applications, allocations and arranging property exchanges and transfers. Housing Officers often work with social and welfare agencies and need to have a basic understanding of the different welfare benefits.

Qualifications and Training

The basic qualifications needed for professional training in housing are three GCSE or five Standard grade passes, including English language and one GCSE at A level or three H grade passes or vocational qualification equivalents. Students over the age of 21 who do not meet these requirements but have relevant work experience may be considered as exceptional entrants. Contact local colleges to discuss this in more detail.

Usually, people who work in housing follow a day-release or distance-learning course to do the Chartered Institute of Housing's professional qualification (PQ). In addition to the course, candidates also need to do the work-based Test of Professional Practice (TPP), normally completed within two years. The PQ can take three or four years to complete, depending on whether you take the graduate or non-graduate route.

Graduates or mature entrant candidates are required to study a one-year graduate foundation course followed by a two-year professional diploma. Non-graduates are required to complete an Edexcel (BTEC) HNC in housing studies followed by a two-year professional diploma.

There are also full-time degree courses, and full- and part-time postgraduate diplomas. The Test of Professional Practice will still need to be undertaken with these alternative routes.

NVQs levels 2, 3 and 4 in Housing are available, and anyone working in housing is eligible to do an NVQ. In 1997, an NVQ in Special Needs Housing was introduced. Currently, a level 4 NVQ will allow candidates to proceed to stage 2 of the Chartered Institute of Housing's PQ (the professional diploma).

Personal Qualities

An interest in improving people's living conditions, good interpersonal skills, effective organisation skills, sensitivity to an individual's needs, and flexibility are all important.

£ Salaries vary from area to area, and from job to job. Trainee posts are offered in the range of £8,500 to £12,000. A standard Housing Officer/Manager post (requiring one to five years' experience) will have a salary of £11,000 to £19,000 (the higher figure includes London weighting).

i Chartered Institute of Housing, Octavia House, Westwood Business Park, Westwood Way, Coventry CV4 8JP; 024 7685 1700

Chartered Institute of Housing in Scotland, 6 Palmerston Place, Edinburgh EH12 5AA; 0131 225 4544

Institute of Housing in Wales, 4th Floor, Dominions House North, Dominions Arcade, Queen Street, Cardiff; 029 2039 7402

Chartered Institute of Housing in Northern Ireland, Carnmoney House, Edgewater Office Park, Dargan Road, Belfast BT3 9JQ; 028 9077 8222

HUMAN RESOURCE ADVISOR/MANAGER

Work in human resources can include working at a strategic level on a range of HR policies, processes and practices in relation to the business needs of the organisation. More commonly, however, HR advisors work on day-to-day issues such as contracts of employment, payroll, training, induction and setting up staff support systems. The role of an HR professional can vary and is largely dependent on the individual organisation's needs and the value that the organisation's senior managers place on the HR function.

Qualifications and Training

A good general education is essential and most HR professionals will have NVQ at level 3 or above, or a first degree in an appropriate area. A degree is not essential. A range of appropriate qualifications include NVQs in Training and Development, Management or Administration, and postgraduate qualifications are also increasingly available. The professional bodies for HR offer a number of training opportunities.

Personal Qualities

A good understanding of business needs is essential at strategic level. An honest, straightforward and approachable manner is essential when dealing with colleagues. HR professionals need to be clear thinking and able to help implement changes effectively.

£ Dependent on qualifications, experience, expertise and the business sector. HR advisors £17,000–£30,000; HR managers £20,000–£50,000.

i The Institute of Personnel and Development, IPD House, Camp Road, Wimbledon SW19 4UX; 020 8971 9000
www.ipd.co.uk

I

Illustrator, see *Artist, Medical Illustrator, Technical Illustrator*

INDEXER

Indexers provide a systematic arrangement of the terms appearing in a book or journal together with the page numbers where they appear in order to aid location of information. They are employed by publishers or authors. Indexers are generally freelancers and work from home.

Qualifications and Training

No formal qualifications are required but a good education is necessary plus subject knowledge in the case of specialist books. Training is by open-learning course.

Personal Qualities

Meticulous attention to detail is essential, plus the ability to work to set requirements and time limits.

£ Payment may be by lump sum or by the hour. The minimum rate recommended by the Society is £14 per hour (1999).

i Society of Indexers, Secretary: Liza Weinkove, Globe Centre, Penistone Road, Sheffield S6 3AE; 0114 201 3060; fax 0114 281 3061
www.socind.demon.co.uk

INDUSTRIAL DESIGNER

Art-school and college-trained designers work within industry with the engineers who have created a product. They are concerned with designing products that look attractive, and are efficient and convenient in use. The competition for the sale of new goods, from suitcases or spectacles to cassette players or cars, has resulted in an increased demand for the services of industrial designers.

Qualifications and Training

Sixteen-year-olds with GCSE or H grade passes may take a two-year foundation course which gives an introduction to art subjects, including drawing, painting and photography. Seventeen-year-old students with at least five GCSEs or H grades and one AS level may take a one-year foundation course. Students may then enter more specialised art or design training.

Students aged 18, preferably having completed a foundation course as above *or* any other passes accepted by the Council for National Academic Awards (all qualifications must include English), may apply for courses at schools of art and design, universities and colleges of higher education for full-time courses lasting three years, or four-year sandwich courses. Students should show a portfolio of their art work when they are interviewed.

Students aged 21 or over may be able to enter college without the normal qualifications required if the college is satisfied with their work and motivation.

Personal Qualities

As well as artistic ability, an understanding of mass-production processes is necessary; the industrial designer should also be able to work as part of a team and to schedule, and recognise the needs of the consumer.

£ £10,000–£11,000.

i Local Jobcentres and Careers Offices

INFORMATION SCIENTIST

(see also Librarian/Information Manager)

The work of the information scientist is akin to that of a librarian and involves collecting, indexing and classifying information for experts such as scientists, engineers or economists. However, in information science more emphasis is placed on current technology, and information is supplied online, on CD-ROM or via other electronic media. Information scientists work for industrial concerns and research organisations in their information departments or 'special libraries'. The information scientist often needs to have specialist knowledge, and must be able to keep up to date with technical information, reading journals and papers, and making a summary of the information in them, indexing and researching for information in other sources, such as other libraries, so that the knowledge can be passed on.

Qualifications and Training

Five GCSE/SCE passes are needed, plus two A levels, or three SCEs including English at H grade; passes must also include maths, a foreign language and a science subject. These can give entry to the three-year full-time course at Leeds Metropolitan University for first degrees in information science.

In Scotland, there are HND courses in information studies at Kirkcaldy College of Technology, Scottish College of Textiles at Heriot Watt University, Queen Margaret College and Bell College of Technology.

Those with a relevant first degree can take a postgraduate course in information science. Full- or part-time courses leading to diplomas or MScs are available. Non-graduates with qualifications equal to a pass degree may enter the City University (London) course.

Personal Qualities

A methodical approach and accuracy, the ability to retain information, and an interest in the appropriate field of research, plus a desire to help people to find the information they want, are all important attributes.

£ £10,000–£14,000.

i ASLIB (Association of Information Management), Information House, 20–24 Old Street, London ECIV 9AP; 020 7253 4488 (career information leaflets available)

Institute of Information Scientists, 44 Museum Street, London WC1A 1LY; 020 7831 8003/8633

The Library Association, 7 Ridgmount Street, London WC1E 7AE; 020 7636 7543

'Information Work as a Career' (ASLIB)

INFORMATION TECHNOLOGY

Information technology (IT) is concerned with all aspects of the handling of information. It is the acquiring, processing, storing and disseminating of textual, numerical, vocal and pictorial information by means of computers and telecommunications.

Qualifications and Training

There are jobs in IT at many different levels. There are openings for those with good GCSE results or equivalents, English being particularly important. Other useful subjects are business studies, commerce, accounting, office practice and physics. For those taking A levels or going on to further study at degree level, subjects such as economics, statistics, electrical or mechanical engineering and electronics should be considered. City and Guilds offers a course called Basic Competence in Information Technology, aimed at sixth-formers. One of the most useful skills for working in IT is the ability to use a keyboard effectively. NVQs at levels 2, 3 and 4 are available in Software Systems Development and Software Systems Design. The British Computer Society offers the European Computer Licence.

Personal Qualities

Workers in IT should be accurate, clear thinking, practical and have the ability to work on their own.

£ Typical salaries are: data preparation £8,500–£13,000; data preparation management £11,500+; word processing £8,500–£15,000+; word processing management £17,250+.

i The British Computer Society, 1 Sanford Street, Swindon SN1 1HJ; 01793 417424
www.bcs.co.uk/
Institute for the Management of Information Systems, 5 Kingfisher House, New Mill Road, Orpington, Kent BR5 3QG; 0700 0023456
www.imis.org.uk

INSURANCE

(see also Actuary)

Apart from statutory obligations, insurance is a way of covering the costs arising from disasters of various kinds. Many people pay into a common pool, and those who incur losses can draw money from the pool. The four main areas are personal lines (motor, household, travel), commercial lines (fire, liability, goods in transit), life assurance and reinsurance. Work undertaken in the office includes assessing risks, policy drafting, underwriting (the acceptance and rating of business) and claims settling, and often involves computers. Sales staff work outside the office, as do surveyors and claims inspectors who assess losses on site. Other aspects of insurance include investment, legal and accountancy work. Insurance companies also operate pension funds for businesses. Lloyd's of London is a group of private insurers and is traditionally connected with international insurance, offering all types of cover.

Broker
As the link between client and insurer, the broker advises on and arranges policies for a wide range of businesses.

Loss Adjuster
They work independently, and are appointed by insurers to negotiate settlement of insurance claims. Most chartered loss adjusters used to operate in private practice 'adjusting' claims to ascertain the proper liability of an insurer. Increasingly, loss-adjusting companies are just as likely to provide cost-effective claims and risk-management services to large corporations, local authorities, health services or brokers.

Agents and Inspectors
Agents call on people in their homes, selling insurance and collecting premiums; inspectors are sales people and may also supervise agents and areas.

Qualifications and Training

Those with three GCSEs at grade C or above, including English and maths, may enter a company and at the same time study part-time at a college for an Edexcel (BTEC)/SQA national certificate or diploma. Most insurance employers run a minimum basic training scheme, and candidates can also attend courses run by the employer or at the College of Insurance, leading to the examinations of the Chartered Insurance Institute. To take the initial qualifying exam of the Institute, candidates need three GCE A level or four SCE H grade passes; *or* two subjects at grade C, GCSE and two A levels or five SCE passes, including three at H grade, both including certain specified subjects; *or* the Edexcel (BTEC)/SQA national certificate or diploma; *or* NC/ND or SNC/SND in business studies or public administration.

Other routes to professional qualifications are available for those entrants without A levels or equivalents. The Chartered Insurance Institute's Certificate of Insurance Practice (CIP) can be taken by applicants over 21 without specific qualifications or by those under 21 with four GCSEs grades A to C or Edexcel (BTEC) equivalent. NVQs are available at levels 2, 3 and 4 for General or Life Insurance and intermediaries. The CII's Insurance Foundation Certificate (IFC) provides the insurance knowledge base for the level 2 NVQs, which then require individuals to prove their competence in insurance disciplines.

Personal Qualities

Absolute integrity is necessary, as well as some mathematical ability and an interest in people. Communication skills in speech and writing are also necessary.

£ Salaries vary from employer to employer depending on qualifications and location. Some examples are: £8,000–£11,000 for clerks at 16 and claims officials; insurance salespeople £12,000+; loss adjusters, underwriters and brokers £10,000–£12,000 to start, but highly paid later.

i The British Insurance and Investment Brokers Association, 14 Bevis Marks, London EC3A 7NT; 020 7623 9043

The Chartered Institute of Loss Adjusters, Manfield House, 376 Strand, London WC2R 0LR; 020 7240 1496 www.cila.co.uk

The Chartered Insurance Institute, Careers Information Service, 20 Aldermanbury, London EC2V 7HY; 020 7417 4793 www.cii.co.uk

INTERIOR DECORATOR

(see also Interior Designer, Painter and Decorator)

Decorators may be the craftsmen who do the work of papering and painting in private homes, or larger buildings, or they may give advice on interior decoration – the colour schemes, including carpets and curtains, as well as the paint, wall coverings and fittings. In this context they may be employed by large stores, manufacturers, architects or specialist shops, and also private individuals and companies.

Qualifications and Training

Craftsmen decorators can learn the trade without formal educational qualifications through apprenticeships, whereby they work towards NVQs awarded jointly by City and Guilds and the Construction Industry Training Board. Advisory decorators can learn by working in a workroom or studio of a store, specialist shop or architect's office as a junior, and taking suitable evening classes and City and Guilds courses. Unlike interior designers, interior decorators do not need to hold art and design qualifications.

Personal Qualities

Manual dexterity is necessary for craftsman decorators; artistic sense is imperative for advisers and useful for craftsmen too.

£ £65–£75 a week at 16; £165+ for craftsmen.

i Interior Decorator and Designers Association (IDDA), 1–4 Chelsea Harbour Design Centre, Lots Road, London SW10 0XE; 020 7349 0800

INTERIOR DESIGNER

(see also Interior Decorator)

Interior designers work for commercial organisations, as well as undertaking private commissions. They are responsible for the interiors of buildings (whereas an architect is responsible for its shell). Interior design can cover materials for floors and ceilings, fitments and fittings and colour schemes along with electrical and spatial planning. The commercial organisations may be offices, a chain of hotels or pubs, stores or banks. Interior designers may work with architects, have their own consultancies, or work in design units within large organisations, or have their own business.

Qualifications and Training

Entry to art school and college via a foundation course is the same as for an industrial designer (*see* page 184). Once at art college, the student may specialise in interior design.

Personal Qualities

A natural aptitude for art is necessary, and the ability to work as part of a design team, and to present work to customers.

£ About £11,000, according to experience and ability.

i Interior Decorator and Designers Association (IDDA), 1–4 Chelsea Harbour Design Centre, Lots Road, London SW10 0XE; 020 7349 0800

Careers in Art and Design (Kogan Page)

INTERPRETER

(see also Translator)

Interpreters communicate between people who do not share a common language. They use two main techniques: simultaneous and consecutive interpreting. Conference interpreters usually work using the simultaneous method in a booth with headphones and communicative technology, allowing them to hear the speaker and interpret to their audience.

Very few openings are available for interpreters, even worldwide. Conference interpreters work at international conferences such as UNO and the EC and at the International Court of Justice, using simultaneous or consecutive interpreting. Some work for international agencies; others are freelance. Demand for conference interpreters in particular languages may fluctuate depending on the political and economic requirements of the day. Interpreters with specialist knowledge, such as engineering or economics, may have the chance to work at conferences on their subject.

Interpreters may also work as guides in tourist centres, and to do this must usually be accredited and trained as guides. Demand for interpreting in the public services (police, courts, public health and local government) has led to the creation of the National Register of Public Service Interpreters covering a wide range of African, Asian, European and Far Eastern languages. This register is supported by the Home Office and the UK legal agencies. The Institute of Translation and Interpreting (ITI) can also help source qualified public service interpreters from its membership, as can numerous other commercial agencies.

Qualifications and Training

To take a degree course, two GCE A levels or three SCE H grade passes, including a foreign language, are normally required. At the newer universities and colleges, training in interpreting and translating is offered, combined with regional studies or technological or business studies, aimed at industry, commerce and international organisations. A list of these courses is offered by the Institute of Linguists and the Institute of Translation and Interpreting (ITI). Such degree courses usually involve work or study abroad.

Those with an Edexcel (BTEC) national award or one A level and three GCSEs may enter for the Edexcel (BTEC) higher national diploma course. Those with SNC/SND with a language pass or three H grade passes including English and at least one foreign language and two Standard grade passes can apply for SQA courses at levels up to postgraduate.

Personal Qualities

Fluency in two or more languages should be allied with a natural feeling for words and phrases and a good ear. It is necessary to be able to think quickly, to remain alert for long periods, and to be socially confident. Subject knowledge is essential, especially for simultaneous interpreting which requires a degree of understanding and anticipation of subject matter and context.

£ Interpreters working in business earn £200 and more per day. Hourly rates for some public service agencies can be comparatively lower.

i Institute of Linguists, Saxon House, 48 Southwark Street, London SE11 1UN; 020 7940 3100; fax 020 7940 3101

Institute of Translation and Interpreting (ITI), 377 City Road, London EC1V 1ND; 020 7713 7600; fax 020 7713 7650 www.iti.org.uk

'Average Rates for Translation' (Institute of Linguists)

Careers Using Languages (Kogan Page)

Great Careers for People Interested in Languages (Kogan Page)

'Some courses in translation and interpreting in the UK', factsheet from ITI (address above)

ITI information pack (send sae with 39p stamp, ref: T/I training and careers pack)

'1998 ITI Rates and Salaries Survey', available from ITI (address above)

INVESTMENT ANALYST

Investment analysts analyse the financial markets in order to advise on the best investments for clients. Investment managers rely on their information.

There are two main types of investment analyst: first, those who work for stockbrokers and undertake their own analysis to provide information for fund manager clients. The aim is to generate 'buy and sell' orders for the stockbrokers for whom they work. This is known as the 'sell side'. Second, there are those who work for investment management institutions. They provide ideas and information to enable their in-house fund managers to make the best decisions for their clients. This is known as the 'buy side'. The majority of investment analysts work on the 'sell side'.

Qualifications and Training

Entrants generally have a degree and often a professional qualification. The most useful degrees are economics, accountancy or statistics. Training is on the job and during this time entrants study for a professional qualification by an examination set by the Institute of Investment Management and Research.

Personal Qualities

Entrants must be able to work as part of a team as well as on their own initiative. Considerable time is spent on the telephone, so communication skills are important. Naturally, a keen interest in world financial and current affairs is essential.

£ Trainees in investment analysis work draw a fairly modest salary, but with experience may earn £50,000+.

i The Institute of Investment Management and Research, 21 Ironmonger Lane, London EC2V 8EY; 020 7796 3000; fax 020 7796 3333
www.iimr.org.uk

INVESTMENT FUND MANAGER

Investment fund managers invest the funds of other people – private clients and institutions, such as insurance companies, charities, independent schools and specialised research institutions. Managers must keep their clients' interests continually under review, offering advice on how to retain their clients' income and when to change investments. Investment fund managers may be employed by the larger institutions or work in specialist firms that tend to serve smaller clients.

Qualifications and Training

Entrants generally should have a degree, the most useful being economics, accountancy or statistics. The regulatory authorities now have rigorous training requirements, including the passing of a basic competence examination, the Investment Management Certificate (IMC), which is operated by the Institute of Investment Management and Research. The Associate examination of the Institute is the formally recognised qualification for investment fund managers.

Personal Qualities

Investment managers must have a keen interest in world financial and current affairs, and be logical and trustworthy.

£ Trainees in investment work draw a fairly modest salary, but with experience may earn £50,000+.

i The Institute of Investment Management and Research, 21 Ironmonger Lane, London EC2V 8EY; 020 7796 3000; fax 020 7796 3333
www.iimr.org.uk

J

JEWELLERY TRADE

Design
Jewellery designers craft a wide variety of items either by hand or using methods of large-scale production. These may be very expensive traditionally styled pieces, using gold or platinum, cheaper costume jewellery using synthetic stones and base metals, or fashion accessories made from beads, plastic, wood, and so on.

Although there are a few openings for designers of expensive jewellery, the more costly costume jewellery, and mass-produced jewellery, there is more scope for original designers on either a freelance or artist/craftsman basis, making fashionable ranges with semi-precious stones.

Manufacture
The jewellery, silverware and allied industries encompass a vast range of specialist skills. Apart from mounting and silversmithing, other skills are needed to support these occupations, such as gem setting, engraving (hand and machine), enamelling, chasing, engine turning, spinning, electro-plating, polishing. Each skill may usually be learnt at specialist companies or within larger companies' departments.

Qualifications and Training

It is advisable for those wishing to follow a career in jewellery design to have had full-time specialist training before looking for employment. Full-time three-year, and some sandwich-based, degree courses in three-dimensional design, with main options in jewellery, silver, metal, etc, are available at a number of colleges and universities.

The minimum entrance requirements are usually two A levels and three GCSEs or equivalents, or satisfactory completion of a one- or two-year foundation course at a college of art and design, together with one A level and four GCSEs or equivalents.

Manufacturing training can be by traditional trade apprenticeships, lasting between three and five years, or Youth Training Credit programmes lasting two years and with competency linked to NVQ level 2 in Manufacturing Jewellery and Allied Products.

The Gemmological Association and Gem Testing Laboratory have two diploma qualifications – the Diploma in Gemmology (taken in two parts), and the Gem Diamond Diploma (one part). These may be studied by correspondence, or as daytime or evening courses at GAGTL and allied technology centres worldwide. There are also two examinations conducted by the British Horological Institute – the certificate for clockmakers and the diploma for salesmen.

Personal Qualities

People in the jewellery trade must have a sense of design and an appreciation of quality. Designers must be prepared to work hard and keep to a busy schedule. Self-employed or independent designers will need determination to keep going and unflagging enthusiasm to sell their products. Manufacturing employees and craftspeople must possess good manual dexterity, creativity, integrity, attention to detail, initiative and self-motivation.

£ Shopworkers earn about £170 a week. Individual craftsmen set their own rates. Apprentice craftsmen earn £70+ a week.

i British Jewellers' Association, 10 Vyse Street, Birmingham B18 6LT; 0121 237 1109

Gemmological Association and Gem Testing Laboratory of Great Britain, 27 Greville Street, London EC1N 8TN; 020 7404 3334; fax 020 7404 8843
www.gagtl.ac.uk/gagtl

National Association of Goldsmiths, 78a Luke Street, London EC2A 4PY; 020 7613 4445
www.jewellers.org.uk

Jobber*, see *Market Maker

JOCKEY

Jockeys are employed by trainers of flat racing and National Hunt (jump) racehorses to ride horses at race meetings. They may ride for one trainer or for several. To become a jockey it is necessary first to work in a racing stable as an apprentice jockey or stablehand.

Only those showing most talent – about one out of every ten – are chosen to ride in a race. The others remain as stablehands, and may be promoted to Head Lad (this title applies to boys and girls).

Stable Lad

Stable lads (who may be boys or girls) do much labouring work: mucking out, fetching straw, filling haynets and sweeping. They must also learn to groom and exercise the horses, and usually become responsible for a certain number of their 'own'. On race days, a stable lad will accompany a horse, groom him, walk him round before the race and lead him into the winner's enclosure if he wins.

Qualifications and Training

No specific educational qualifications are needed to become a jockey. Some experience of riding is useful but serious training is given by the stable. The racing industry has introduced NVQs, levels 1, 2 and 3 in Racehorse Care and Management. Flat-racing apprenticeships start at 16 and last until the age of 24. National Hunt apprenticeships start at 17–18 and last until the age of 25.

There is a nine-week training course available at the British Racing School in Newmarket, funded by racing, and open to school leavers who wish to work in a racing yard. Pupils are taught to ride, look after horses and carry out elementary stable management. The Northern Racing School at Doncaster runs a 12-week course for those coming into the industry to train as stable staff. Both schools run a Youth Training scheme.

Personal Qualities

Apprentice jockeys must be prepared to work long hours in all weather conditions. At 16, flat-racing apprentices should weigh 7–8 stone (44–51kg), girls 8–9 stone (51–57kg); National Hunt jockeys may be heavier. Jockeys need strong hands and arms and must be able to deal with nervous horses in a calm, confident and unemotional way. Jockeys must also be able to work within the strict, rather conservative traditions of the racing world.

£ Apprentice jockeys and stablehands over 19 and with a year's experience earn about £140 a week. Apprentice and conditional jockeys receive their normal wage plus half the riding fee when racing. Racing jockeys' salaries vary according to their success; there is a rate per ride plus a percentage of the prize money.

i British Racing School, Snailwell Road, Newmarket, Suffolk CB8 7NU; 01638 665103

National Trainers' Federation, 9 High Street, Lambourn, Hungerford, Berkshire RG17 8XN; 01488 71719 www.martex.co.uk/racehorsetrainers

Stable Lads' Association (SLA), 4 Dunsmore Way, Midway, Swadlincote, Derbyshire DE11 7LA; 01283 211522

The Northern Racing School, The Stables, Rossington Hall, Great North Road, Doncaster DN11 0HN; 01302 865462

Joiner,* see *Carpenter and Bench Joiner

JOURNALIST

The title 'journalist' covers a variety of jobs.

Reporter

Reporters find, research and write news articles and features for newspapers, magazines, special-interest periodicals, news agencies, radio and television. They work irregular hours to meet deadlines and must be able to produce accurate, interesting and readable copy quickly, often in noisy offices or even public places. Reporters cover all kinds of stories, from weddings and council meetings (at local level) to world events and sensational murder cases (for the national papers). Some opportunities exist for foreign correspondents and freelance journalists.

Sub-Editor

Sub-editors reduce or, if necessary, re-write articles to an appropriate size depending upon importance and position in the paper. They also deal with continuing stories which come in a bit at a time, write the headlines and, in between editions, may amend stories to accommodate sudden developments or change the page layout if required. Sub-editors may specialise, for example, dealing only with the sports-page production or page design.

Fashion Editor
The Fashion Editor on a newspaper or magazine is responsible for researching and anticipating the latest fashion trends and presenting them in articles which will appeal to readers.

Feature Writer/Columnist
Feature writers suggest subjects for research and produce longer than average articles dealing with topics not necessarily of current news value but of general interest, such as an interview with a public figure or an article about tax relief, motoring, and so on. Columnists write about subjects from their own personal point of view.

The Editor
The Editor of a publication is responsible for its policy, its content and the appointment and organisation of the staff.

Qualifications and Training

Most journalists begin their career by serving for two or three years on a provincial newspaper. Each year, approximately 800 school-leaver entrants, with at least five GCSEs and two A level passes, and from the one-year National Council for the Training of Journalists (NCTJ) pre-entry course, find positions. Direct entrants undertake a qualifying period of two years (pre-entry trainees 18 months) of on-the-job training and experience in full-time employment. Part of the learning process is spent on block-release courses at colleges approved by the NCTJ or tuition on in-house schemes, the rest of the time being taken up with work as a junior reporter. Preliminary exams lead finally to the exam for the national certificate awarded by the NCTJ. (This equates to level 4 NVQ.) There are also a number of degree courses, postgraduate courses usually lasting one year, and two 18-week NCTJ postgraduate courses.

Personal Qualities

Journalists must possess powers of self-expression, observation, accuracy, patience and tact. They must take pride in their work, be resourceful, willing to travel and to work under pressure and irregular hours; stamina is required, as is confidence, great curiosity and the ability to put people at their ease. It helps to be able to write fast in long hand, and to learn shorthand and word-processing skills.

£ Salaries vary greatly. Trainees on a small weekly paper earn about £7,000+. In London trainees start at about £10,000+. Generally, trainee journalists' salaries are lower than average, but increase rapidly with experience, specialist knowledge and seniority.

i Chartered Institute of Journalists, 2 Dock Offices, Surrey Quays Road, London SE16 2XU; 020 7252 1187

National Council for the Training of Journalists, Latton Bush Centre, Southern Way, Harlow, Essex CM18 7BL; 01279 430009

Careers in Journalism (Kogan Page)

K

KENNEL WORK

(see also Dog Groomer)

Kennel staff ensure that the animals in their care have clean accommodation, are fed a regular and nutritious diet, are clean, well groomed and given sufficient exercise. Where animals are sick or recovering from an operation, the kennel staff must also be able to provide adequate nursing care.

There are a number of different types of kennel – greyhound kennels train dogs for racing, hunt kennels for hunting – and involve a lot of outdoor work, exercising the dogs, and perhaps travelling to meetings. There are quarantine kennels licensed by the Ministry of Agriculture, Fisheries and Food and breeding kennels where duties will also include weaning and training puppies, preparing dogs for shows, and possibly handling them. Boarding kennels look after animals while their owners are away. Some of the racing and quarantine kennels are large operations situated near racing stadia, airports and ports but others may be smaller, family-run concerns.

Qualifications and Training

No formal qualifications are needed to work in kennels, and most employers prefer school leavers to train on the job – this is best done via a Youth Training course. Indeed a good entry route is via work experience while still at school. The NVQ level 2 qualification in Animal Care is nationally recognised by the industry and this is a good base for further study. Many training organisations and agricultural colleges throughout the country offer this qualification. Entry requirements vary depending on the institution.

Personal Qualities

Good health, general fitness and stamina are required for this manual, physically demanding outdoor work. Kennel staff must be unsentimental about animals but at the same time have a genuine concern for their well-being; they require patience and a placid but firm nature. A willingness to work long days, weekends and public holidays is also required.

£ £80–£120+ a week.

i Animal Care College, Ascot House, High Street, Ascot, Berkshire SL5 7JG; 01344 628269

Animal Care and Equine National Training Organisation, 2nd Floor, The Burgess Building, The Green, Stafford ST17 4BL; 01785 227399; fax 01785 229015

Our Dogs, 5 Oxford Road, Station Approach, Manchester M60 1SX; 0161 228 1984 (weekly magazine featuring job offers and advertisements from kennels. Also publishes *Cats*)

Local Jobcentres and Careers Offices

Careers Working with Animals (Kogan Page)

Running Your Own Boarding Kennels (Kogan Page)

L

LABORATORY TECHNICIAN

(see also Biomedical Scientist)

Laboratory technicians support scientists, technologists, lecturers and medical staff by enabling practical work to be carried out in laboratories and related areas. Their work may include: preparation, cultivation, maintenance, use and disposal of specimens and samples used for analysis or other work. Care of animals, insects and plants, design, construction, maintenance and use of equipment, obtaining, evaluation and reporting on results. A range of materials, procedures and equipment may be used including sophisticated instruments with dedicated computers.

Laboratory technicians work in a range of industries, including petrochemical, food, textiles, pharmaceutical, for national and local government, for research organisations, in all sectors of education and in medical services.

Qualifications and Training

The minimum entry requirement is likely to be four or five GCSEs at grade C or higher, or equivalent, including maths and science. Training is usually provided on the job. NVQs are available for laboratory technicians working in the chemical and pharmaceutical industries and in education.

The Institute of Science Technology offers its own vocational qualifications at Preliminary and Core levels through a network of registered centres.

Personal Qualities

Laboratory technicians must be practical, numerate, methodical, conscientious, discreet and accurate. Good colour vision is essential.

£ £7,000–£9,000 depending on age and qualifications.

i Institute of Science Technology, Stowe House, Netherstowe, Lichfield, Staffordshire WS13 6TJ; 01543 251346; fax 01543 415804; e-mail *ist@ismstowe.demon.co.uk* www.inscite.demon.co.uk

Working as a Laboratory Technician (Batsford)

LAND AGENT

(see also Surveyor/Surveying Technician)

Land agents work for estate owners and sometimes for large institutional owners. Their work overlaps to some extent with that of agricultural surveyors in that they are both concerned with the use and development of land and may advise owners on agricultural methods, forestry, accountancy and the building or improving of farm buildings. In addition the land agent may be responsible for stocking and for employing estate staff, as well as attending to the owner's personal business matters.

Qualifications and Training

Formal qualifications are not always necessary for a land agent who is employed by a private owner. However, it is advisable to become professionally qualified as a surveyor (*see* Surveyor/Surveying Technician).

Personal Qualities

Necessary requirements include a love of the land and being out of doors, a practical approach and the ability to direct one's own work.

£ A school leaver could expect about £8,000, whereas a newly qualified surveyor with professional competence would receive about £15,000–£20,000.

i The Royal Institution of Chartered Surveyors, 12 Great George Street, London SW1P 5AD; 020 7222 7000

LANDSCAPE DESIGNER

Landscape designers are trained in the planning and design of all types of outdoor spaces. They use design techniques based on their knowledge of the functional and aesthetic characteristics of landscape materials, and of the organisation of landscape elements, external spaces and activities. Their work ranges from large-scale landscape planning to the preparation of schemes for the short- and long-term development of individual sites. It also includes the preparation of detailed designs, specifications, contract drawings and the letting and supervision of contracts.

Some practitioners are also qualified in other disciplines such as planning and architecture and the landscape designer draws on many fields in order to promote new landscapes, and sustain existing ones.

Qualifications and Training

The recognized professional qualification for landscape designers is Member of the Landscape Institute (MLI), entitled to use the title Chartered Landscape Architect (Design Division). Associate Membership, the first step towards achieving this, is gained after completing an accredited degree. Two years' relevant work is required as an Associate Member before taking the Institute's Professional Practice Examination and thus progressing to full Professional Membership. A list of accredited courses is available from the Landscape Institute.

Personal Qualities

Necessary requirements are creativity, imagination, a practical outlook, interest in the landscape and an enthusiasm for working outdoors.

£ A recent graduate could expect to earn between £11,000–£17,000. A recently qualified Chartered Landscape Architect could expect to start on approximately £17,000.

i The Landscape Institute, 6/8 Barnard Mews, London SW11 1QU; 020 7738 9166; fax 020 7738 9134
www.l-i.org.uk

Careers Working Outdoors (Kogan Page)

'Professional Careers in Landscape Architecture' (The Landscape Institute)

LANDSCAPE MANAGER

Landscape managers employ management techniques in the long-term care and development of new and existing landscapes and also in determining policy and planning for future landscape management and use. They have particular expertise in the management and maintenance of landscape materials, both hard and soft, based on established principles of construction, horticulture and ecology. In addition, the landscape manager will have a thorough knowledge of budgetary control procedures, property and resource management, especially related to manpower and machinery and of letting and administration of contracts.

Qualifications and Training

The recognised professional qualification for landscape managers is Member of the Landscape Institute (MLI), entitled to use the title Chartered Landscape Architect (Management Division). Associate Membership, the first step towards achieving this, is gained after completing an accredited degree or a relevant degree and a period of relevant work experience. Two years' relevant work is required as an Associate Member before taking the Institute's Professional Practice Examination and thus progressing to full Professional Membership. A list of accredited courses is available from the Landscape Institute.

Personal Qualities

Desirable qualities are an interest in the landscape, good organisational and interpersonal skills, consistent application and a practical outlook.

£ A recent graduate could expect to earn between £11,000–£17,000. A recently qualified Chartered Landscape Architect could expect to start on approximately £17,000.

i The Landscape Institute, 6/8 Barnard Mews, London SW11 1QU; 020 7738 9166; fax 020 7738 9134

'Professional Careers in Landscape Architecture' (The Landscape Institute)

LANDSCAPE SCIENTIST

Landscape scientists have a specific understanding of the principles and process of natural biological and physical systems. They relate their environment training and experience to the solution of practical landscape problems, providing both traditional and innovative input to landscape design, planning and management work. Their scientific training in subjects such as ecology, conservation, biology, soil science, botany or related subjects, together with the ability to apply these skills to a variety of landscape issues, makes them key participants in the field of environmental impact analysis. Evaluation of the significance, effects and possible amelioration of major and minor planning proposals, along with creating new habitats and environments in association with mineral workings, forestry and agriculture are significant roles of the landscape scientist. Smaller-scale ecological and habitat surveys, species assessments, wildlife management plans and the appraisal and preparation of conservation schemes are frequents tasks. Some are involved in research and teaching but this work is directly applied to real landscape situations and the practical training of landscape designers, managers and scientists.

Qualifications and Training

The recognised professional qualification for landscape scientists is Member of the Landscape Institute (MLI), entitled to use the title Chartered Landscape Architect (Science Division). Associate Membership, the first step towards achieving this, is gained after completing a relevant degree and a period of relevant work experience. Two years' relevant work is required as an Associate Member before taking the Institute's Professional Practice Examination and thus progressing to full Professional Membership.

Personal Qualities

Desirable qualities are enthusiasm for the subject, technical commitment, a practical and realistic outlook and good communication skills.

£ A recent graduate could expect to earn between £11,000–£17,000. A recently qualified Chartered Landscape Architect could expect to start on approximately £17,000.

[i] The Landscape Institute, 6/8 Barnard Mews, London SW11 1QU; 020 7738 9166; fax 020 7738 9134
'Professional Careers in Landscape Architecture' (The Landscape Institute)

LAW COMMISSION (RESEARCH ASSISTANT)

The statutory Government advisory body on law reform, the Law Commission is currently working on projects in a variety of fields including common law, company and commercial law, crime and property law, and on general revision of statute law. The work is carried out in small teams, each under the direction of a Commissioner, consisting of qualified lawyers and research assistants. Draft Bills are prepared by Parliamentary Counsel on loan to the Commission. Extensive consultation and investigation takes place before proposals are formulated; a sizeable proportion result in legislation. Projects range from major investigations of controversial areas of law to the consideration of a specific problem.

Qualifications and Training

Law graduates (upper second class honours minimum), and graduates of other disciplines who have completed the Legal Practice Course or the Bar Vocational Course, are recruited annually to work as research assistants. The work offers a unique opportunity to take part in the creation of new legislative measures, as well as the in-depth development of skills in a particular area of law. Former research assistants have found their experience a valuable asset in their subsequent legal careers, whether in practice or in academic posts. The initial appointment is for one year with the possibility of extension for a further period up to a maximum of three years in all.

Personal Qualities

Entrants should have a good knowledge of and genuine interest in the law, and should be able to think and write clearly.

[£] About £13,500.

[i] The Law Commission, Conquest House, 37–38 John Street, Theobalds Road, London WC1N 2BQ; 020 7453 1210

LAW COSTS DRAFTSMAN

The way a solicitor's bill is drawn up is complicated: different fees are charged depending on the experience and seniority of the solicitor involved, the solicitor may have had to pay travelling expenses and court fees, and a Barrister might have been engaged. Some bills are paid direct by clients, others out of public funds if the client is entitled to legal aid.

To save time and expense, many solicitors now employ a law costs draftsman to prepare their bills for them. Some law costs draftsmen work in solicitors' offices, others in independent firms and others work at home, going into a legal office to pick up the files.

Qualifications and Training

No formal educational requirements are necessary but four GCSEs or equivalent, to include English, would be beneficial. A good head for figures and a good standard of written and spoken English are necessary. Training is required but some begin the work with a background in accounts and others have previously worked as legal executives.

Personal Qualities

Law costs draftsmen need to be patient, able to cope with detail and be methodical and careful in their work.

£ From £11,000–£16,000, but in this work there is a range of payments and some people may earn much more than this.

i Association of Law Costs Draftsmen, c/o S A Chapman, Church Cottage, Church Lane, Stuston, Diss, Norfolk IP21 4AG; 01379 741404
www.btinternet.com/nalcd

LEATHER PRODUCTION

Leather is produced from skins and hides to make shoes, bags, gloves, clothes, upholstery and saddlery. Modern leather production is based on up-to-date science (particularly chemistry) and technology with a responsible regard for environmental factors. There is a worldwide shortage of well-qualified leather technologists.

Qualifications and Training

Training for leatherworkers is on the job, and vocational qualifications are available for operatives and craftspeople through part-time, full-time and open-learning courses. Technicians require a good general education and GCSEs should include maths, science and English. Recognised qualifications include NVQs in Leather Production, BSc in leather technology and MSc in leather technology. Entry to a specific course is dependent on the entry requirements of the institution.

Personal Qualities

Operatives and craftsmen must be physically fit and possess stamina. Technologists must have a practical, responsible approach to their work and be prepared to travel abroad if required.

£ The basic salary for leatherworkers is £140 for a 40-hour week and increases through piecework or incentive bonus to between £175 to £400. A leather technologist could expect an annual salary of approximately £16,000.

i BLC, Leather Technology Centre, Leather Trade House, Kings Park Road, Moulton Park, Northampton NN3 6JD; 01604 679999; fax 01604 679998
www.blcleathertech.com

British School of Leather Technology, University College, Northampton, Bo Green Road, Northampton, NN2 7AL; 01604 735500; fax 01604 711183
www.leathernet.com/bslt/

LECTURER

Higher Education

Lecturers in universities, and other higher education institutions (HEIs) teach mainly undergraduates. As well as teaching, many carry out their own research, write articles and books, give outside lectures and, in some cases, broadcasts. Competition is fierce and it is unlikely that a new graduate will be able to enter higher education as a first job.

Further Education
Lecturers in this field may teach anyone over the age of 16. The range of subjects taught in further education is diverse and growing rapidly. Most lecturers have a particular expertise but are increasingly expected to teach outside of their specialist area. They may work on vocational and/or academic courses. In order to meet the demands of their clients, further education colleges offer courses on a full- or part-time basis. These include evening courses and short courses.

Qualifications and Training

Lecturers in HEIs must have first or upper second class degrees; many have postgraduate qualifications, and some have further degrees. In the new universities, lecturers may be drawn from industry or commerce.

Qualifications for lecturers in further education vary, depending on the subject taught. A degree, a professional qualification and a teaching qualification are all acceptable and desirable. There are one-year full-time and two-year part-time courses available for those intending to teach in further education.

Personal Qualities

All teachers/lecturers must have a high level of knowledge of, and enthusiasm for, their subject, combined with a desire to communicate this to others. They must have the ability to organise and deliver their material in a way that is understandable to their students.

£ Starting salaries in higher education are from £14,600 upwards; salaries in the new universities are comparable for similar levels of work. Full-time lecturers in further education can expect a starting salary of about £12,000.

i Department for Education, Sanctuary Buildings, Great Smith Street, London SW1P 3BT; 020 7925 5555 www.dfee.gov.uk

Department of Education for Northern Ireland, Rathgael House, Balloo Road, Bangor, Co Down BT19 7PR; 028 9027 9279

NATFHE – The University and College Lecturers' Union, 27 Britannia Street, London WC1X 9JP (written enquiries only)

The Scottish Office Education Department, Victoria Quay, Edinburgh EH6 6QQ; 0131 556 8400

LEGAL CASHIER/ADMINISTRATOR

Legal cashiers and administrators work in solicitors' offices and are responsible for dealing with the accounts and administration. Legal cashiers may work as the sole bookkeeper, administrator or manager, or, in a big firm, be responsible for a large number of staff.

The Institute of Legal Cashiers and Administrators keeps a register of vacancies, providing a free service to solicitors and members.

Qualifications and Training

The Institute of Legal Cashiers and Administrators has three levels of qualification: Diploma, Associateship and Fellowship. It offers correspondence courses leading to the Diploma and Associateship examinations. Formal academic qualifications are not required to take these. The diploma is a qualification in its own right and covers the maintenance of a solicitor's internal financial records. It is particularly aimed at those without bookkeeping knowledge. The Associateship is for those who wish to make a career as a legal cashier or administrator and enables them to advise and manage financial and administrative affairs in any solicitor's office. The Fellowship, available to Associates, is the highest qualification, offering a deeper insight into the profession.

Personal Qualities

Entrants must have a high standard of integrity and reliability and be very discreet.

£ £10,000–£16,000.

i The Institute of Legal Cashiers and Administrators, 2nd Floor, 146–148 Eltham Hill, Eltham, London SE9 5DX; 020 8294 2887

LEGAL EXECUTIVE

A Legal Executive is a professional lawyer employed in a solicitor's office or in the legal departments of commerce and central local government. The training and academic requirements in a specified area of law are at the same level as those required of a solicitor. Consequently, with few exceptions, a Legal Executive is able to carry out tasks which are similar to those undertaken by solicitors. The main areas of specialisation are conveyancing, civil litigation, criminal law, family law and probate. In addition to providing a worthwhile career in its own right, the Legal Executive qualification provides access to those wishing to qualify as solicitors via the Institute route.

In Scotland, the term Legal Executive is not used, but solicitors engage assistants to do similar work.

Qualifications and Training

The minimum entry requirement is four GCSEs to include English, but A level students and graduates are welcome. As an alternative, the Institute accepts a qualification in vocational legal studies and has special arrangements for students who are over 21 years of age. In the main, training is on a part-time basis so that there is potential for trainees to 'learn while they earn'. For those already working in a legal environment, but with no formal legal qualifications, an NVQ (level 4) in Legal Practice is available and ILEX is the awarding body.

Personal Qualities

An ability to communicate, both verbally and in writing, with people at all levels, absolute discretion and trustworthiness, together with a meticulous attention to detail, are essential.

£ Varies according to age and qualification, and the type of work undertaken. Currently, the commencing salary is likely to be in the order of £11,200, rising to £25,000–£40,000 when qualified. Many established Legal Executives receive salaries in excess of £50,000.

i The Institute of Legal Executives, Kempston Manor, Kempston, Bedford MK42 7AB; 01234 841000; e-mail *info@ilex.org.uk* www.ilex.org.uk

Careers in the Law (Kogan Page)

LEISURE AND AMENITY MANAGEMENT

(see also Sport and Recreation Facility Management)

People employed in this field may work in leisure centres, outward bound centres, theatre and arts centres, historic houses and ancient monuments, country areas offering nature trails, fishing and camping facilities to the public, or even be in charge of bingo or dance halls. Managers, as well as being interested in their particular leisure activity, must be responsible for the administrative and financial running of the enterprise. Many in this field are employed in local government, but there are also opportunities in private sports centres, health and fitness clubs and tourist attractions.

Qualifications and Training

The Institute of Leisure and Amenity Management (ILAM) offers four levels of qualification based upon the completion of work-based projects: the ILAM first award for candidates who are new to the industry and who hold junior positions within leisure organisations; the ILAM Certificate in Leisure Operations, for candidates who have a working knowledge of the industry and hold junior supervisory positions; the ILAM Certificate in Leisure Management for candidates with a good understanding of the industry and who hold junior or middle management jobs; the ILAM Diploma in Leisure Management for candidates who have successfully demonstrated their managerial ability at a senior level.

HND courses are available and a range of degree courses in leisure studies/recreation management and sports sciences. GNVQs are available in Leisure and Tourism at levels 2 and 3.

Personal Qualities

A strong interest in the particular area of leisure is necessary, as is the ability to organise, administer and manage people.

£ An assistant manager would probably earn £15,000–£20,000, depending on the size and type of establishment.

i Institute of Leisure and Amenity Management, ILAM House, Lower Basildon, Reading, Berkshire RG8 9NE; 01491 874800 www.ilam.co.uk

LIBRARIAN/INFORMATION MANAGER

Librarians and information managers anticipate the information needs of their clients, acquire that information by the most efficient means possible on behalf of their clients, and may well analyse it and repackage it for the client. Information may come in the form of a book or journal, or may be extracted from databases in-house, on CD-ROM or online. Ideally, librarians and information managers are skilled navigators and facilitators on the Internet.

The information is organised to make it accessible to users by indexing, cataloguing and classifying. Librarians and information managers promote and exploit the library's collection to the library or information source users and assist them with any enquiries. They work in public libraries and schools, universities and colleges, in government, in the law, in hospitals, business and industry, and also in accountancy and engineering, professional and learned societies, and in virtually all areas of economic activity.

Qualifications and Training

Library assistants are usually required to have four to five GCSEs or equivalent, to include English language; training is on the job. Part-time or distance-learning vocational courses leading to City and Guilds and SVQ qualifications are available to Library Assistants in post. NVQs levels 2 to 4 in Information and Library Services are also available. To qualify as a professional Librarian or Information Officer and gain Chartered Membership of the Library Association, a degree or postgraduate qualification accredited by the association is necessary.

A number of colleges and universities offer degrees in archive administration, information management and information and library studies for individuals with A levels or equivalents. A list of courses and colleges is available from Aslib (address below).

Personal Qualities

Librarians and information managers need to be well educated, with an outgoing personality, and able to communicate with people at all levels with clarity, accuracy and tact. They need intellectual curiosity and breadth of knowledge and a logical and methodical approach to organising and subsequently seeking out and presenting information. A good memory is also useful. Management skills and an interest in working with computers are important assets.

£ Depending on age and experience, library assistants' salaries range from £8,000 to £16,500; newly qualified librarians earn from £11,900 to £16,500, and middle managers from about £17,000–£27,000. The most senior qualified library managers of large services can earn above £32,000.

i Information Services, The Library Association, 7 Ridgmount Street, London WC1E 7AE; 020 7636 7543; fax 020 7436 7218

Aslib Professional Recruitment, Staple Hall, Stone House Court, London EC3A 7PB; 020 7903 0000
www.aslib.co.uk/aslib/

Linguist, **see** *Interpreter, Translator*

LITERARY AGENT

Literary agents act as middlemen between authors and publishers, film producers and theatre managements. Initially they read authors' manuscripts and decide whether or not to accept an author as a client. Once accepted, an author may be guided by an agent about ideas for books and changes to existing manuscripts. The agent then finds a publisher or producer for the author's work and negotiates the best possible terms. The agent deals with the publisher on all matters that will affect the client, including the contract, manuscript delivery, follow-up titles, advertising, publicity, paperback, television and film rights, and obtaining payments when due.

Some literary agents also act for foreign publishers attempting to find British publishers who will bring out an English edition of a book already published abroad. Like publishers, agents tend to specialise in such areas as fiction, general non-fiction and specialist publishing.

Qualifications and Training

No particular educational qualifications are necessary. Experience of the book trade is the most important factor, and most literary agents have gained this by working in a publishing house. Foreign languages are an asset, particularly in the international field.

Personal Qualities

Agents need shrewd literary judgement and a knowledge of worldwide market conditions, negotiating and legal skills, business and financial ability. They must be hard working, persistent, adaptable and sympathetic towards their authors.

£ Agents receive a percentage of the money earned by the author – usually in the 10–20 per cent range.

i *The Writer's Handbook*, ed Barry Turner (Macmillan) (annual publication); *Writers' and Artists' Yearbook* (A&C Black)

LOCAL GOVERNMENT

Local authorities provide a range of services to the community. They provide the services that affect the daily lives of people living in their area, from sports centres to refuse collection; schools to homes for the elderly; bus services to libraries. They also have responsibility for ensuring that food sold in shops and restaurants is fit to eat; that streets are lit; and that land is developed with environmental considerations and the needs of the local population in mind. Consequently there are many varied areas of work to consider and over 500 different careers to choose from.

Local government employs over two million staff in England, Scotland and Wales, some of whom are administrators who supervise, coordinate and organise the provision of services to the community. They also employ professional and technical staff, for instance, architects, accountants, engineers and electricians.

Qualifications and Training

There are a variety of paths to follow to obtain a position in local government. GCSE and A level passes may be necessary, or a degree, and some posts require professional qualifications. Work experience and appropriate NVQs are recognised as equivalent in value.

Training is seen as an important commodity in local government and as such is available in abundance in the form of internal and external courses.

Personal Qualities

These vary according to the job to be performed, but in general local government employees should be able to communicate effectively both with colleagues and the community at large, work well in a team and be professional in their approach.

£ Salaries in local government can be competitive. There may also be a variety of benefits, including relocation packages, as well as flexible working arrangements.

i Local Government Opportunities, Improvement and Development Agency for Local Government (IDeA), Layden House, 76–86 Turnmill Street, London EC1 5QU; 020 7296 6600

Personnel Officer of individual local authorities

'Careers and Training in Local Government', *Local Government Careers Explorer*, IDeA Web site www.lgnto.gov.uk/lgo

LOGISTICS

When a customer places an order a chain reaction – the supply chain – is started. The supply chain ensures that the product that has been ordered, whether it is a car for an individual, or a thousand bars of chocolate for a retailer, reaches the customer who placed the order.

Logistics is the management of the supply chain. The professionals working in logistics are responsible for warehouse management, distribution and transport management, inventory (stock) control, information systems, logistics planning and analysis and supply-chain management.

Qualifications and Training

Logistics professionals will be expected to have achieved GCSEs or GNVQs and A levels, or Advanced GNVQs, a degree and/or a professional qualification.

First degree courses (BSc) in logistics are available, but companies accept trainee managers from various disciplines. Many offer further on-the-job training linked to the professional qualifications of the Institute of Logistics and Transport. An MSc in logistics is a pre-requisite in some companies. The alternative is to follow the professional qualification route, commencing with the foundation programme of the Institute of Logistics which is offered by selected colleges of further education.

Personal Qualities

Logistics can offer early responsibility, so trainee managers should be responsible, able to motivate others and enjoy a challenge. Organisational, numeracy and man-management skills are essential. Foreign-language skills are an advantage.

£ The average for a graduate management trainee is £15,000. Managers' salaries are variable, rising as high as £100,000 for Directors with board-level responsibility.

i The Institute of Logistics and Transport, Supply-Chain Centre, PO Box 5787, Corby NN17 4XQ

LORRY DRIVER

This work ranges from driving conventional flat-bodied lorries that can carry a variety of loads to driving lorries designed for one purpose, such as car and animal transporters and milk tankers. Drivers who work for large firms may often take a load from A to B then carry one back from B to A in the UK or across Europe. As well as driving, lorry drivers may have to help with the loading and unloading of goods. Drivers of potentially dangerous products must know how to handle them safely, and special training is required.

Qualifications and Training

No formal educational requirements are necessary, but drivers must have a good enough education to be able to do simple sums, read maps, follow instructions and handle documents concerned with the delivery of goods. An LGV licence is essential. Some firms will not take on drivers until they are 25, when the cost of insurance is reduced. Some companies, particularly those with specialised loads, run short training courses. NVQs have been developed.

Personal Qualities

It is unusual for drivers to have a mate, so much of their time is spent on their own. They must be self-reliant, physically strong, responsible, and careful drivers. The job involves nights spent away from home.

£ £150–£230 a week. Travelling outside Europe or with a dangerous load merits an extra payment of about £250 a week.

i Centrex Training and Conference Centre, Highercall, Telford, Shropshire TF6 6RB; 01952 770441

Loss Adjuster,* see *Insurance

M

Make-up Artist, see *Broadcasting, Film Production*

MANAGEMENT CONSULTANT

Management has been defined as the art of getting results through other people, and consultancy as giving professional advice. Management consultants are employed to provide a higher degree of expertise than is available in a particular company; to recommend business solutions and assist in their implementation; to assist in cultural change; and to provide expertise to solve specific business issues.

Firms of management consultants specialise, tending to divide their activities into the following areas: organisation development and policy formation – long-range planning and re-organisation of a company's structure; production management – production control arrangements; marketing, sales and distribution; finance and administration – installation of budgetary control systems; personnel management selection; management of information systems – the provision of software, systems analysis; economic and environmental studies – urban and regional development planning, work for overseas organisations.

Qualifications and Training

Management consultants tend to have qualifications in at least one of the following: accountancy, engineering, marketing, industrial relations, human resources, social sciences, and operating experience in one of these fields.

On joining a firm, a new entrant will receive training and after six months is eligible to join the Institute of Management Consultancy (IMC) as an Associate. Associates are entitled to become members after three years' continuous work as an Associate.

Personal Qualities

Management consultants must have the integrity to put clients' interests first, the ability to communicate, an enquiring mind, clarity of expression and the ability to get on with people at all levels.

£ Varies from practice to practice depending on the number and type of clients, but generally is at a level commensurate with qualifications and experience.

i www.consultancies.com
Directory of Management Consultants in the UK (member firms and their services to clients, available from Management Information Publishing Ltd; 020 7253 5530)
Institute of Management Consultancy (IMC), 5th Floor, 32–33 Hatton Garden, London EC1N 8DL; 020 7242 2140
Management Consultancies Association, 11 West Halkin Street, London SW1X 8JL; 020 7235 3897
www.mca.org.uk
Institute of Management Services, 1 Cecil Court, London Road, Enfield EN2 6DD
www.imgtserv.co.uk

Mapping*, see *Cartography, Ordnance Survey Work

MARINE BIOLOGIST

Marine biology is a relatively new and expanding area of biology, and as yet offers few job opportunities. It is a science that studies the ecology of the sea and coastal waters and is particularly concerned with food stocks and the effects of pollution. Marine biologists are employed by the Ministry of Agriculture, Fisheries and Food, the Natural Environment Research Council and in the marine laboratories of some private organisations.

Qualifications and Training

Two or three A level or three H grade passes in biology, chemistry and maths or another science (or similar suitable subjects), plus GCSE level or equivalent in maths and physics are necessary for entry to a first degree course in biology at university or college of higher education. Some universities offer first degree courses in marine biology, but it may be advisable to take a broader degree in applied biology first.

Personal Qualities

Biologists need the same characteristics as all scientists: patience and the willingness to repeat experimental work and measurements to check results, a methodical way of working, good observation and accuracy.

£ £10,000+.

i Institute of Biology, 20–22 Queensberry Place, London SW7 2DZ; 020 7581 8333 (enclose an sae)

Marine Biological Association of UK, The Laboratory, Citadel Hill, Plymouth PL1 2PB
www1./npm.ac.uk/mba

The Scottish Association for Marine Science, PO Box 3, Oban, Argyll PA34 4AD; 01631 562244

A range of career guidance leaflets are available from the Institute of Biology (address above), including 'Careers in Biology' (send £4.50)

Marine Engineering, **see** *Engineering*

MARKET GARDENING

(see also Gardener, Horticulturist)

Crops grown in market gardens are vegetables, salad crops – such as lettuces and tomatoes – and flowers and ornamental plants. The work consists of preparing the soil, and working by hand on such jobs as transplanting young plants and thinning growing plants, and grading, washing and packing the produce after harvesting so that it can be sold.

Qualifications and Training

Qualifications in horticulture are desirable but not always necessary. Training programmes are provided through apprenticeship, and it is also possible to gain NVQ qualifications. Those with A levels and/or NVQ practical work experience can apply for entry to an agricultural college, which will provide a full training in horticulture.

Personal Qualities

The enjoyment of growing plants is important, as is an ability to use the necessary machinery, plus physical strength, and a willingness to work outdoors, whatever the weather.

£ £115–£150 a week for trained staff.

i Institute of Horticulture, 14–15 Belgrave Square, London SW1X 8PS; 020 7245 6943
www.horticulture.demon.co.uk
'Come into Horticulture' and 'Education and Training Courses in Horticulture' (available free from the Institute of Horticulture, address above)

MARKET MAKER

Jobbers, now known as market makers, conduct their business on the Stock Exchange, the market where industrial and commercial organisations raise finance through the sale of stocks and shares to individuals or institutions willing to invest capital. They are employed by merchant banks. Market makers aim to make their profits by buying and selling securities to other market makers and stockbrokers, and some now deal direct with the public. It is usual for firms to employ individual market makers who have specialist knowledge of all the factors which may influence prices, and the ability to judge and predict the performance of companies within that particular field.

Qualifications and Training

Market makers are recruited at GCSE, A and degree level, usually starting in a clerical position and progressing to working alongside a senior member and then alone on the floor of the Exchange. To become a partner in a firm it is necessary to be elected as a Member of the Stock Exchange. Candidates for election must be aged at least 21, have three years' experience or more with a member firm, and have passed the Stock Exchange examination. This may only be taken by employees of member firms or firms allied to stockbroking. Candidates must have five GCSEs or appropriate professional qualifications such as a national certificate in business studies with four individual credits or a Edexcel (BTEC) national award.

'Market maker' is a new title and the structure of the career may change over the next few years.

Personal Qualities

An ability to keep abreast of current affairs and any factors that may affect the price of shares, and to make decisions very quickly, and a willingness to take calculated risks. They must be able to work hard and to conduct business verbally. A good memory and a flair for dealing with people are helpful.

£ Salaries are low initially, but there are eventual opportunities to earn upwards of £60,000.

i Contact individual merchant banks

MARKETING

(see also Advertising, Events Officer, Retailing)

Marketing is concerned with undertaking market research, identifying consumer needs and demands relative to product or service, price, place and time, organising their production and promoting them to the appropriate customer segment. It includes new-product development, packaging, advertising, pricing, sales, distribution and after-sales service.

People usually come into marketing either from sales or from the market research side, or they may have worked for an advertising agency before joining the marketing team of a manufacturing company.

Direct Marketing

Direct Marketing covers a wide spectrum of marketing activity. It consists of simple customer mailing lists, databases recording customers' buying patterns and increasingly, selling on the Internet. Direct selling can provide opportunities for copywriters (compiling brochures and catalogues, writing accompanying letters and advertisements, and so on) and telephone salespeople. The latter will either follow up by phone the leads produced by the responses to the company's catalogues, brochures and advertisements, or call other prospective customers who may not have been approached.

There are also opportunities for web designers who would have a focus on the marketing strategy of the company as a whole.

Market Research

Market research is essential in the early stages for obtaining data on what customers want, with the object of avoiding losses on unwanted and unpopular products. Market research can be desk or field research. Market researchers carry out sample surveys in which potential customers are personally interviewed, or the necessary information is gained through postal questionnaires, analysis of manufacturers' records and research into statistics. The interviewers are known as field workers, and their work, and that of the analysis personnel, is organised by the Research Executive, who is in overall charge of the project for a Marketing Executive or client, and is responsible for interpreting the results.

Qualifications and Training

Entry qualifications can vary considerably, depending on the products or services being sold. Good GCSEs would probably be the minimum but employers are increasingly demanding an appropriate degree or diploma, such as the Chartered Institute of Marketing's internationally recognised graduate Diploma in Marketing. Colleges and universities, and education and training organisations such as the Chartered Institute of Marketing, offer a wide range of marketing courses, or courses including marketing options. Additionally, most companies give some sort of in-house training in product knowledge, selling techniques, customer relations, order processing procedures, and so on.

Market Research

A degree, preferably in a social science (such as economics, maths, business studies, statistics, psychology and sociology), or Edexcel (BTEC)/SVQ higher national diplomas or equivalent is normally required by companies for training research executives. A science or technological degree or diploma is also of value. Training is usually on the job, or through training courses.

The Market Research Society offers training through lectures, weekend courses and summer and winter schools, and awards its own diploma. Courses in market research are also available through further education centres.

No special qualifications are required by field workers, and companies themselves will give training. Those with several GCSEs, or equivalents, including maths, can apply for training as analysis personnel, and may be trained as punch operators, tabulating machine operators or computer programmers.

Personal Qualities

All types of skills and abilities can be usefully employed in marketing; however, outgoing personality, good appearance, resilience, tact and a certain toughness are required in all selling jobs.

Field workers working in market research must be good at getting on with people of all types. Analysis personnel should be able to work with figures and maintain accuracy. The research executives need to understand figures as well as being capable of setting up a survey to cater for the client's or marketing executive's needs, administering it and reporting on the results.

£ Many salespeople have the added financial incentive of commission paid on sales made, and marketing people can command a rewarding remuneration package, but the hours are often long.

In market research, £10,000+ for permanent staff, analysis personnel and for trainee executives. Field workers are paid a day rate of £30+ for a six- to seven-hour day; from £3 per hour for market research.

i Chartered Institute of Marketing, Moor Hall, Cookham, Maidenhead, Berkshire SL6 9QH; 01628 427500
www.cim.co.uk

Market Research Society, 15 Northburgh Street, London EC1V 0AH; 020 7490 4911 (send A4 sae)

Careers in Marketing, Advertising and Public Relations (Kogan Page)

How to Get On in Marketing, Advertising and Public Relations (Kogan Page)

Market Research,* see *Advertising, Marketing

MASSAGE THERAPIST

Massage is a way of kneading and rubbing the body in order to relieve aches, and tone muscles to encourage relaxation. There are many different types of massages but they all serve the same purpose. Masseurs work in a range of settings such as health centres, hospitals, beauty clinics or as freelancers. The growth in alternative therapies has increased the demand and acceptance of massage therapy.

Qualifications and Training

There is a wide range of massage courses available and most specialise in specific types of massage, although there are some general massage courses too. Every mode of delivery is available, from part-time and full-time, to weekend and block courses. There are also some postgraduate courses in sports therapy, electrotherapy and manual lympathic drainage. NVQs are available from levels 2 to 5 at a range of institutions and further education colleges.

Personal Qualities

Masseurs must be physically strong, have good interpersonal skills and the ability to make people feel comfortable. They must also be good listeners and have excellent personal hygiene habits.

£ Varied, depending on employer and demand of customers.

i The Northern Institute of Massage, 100 Waterloo Road, Blackpool FY4 1AW; 01253 403548

Alternative Therapies, 16 Duke's Wood Drive, Gerrards Cross, Bucks SL9 7LR; 01753 890202

London School of Sports Massage, 28 Station Parade, Willesden Green, London NW2 4NX; 020 8452 8855

Materials Manager, **see** *Purchasing Officer*

MATERIALS SCIENTIST

Materials science is the study of a wide variety of materials, including plastics, glass, ceramics, natural materials and metals, that are used in modern technology. The scientist or technologist is responsible for selecting materials for a specific job, or for finding uses for materials. There are opportunities in many industries, including the car and electronics industries, and in nuclear power, research, development and production work.

Qualifications and Training

Technicians should have a good education to GCSE level to include studies in maths, a science and English in order to take the technician's certificate in metal finishing. An Edexcel (BTEC) certificate and diploma are available in metals technology with the technician's certificate counting towards the units.

Two GCE A level or three SCE H grade passes in maths, physics or chemistry; or Edexcel (BTEC) awards or equivalents, are necessary for entry to the universities that offer courses leading to degrees in: metallurgy, science and engineering of metals, and metallurgy and materials science. The necessary practical experience is gained through apprenticeships or trainee posts by both technicians and scientists.

Personal Qualities

An interest in the scientific and technological problems posed, and the ability to find constructive solutions, must be allied to the scientific qualities of orderly and logical thought.

£ This varies, depending on the level of employment and its nature, but is around £12,000–£13,000.

i The Institute of Materials, 1 Carlton House Terrace, London SW1Y 5DB; 020 7839 4071

The Institution of Mining and Metallurgy, 44 Portland Place, London W1N 4BR; 020 7580 3802

MEAT INDUSTRY

(see also Butcher)

As well as retail and supermarket work as a butcher, or working for large organisations such as hotels, there are other openings in the meat industry. Some wholesale establishments selling pre-packed meat need teams of butchers for boning, cutting and packing the meat, or processing it into pies. Wholesale butchers do not meet the general public but deal with other butchers and retailers.

Workers are also needed in abattoirs, to handle and kill the animals, and to inspect and deal with the meat.

Qualifications and Training

A good general education is necessary but there are no formal educational requirements. Training is on the job and courses are available at further education establishments and approved training organisations, leading to NVQs levels 1 to 4, and exams of the Meat Training Council (formerly the Institute of Meat). Some Modern Apprenticeships are available; details from the Meat Training Council.

Personal Qualities

An above-average attitude to hygiene is vital. In addition, workers in the meat industry must be strong enough to cope with heavy lifting and fit enough to work in cold conditions.

£ About £60 a week at 16; £250 when trained.

i Meat Training Council, PO Box 141, Winterhill House, Snowdon Drive, Milton Keynes MK6 1YY; 01908 231062 www.meattraining.org.uk

National Federation of Meat and Food Traders, 1 Belgrove, Tunbridge Wells, Kent TN1 1YW; 01892 541412

Scottish Federation of Meat Traders Association, 8 Needless Road, Perth PH2 0JW; 01738 637472

Mechanical Engineer, **see** *Engineering*

MEDICAL ILLUSTRATOR

The work done by the medical illustrator is used both as a record for doctors and other medical staff and to illustrate medical journals and textbooks for teaching purposes. Both photographers and artists are classed as medical illustrators, and they normally work in hospitals, though there is also some freelance work. The field is very small, however, and competition is strong.

Qualifications and Training

The basic entry qualification to the degree in medical illustration is an HND or equivalent in photography, art or graphics. Candidates without the HND but with prior experience may be able to have their experience accredited. The BSc in medical illustration is a part-time work-based course offered by Caledonian University, Glasgow.

To become a medical photographer, four GCSEs at grades A to C including English and a science are necessary for entry into the profession as a trainee medical photographer. However, if entrants prefer to obtain qualifications at a college, A levels may be necessary. There are many courses in photography available that lead to an Edexcel (BTEC) professional qualification, or a degree in photographic science, photography or media studies (photography).

It is also possible to take a course directly in medical photography which includes on-the-job training in hospitals. This latter course is offered by the School of Medical Photography, Institute of Health Care Studies, Cardiff; Glasgow College of Building and Printing; and Berkshire College of Art and Design.

Personal Qualities

As well as having a natural artistic ability, the medical illustrator must be prepared to draw, or photograph, any part of the body in any condition.

£ About £8,500.

i British Institute of Professional Photography, Fox Talbot House, Amwell End, Ware, Hertfordshire SG12 9HN; 01920 464011

Institute of Medical Illustrators, Bank Chambers, 48 Onslow Gardens, London SW7 3AH

MEDICAL TECHNICAL OFFICER (CARDIOLOGY) (CARDIAC CLINICAL SCIENTIFIC OFFICER)

Medical technical officers set up, operate and are responsible for the application of increasingly specialised equipment used to diagnose, monitor and treat various heart conditions; for example, measuring blood flow in a specific part of the heart or reprogramming a cardiac pacemaker. Their work ranges from out-patient clinics to operating theatres, cardiac catheterisation laboratories and intensive/coronary care units. The more routine procedures are often handled by a cardiographer, who is less qualified.

Qualifications and Training

Four GCSEs or equivalent passes (English language, maths, double science) are necessary from candidates just leaving school. Training involves a minimum period of two years, but typically four, on a block- or day-release basis leading towards Edexcel (BTEC) national and higher national certificate qualification in medical physics and physiological measurement. Alternatively, an increasing number of trainees are registering for a four year part-time BSc (Hons) clinical science (cardiology) degree or 'topping-up' Edexcel (BTEC) qualifications with degree courses post-HNC. A number of trainees are recruited already holding relevant Edexcel (BTEC) qualifications or university degrees.

Personal Qualities

Candidates need technical skills and interest as well as a high sense of responsibility and an ability to communicate sympathetically with patients.

£ Trainee £6,693–£8,179; once qualified, depending on grade, £9,064– £25,908.

i Public Relations Officer, Society for Cardiological Science and Technology, British Cardiac Society, 9 Fitzroy Square, London W1P 5AH

MEDICINE

Most doctors work for the NHS in some capacity, in hospital services, general practice or in public health medicine and community health. Some doctors work exclusively in private practice, but this is unusual.

General Practitioner (GP)

Family doctors, or GPs, may form a long-standing relationship with their patients. They must be able to diagnose and deal with a broad spectrum of illnesses and disorders, mainly those common within the community, but also be able to recognise those that are rare. Increasingly, doctors are asked to help their patients to cope with personal and emotional problems. About 90 per cent of GPs now work together in group practices, giving both better working conditions and allowing some specialisation.

Public Health and Community Health
Public health doctors are mainly concerned with preventive medicine and environmental health. They may have overall management over paramedical services, such as health promotion. Community health doctors deal with child health, family planning, social services, special hostels and day centres and other roles as advisers to the authority. The career structure is similar to that within a hospital.

Hospital
A hospital doctor begins as a House Officer (up to one year), then progresses to Senior House Officer (about three to four years), Registrar (about three years), and Senior Registrar (three or more years), and finally (usually) to Consultant in a particular specialty. Consultancy posts are quite limited. The choice of specialty must be made early; the main groups are surgical specialties, medical specialties (patients who do not need operations), pathology (concerned with disease and its effect on the body) and psychiatry. Other large specialties are obstetrics and gynaecology, anaesthetics and radiology.

Research and Teaching
Research work is carried out in universities, hospitals, public health laboratories, and other research establishments and pharmaceutical manufacturing companies. There are opportunities too for teaching in universities. Teaching may involve very little or no contact with patients, or it may be similar in content to hospital doctors' work.

Occupational
This aspect of medicine is one in which part-time work is possible. Medical check-ups are given to people at their place of work. In addition, doctors may also research the effects of occupational and environmental conditions on the health of staff.

Qualifications and Training

Medical training in the UK is designed to meet the needs of the NHS and its length and structure may differ from those in countries with different health care systems.

A minimum age of 18 and excellent A level passes in chemistry and two other science subjects (biology, physics or maths) are necessary for entry to medical school. Most medical school courses last five years. Some, however, offer a six-year course, which includes a pre-medical year. This year, intended as a foundation year in basic sciences, gives students with good non-science grades and some non-science graduates a way into the medicine degree course.

After obtaining medical qualifications most graduates go on to specialise in a specific medical field, such as genetics, haematology, or paediatrics.

Personal Qualities

Those who want to become members of the medical profession must have a caring and responsible attitude to other people, as well as ability in scientific subjects.

£ House Officer (posts in this grade are tenable for six months), £16,710; Senior House Officer from £20,845; Registrar from £23,300; Senior Registrar from £26,840; Specialist Registrar from £23,300. The average net intended income for a GP is £52,600.

i British Medical Association (BMA), BMA House, Tavistock House, London WC1H 9JP; 020 7387 4499
www.bma.org.uk

Careers in Medicine, Dentistry and Mental Health (Kogan Page)

Member of Parliament,* see *Politics

MERCHANT NAVY

The Merchant Navy carries passengers and cargoes of all kinds and is made up of a large number of independent organisations. Some operate exclusively in UK coastal waters, others around Europe and the Baltic ports, while the deep-sea trade sends ships around the world, including the Far East and South America. Crews on these ships can be away from home for several months at a time, with long periods of leave. Most shipping organisations belong to the Chamber of Shipping, which has set up the National Sea Training Centre, part of the North Kent College, where school leavers are trained as deck, engineering or catering ratings. Only a small number of shippers offer their own training. Ratings are being recruited by a number of companies.

Although the three main areas of deck, engine room and catering are still important, there is now, as regards ratings, a move towards less specialisation. Currently the Merchant Navy is looking for deck and engineering officer cadets only. Ratings are not being recruited.

Deck

Ratings work on the securing of cargo, making the ship ready for sea, handling the mooring ropes and anchors and doing maintenance jobs when the ship is at sea, all under the supervision of the deck officers. In addition to these tasks, deck officers are also responsible for navigation and watch-keeping. Ratings may train to become officers.

Engine Room

Ratings may share the work of cleaning, maintenance and lubrication with deck ratings; the bulk of the work in the engine rooms of modern ships is done by officers, who are responsible not only for the ship's engines, but also for the electrical system, air-conditioning, refrigeration and safety systems.

Purser

Pursers are usually employed by ferry and passenger ship companies to look after the comfort of passengers. They arrange entertainment for them and provide banking services. In addition, they deal with accounts and clerical work and handle customs and immigration.

Catering

The two sides to catering are cooking and stewarding, with promotion possible in both, and the opportunity to switch from one to the other.

Qualifications and Training

No formal qualifications are required for deck, engineering or catering ratings at the National Sea Training Centre, but education to GCSE standard with particular reference to maths and English is expected; candidates, boys or girls, should be aged 16 to 18, and must be sponsored by a shipping company. Courses are 13 weeks for deck ratings, 11 weeks for catering ratings. On completion, the trainees will have been assessed for City and Guilds certificate Part I. Part II may be taken after service at sea.

Candidates with four GCSEs to include maths, science (preferably physics) and an English subject can apply for a sponsored training scheme for deck officers combining training at a Nautical Training Centre and at sea. The same requirements apply for trainee engineering officers but they spend one year less at sea than trainee deck officers.

Those holding A level, H grade or equivalent qualifications including maths or a suitable science subject with a strong element of physics can enter accelerated training schemes which can be completed within three years.

For those interested in a career in the European Trading Area, three GCSEs or equivalent in maths, a science and preferably a language are necessary.

Gradually, NVQs have been introduced into the Merchant Navy, ranging from level 1 for a junior rating to level 4 for the most senior officer.

There are cadetship schemes available for deck and engineer entrants. These combine periods at sea with courses of training in a nautical college.

Personal Qualities

Physical fitness is very important, and candidates who have to wear glasses or contact lenses need a certain standard of sight without aids to be acceptable as deck officers or ratings. Colour blindness is also unacceptable for deck officers and ratings, and radio officers. A ship carries an enclosed, isolated community, and so the ability to get on well with other people and the ability to adapt to new conditions are also important.

£ Starting salaries vary between sponsoring companies.

i The Marine Society, 202 Lambeth Road, London SE1 7JW; 020 7261 9535 (information on careers at sea and on grants and loans)
www.marine.society.org.uk

The Chamber of Shipping, Carthusian Court, 12 Carthusian Street, London EC1M 6EZ; 020 7417 2800
www.british-shipping.org.uk

National Sea Training Centre, North West Kent College, Dering Way, Gravesend, Kent DA12 2JJ

METALLURGIST

Metallurgists are involved with the extraction of metals from ores, and their purification, and often nowadays with reclaiming them from scrap. They are also concerned with the development of new alloys and with the processing of metals during manufacture.

Qualifications and Training

GCSE passes in a science subject, maths and English, or an English subject, or SCE Standard grade passes in chemistry, physics or maths, are required for entry to Edexcel (BTEC) two-year courses for a certificate or diploma in metallurgical studies.

Candidates who have successfully completed the two-year course and those with GCE A level or SCE H grade passes in maths, physics or chemistry may study for the Edexcel (BTEC) higher certificates and diplomas.

Two or three (preferably) GCE A level or three SCE H grade passes in maths, physics or chemistry qualify for entry to full-time, sandwich or part-time courses leading to degrees in metallurgy. Those with Edexcel (BTEC) higher awards may also gain admission to degree courses.

Graduates with two years' supervised training and two years' professional experience can apply for corporate membership of the Institute of Materials. Edexcel (BTEC) awards plus at least three years' training and practical experience qualify for associate membership of the Institute of Materials.

Personal Qualities

Metallurgy demands an interest in scientific and technological subjects, and an ability to solve practical problems and work with other people on specific projects.

£ Salaries vary, but are about £9,000–£13,000+ with a degree.

i The Institute of Materials, 1 Carlton House Terrace, London SW1Y 5DB; 020 7839 4071

The Institution of Mining and Metallurgy, 44 Portland Place, London W1N 4BR; 020 7580 3802

METEOROLOGIST

The Meteorological Office (the Met) is an executive agency within the Ministry of Defence. It is a centre of excellence for the production of numerical weather forecasts, climate prediction and related studies. It serves the different and varying needs of defence, other areas of Government, civil aviation, industry, commerce and the general public.

Qualifications and Training

From time to time there are vacancies in administration for which a minimum of five GCSEs to include English language are required. Most vacancies arise in the forecasting, research and IT areas for which a first or upper second degree is necessary in maths, one of the physical disciplines, computer science or meteorology.

Personal Qualities

Candidates need to be adaptable and prepared to work in more than one specialist area. Good communication and computing skills are necessary.

£ Graduates' salaries range from £14,834–£15,950.

i Local Jobcentres and Careers Offices

Meteorological Office College, Shinfield Park, Reading, Berkshire RG2 9AU; 01344 855205

MICROBIOLOGIST

Microbiology is the study of microscopic living organisms, including bacteria, viruses, fungi, protozoa and algae, which affect almost every aspect of our lives. There is a range of job opportunities for microbiologists in medical research, the food, agricultural and pharmaceutical industries. Microbiologists also find employment with environmental companies, in hospitals, research institutes and universities. Microbiologists have a role in the biotechnology field, specialising in subjects such as fermentation, bioprocessing, recombinant DNA technology and molecular biology.

Qualifications and Training

Minimum requirement for entry to a full-time first degree course is usually five GCSE passes at C and above plus two (preferably three) A levels or three H grade passes in science subjects (biology, chemistry, maths or physics). Some universities and colleges of higher education will accept two science subjects with an arts or language. Although courses are offered in specific areas of microbiology, many students prefer to choose a general biological sciences degree which allows specialisation as they progress through the course. It is also possible to obtain qualifications via part-time study while working in a laboratory.

Personal Qualities

Microbiologists have enquiring minds, work accurately and enjoy solving problems. Good communication skills are needed since microbiologists have to describe their work to other people. Most scientists work in a multi-disciplinary group so it helps to be a good team worker.

£ Usually in the range of £10,000–£15,000, depending on the area of microbiology chosen.

i Society for General Microbiology, Marlborough House, Basingstoke Road, Spencers Wood, Reading RG7 1AE

Careers in Microbiology (free booklet from the above)

MIDWIFERY

(see also Nurse)

Midwives (who may be female or male) provide care and advice to mothers and fathers before, during and after birth; they are either by the NHS in hospital and/or community settings, including home births, or by private hospitals, or work independently.

The midwife provides for the care of women during normal pregnancy and birth, and provides care for the woman and her baby up to 28 days following the birth. The midwife will also provide care to women who have complications. The midwife is an integral part of the multi-disciplinary team that is responsible for delivering care, working closely with obstetricians and other health professionals in ensuring the well-being of mothers and babies.

Qualifications and Training

A three-year diploma or degree programme of midwifery education leading to qualification as a registered midwife (RM) is available at various centres nationwide. Candidates need to have a minimum of five GCSEs (grade A to C), or equivalent, including English and a science subject, and must be at least 17 and a half years old (17 in Scotland). Programmes of preparation are also available for nurses who are registered as General Nurses (RGN) or Registered Nurses (RN, adult). Such programmes are of 18 months' duration. Both courses include theory and practical components. Students will spend time in a variety of placement areas, including hospital and community.

Personal Qualities

An understanding of people, practical ability, common sense and good interpersonal skills are essential. Midwives must engage in continuous professional development throughout their career to be able to provide safe and effective care to mothers and their babies.

£ Staff midwives within the NHS start between £13,877– £17,830; midwifery sisters and community midwives earn between £18,156 and £24,515.

i England: NHS Careers, PO Box 376, Bristol BS99 3EY; 0845 60 60 655 Scotland: CATCH, PO Box 21 Edinburgh EH2 1NT; 0131 247 6622

Northern Ireland: School of Nursing & Midwifery, The Queen's University of Belfast, 1/3 College Park East, Belfast BT7 1LQ; 028 9027 3745

Northern Ireland: School of Health Sciences, University of Ulster, Cromore Road, Coleraine BT52 1SA; 028 7032 4316

Wales: Welsh National Board for Nursing, Midwifery and Health Visiting, 2nd Floor, Golate House, 101 St Mary Street, Cardiff CF10 1DX; 029 2026 1400

Careers in Nursing and Related Professions (Kogan Page)

MILKMAN

A milkman delivers milk and other products such as fruit juice, eggs and bread to customers, keeping an account for each customer and taking payment for goods delivered once a week. The work involves beginning early in the morning but, with experience, a milkman may finish work just after lunch.

Qualifications and Training

Formal academic qualifications are not necessary but applicants' numeracy is tested. Applicants must be able to drive. Training is on the job. NVQs are now available in Dairy Retailing.

Personal Qualities

Milkmen must be physically strong, prepared to be out of doors and ready to drive in all weather conditions, honest, friendly and reliable.

£ About £170 a week.

i National Dairy Council, 5–7 John Prince's Street, London W1M 0AP; 020 7499 7822
National Dairymen's Association, 19 Cornwall Terrace, London NW1 4QP; 020 7935 4562

MILLINER

Expensive 'model' hats are designed by a milliner and made up by the workers in a small retail workroom or factory attached to a boutique or fashion house. Hats for the wholesale trade are mass produced by machine, though some may be hand finished. The designs used are bought from model milliners and passed on to copyists, who work out how the hat can be adapted to machine production.

Qualifications and Training

Training may be obtained as a junior in a retail workroom or factory, supplemented, if possible, by evening classes. Academic qualifications are not necessary, except for those who wish to design millinery, when a full fashion training is required. Full-time courses are also available that include instruction in hat making, among other topics. NVQs are available for some functions of hat making.

Personal Qualities

Those making hats in a retail millinery workroom need manual skill and patience – a hat may take up to three days to complete. The production side of wholesale hat making requires an understanding of technology in the senior posts. Designers and copyists should have fashion sense and artistic creativity.

£ Rates of pay are generally low.

i CAPITB Trust, 80 Richardshaw Lane, Pudsey, Leeds LS28 6BN; 0113 239 3355
www.careers-in-clothing.co.uk
British Hat Guild, The Business Centre, Kimpton Road, Luton, Bedfordshire LU2 0LB; 01582 23456

MINICAB DRIVER

Minicabs are private hire vehicles, which means that instead of being able to ply for hire in the streets, the drivers can operate only if they have first been contacted by the customer, by telephone. Owner-drivers of private hire vehicles often obtain their business through a taxi firm, which passes on enquiries from customers, and charges the owner-driver for the service. Drivers often stay on the taxi firm's premises waiting for calls, or receive them on their radio. Their outgoings include the taxi firm's charge plus bills for servicing and repairs to the vehicle.

Qualifications and Training

Not all areas require hire vehicles or their drivers to be licensed. In areas where a licence is necessary, the vehicle has to undergo testing and the driver must be over 21, with at least a year's driving experience and a group A licence. (Normally people under 25 do not apply, because of the high cost of insurance for the under-25 age group.) A character reference and medical test are also necessary.

Personal Qualities

Minicab drivers must be able to cope with long and unsocial hours, and get on with a wide range of passengers, dealing with difficult ones as necessary.

£ Dependent on the number of hours worked, rates paid and passengers carried.

i Local minicab firms and local newspapers

Mining Engineer, **see** *Engineering*

MODEL

Models work as 'live' or photographic models, generally showing clothes or accessories. Photographic and advertising models rely on an agent to get them work and handle the fees. Competition is intense and very few models get to the top of the profession.

Fashion
Models employed full-time by couturiers, wholesalers or fashion stores are 'live' models. They have the garments draped and pinned on them during the design stages, and show the garments to the public. Live models must be tall, at least 5ft 10in (178cm).

Photographic modelling involves posing in garments chosen to be illustrated in magazines, newspapers, catalogues or on advertising posters. This work is often out of season for the type of garments being modelled – furs are photographed in August, for example – but some of the work is done abroad. Expenses include the provision of accessories, a good basic wardrobe and hairdressing.

Qualifications and Training

Private model schools run training courses for live and photographic modelling. Reputable schools will only take entrants whom they think will succeed, and will introduce them to agencies at the end of the training period (four to six weeks).

Personal Qualities

A model must be able to work hard, be punctual and reliable, get on well with people, and have a great deal of common sense. Competition is intense, and only the more intelligent, who can interpret what the stylist and photographer want, will get to the top. A female model should be at least 5ft 8in tall and more or less 34–24–34. A male model should be at least 6ft tall, chest 38/40, waist 30/32, inside leg 33in. They should have clear skin, good hands, nails and teeth, healthy hair and attractive features.

£ Starting salaries are low; with experience, in the region of £25,000 a year, and the sky's the limit for top models. The highest salaries are often earned abroad.

i Association of Model Agents, 122 Brompton Road, London SW3 1JE; info line 0891 517644 (send sae for information)
Careers in Fashion (Kogan Page)

MODELMAKER

Models can be made to represent almost anything: towns, office blocks, oil terminals, shopping centres, motorways, houses, cars and planes. Models are often scaled-down versions of the real thing, but sometimes they can be enlargements. They are used to show what the real thing will look like and, if they are working models, may be used as testers. Models are often used too in television and films. Modelmakers work for firms specialising in such work, or sometimes branch out on their own.

Qualifications and Training

Formal academic qualifications are not necessary. Modelmakers may teach themselves or learn at evening class; some large firms offer apprenticeships. Edexcel (BTEC) courses are available in modelmaking at Kingsway College, Hertfordshire College of Art and Design, University of Sunderland, Rycote Wood College, Barking College of Technology, Kent Institute of Art and Design, and South Devon College of Arts and Technology.

Personal Qualities

Patience, manual dexterity, a good sense of design, shape and colour are necessary. Modelmakers must be prepared to do one job for a considerable length of time: a project such as a model town could take up to a year to complete.

£ Low when training, and with experience £170+ a week; good modelmakers may earn much more.

i Local Jobcentres and Careers Offices

MOTOR BODY REPAIRER

(see also Vehicle Technician)

The motor body repairer works in a highly mechanised industry where most of the body parts are pressings, forgings or castings. Body-building and repairing are allied to the other specialist skills of painting and industrial finishing, and trimming. Often, a motor mechanic will specialise in several areas of work.

Qualifications and Training

No formal educational qualifications are necessary, but GCSEs or equivalent in maths, English and a science are advantageous. Mechanics and body repairers usually take part in a training scheme whereby different skills are learnt and tested. When an employer deems that a sufficient standard has been reached, trainees may apply for the national craft certificate awarded by the Road Transport Industry Training Board. An NVQ is available in Vehicle Body Repair, level 3.

Personal Qualities

A good standard of physical fitness, a sense of responsibility (since the safety of drivers and passengers is involved) and an aptitude for dealing with machinery and tools are required.

£ £70+ per week to start with; £160+ with experience.

i Local Jobcentres and Careers Offices

MOULDER

Moulders or coremakers work in the foundry industry making the mould or core later to be used to make a variety of other objects. If there is any damage to the mould, the moulder will be required to repair it using various hand tools. This is a highly skilled job offering variety – no two moulds or cores are exactly the same.

Qualifications and Training

Formal academic qualifications are not required. Training lasts for three and a half years during which, depending on the employer, time will be spent at a training centre and day or block release allowed for study leading to a City and Guilds or regional examining body qualification.

Personal Qualities

Care, patience, manual dexterity and some initiative are all required. An understanding of the casting process and the properties of sands and metals is also useful.

£ £70+ per week to start with; £180+ when trained.

i Local Jobcentres and Careers Offices

MUSEUM AND ART GALLERY WORK

Art galleries and museums of various kinds (general, archaeology, social history, natural history, transport, science, local history) are administered by the Government, local authorities, universities, private organisations or individuals. The Director (or Keeper, or Curator) is responsible for running the museum. In large museums there are many staff, with a Curator at the head of each department. Curators are involved in all aspects of running the museum or department: display, cataloguing, advising on new acquisitions, and even lecturing. In addition they must involve themselves in education work and marketing.

Qualifications and Training

No special qualifications are required for attendants and wardens. There are different levels of entry for Curators or Conservation Officers: four GCSEs including English, or, in Scotland, three Standard grade passes or equivalent including English. Relevant work experience is helpful. Curators may also join after obtaining a degree, and for those applying for higher grades, a degree plus relevant postgraduate experience are necessary.

Training courses at different levels, including postgraduate, are available as in-service training schemes for museum and art gallery work. Postgraduate courses are also available at some universities and colleges. A postgraduate qualification improves a person's chances of finding museum work.

Personal Qualities

Staff must have an interest in the objects under their care and they should have the ability to make the information they offer interesting and clearly understood.

£ Salaries in this sector vary widely and are dependent on the type of organisation. It would be misleading to state an average salary.

i The Museums Association, 42 Clerkenwell Close, London ECIR 0PA; 020 7608 2933

Cultural Heritage National Training Organisation (CHNTO), 1st Floor, Glyde House, Glydegate, Bradford BD5 0UP; 01274 391056/391087

Careers in Museums, Heritage and Conservation (booklet available free from CHNTO for £2.50)

MUSIC THERAPIST

Music can be of great help to physically and mentally disabled and maladjusted people, who can benefit from listening to music, and from making it. Both music teachers and performers, who are interested in helping these people, may work in the field of music therapy.

Qualifications and Training

Those who have completed a three-year course in music, or are experienced professional musicians, may take a one-year full-time course in music therapy. There is also a part-time training course available.

Personal Qualities

Working with handicapped people requires patience and sympathy, and a genuine desire to help them. Music therapists also need good keyboard and improvisatory skills.

£ Salaries are in the region of £12,000–£13,000.

i British Society for Music Therapy, 25 Rosslyn Avenue, East Barnet, Hertfordshire EN4 8DH; 020 8368 8879

The Incorporated Society of Musicians, 10 Stratford Place, London W1N 9AE; 020 7629 4413 (free basic career leaflet)

MUSICAL INSTRUMENT TECHNOLOGIST

(see also Piano Tuner)

The instrument technologist is concerned with making and repairing instruments of all kinds, from pianos to guitars. Good training and practical skill are essential, and ensure plenty of work for the technologist.

Qualifications and Training

Manufacturers of musical instruments will train technologists through apprenticeship schemes.

Three GCSEs or equivalent are required for entry to the three-year full-time course at the London Guildhall University, leading to a college certificate. There is an Edexcel (BTEC) national diploma in musical instrument technology, entry requirements being GCSEs in maths, physics and English. Holders of the diploma or those with five GCSEs plus one A level may take the Edexcel (BTEC) HND in musical instrument technology. Practical ability is required for candidates for full-time courses in instrument manufacture, repair and maintenance offered by Newark and Sherwood Technical College, leading to City and Guilds or college certificates. There are also courses at: the London Guildhall University; Merton Technical College, Morden; Stevenson College of Further Education, Edinburgh; City of Leeds College of Music; and Anniesland College, Glasgow.

Personal Qualities

Practical skills are necessary for this work, but special ability in music is not important.

£ Around £170+ a week when trained, but are low without experience.

i Crafts Council, 44a Pentonville Road, London N1 9BY; 020 7278 7700
Institute of Musical Instrument Technology, 8 Chester Court, Albany Street, London NW1 4BU
Institute of Contemporary Music; 020 7378 7986

MUSICIAN

A musical training, leading to a degree or equivalent qualification, opens the door to a wide range of careers in music, including performing, teaching, administration, management, broadcasting, recording, journalism, publishing, promotion, librarianship and the retail trade.

Performer

Many professional musicians work on a freelance basis as soloists, orchestral players, commercial session musicians and in a variety of chamber music ensembles including classical, rock, dance and jazz groups. A performer's working life often includes some teaching, masterclasses or community education work alongside regular and vital practice.

Some musicians arrange their own engagements, others have agents or use a diary service to find work. For all performers, membership of a professional association or union is desirable.

There are opportunities, particularly for those who play an instrument, to join the Army, RAF or Royal Marines as a bandsman.

Composer

There are a few thousand composers yet few earn even a substantial part of their income from composing. The most lucrative area is writing music for TV, films, videos and for the commercial market, but some composers also find time to write their own music and get it performed. Professional advice on copyright (from a solicitor or professional association) is essential.

Teacher

Inspiring others to learn can be a most rewarding career. With music now placed as one of the foundation subjects in the National Curriculum there is an increasing demand for music teachers. Opportunities range from private instrumental teaching to class teaching at primary, secondary and tertiary levels. Private teachers set up and develop their own independent, studio-based business. Class teachers and some visiting instrumental teachers working in maintained schools require Qualified Teacher Status.

Qualifications and Training

Entry to undergraduate courses of study usually requires a minimum of five GCSEs and one or more A levels, preferably including music. Full-time courses of study over three or four years, usually leading to a degree, are available at conservatoires (performance-based), universities (more academic) and colleges of higher education (more broad spectrum). Singers require a longer training, often over six years. Conservatoires and universities also offer a range of postgraduate courses. Teachers require an appropriate teaching qualification, such as a PGCE (Postgraduate Certificate in Education).

Personal Qualities

An innate love of music, a positive and persuasive personality, robust physical and mental health, stamina, patience and excellent communication skills are essential for any career in music. Competition is fierce for performers and only a very few talented musicians can establish a successful solo career. The ability to get on well with others helps to ensure good relationships with colleagues, managers and promoters to support career development.

£ Financial rewards are too varied to give an accurate indication.

i The Incorporated Society of Musicians, 10 Stratford Place, London W1N 9AE; 020 7629 4413; fax 020 7408 1538
www.ism.org.uk

N

NANNY

(see also Nursery Nurse)

A nanny's job today is generally much less formal than it used to be. Instead of being confined to nursery quarters, a nanny now often lives as part of the family, and rarely has to wear the neatly starched uniform of the past. A nanny is often employed by working parents who are out for most of the day, and is in sole charge of feeding, changing and supervising the children, often accompanying them to school or playgroup or on social outings. As a rule, domestic work is not a nanny's responsibility, although sometimes she is asked to keep the children's rooms tidy and care for their clothes as well as preparing simple meals.

Some posts are residential, in which case a nanny may be 'on call' for late or night feeds, but employers are expected to provide adequate private accommodation and a reasonable number of free evenings. Other nannies are employed on a daily basis, working set hours and returning to their own homes at night. A nanny may often remain in one family for a number of years while the children grow up; others are taken on as a temporary measure, to take charge during a mother's illness or for the birth of a new baby, for instance.

Qualifications and Training

A nanny is generally expected to hold the Diploma in Nursery Nursing of the NNEB (the National Nursery Examination Board award) or to be registered with the Scottish Nursery Nurses Board, the Scottish equivalent. There are no minimum academic standards laid down for entry to this course, which can be followed at most colleges of further education. A good standard of English is usually required, however, and candidates who have no formal GCSE qualifications may have to take a written test before admission. This course aims to equip students to work with children from birth to the age of seven and much emphasis is laid on practical experience and observation. It can be followed full-time or on a day-release basis. In addition there are a number of private, fee-paying colleges which specialise in preparing students for private employment. These have their own entrance requirements.

Personal Qualities

A nanny, naturally, has to love children and be able to gain their confidence and encourage their development. Competence in all the basic tasks of looking after children is crucial and employers generally ask for references to prove reliability. Tact and consideration are important too, since a nanny has to live in intimate contact with the whole family. Patience, common sense and a sense of humour are invaluable when dealing with children. Knowing how to drive is frequently an advantage.

£ Salaries vary according to the type of post involved. A live-in nanny receives board and lodging as well as a salary. Daily nannies earn from £75 to £250 a week and live-in nannies from £60 to £230; larger sums are paid for work in London and abroad.

i Local Jobcentres and Careers Offices

Council for Awards in Children's Care and Education (CACHE), 8 Chequer Street, St Albans, Hertfordshire AL1 3XZ; 01727 847636 (enclose sae)

Careers Working with Children and Young People (Kogan Page)

NATUROPATH

Naturopathy is not offered by the NHS, so naturopaths work in private practice. Naturopaths believe in treating the whole patient, and in encouraging the body to cure itself. They do not believe in giving drugs which, they feel, treat local infections or one set of symptoms without dealing with the actual cause of a problem. A naturopath uses treatments designed to correct total body chemistry; diet is seen as a major factor and patients are encouraged to eat more natural and unspoilt food. Fasting, or partial fasting, may sometimes be recommended to eliminate toxic substances. Hydrotherapy is used to stimulate the blood to a specific area of the body or to draw it away from another (by applying cold packs to combat throbbing headaches, for example).

Naturopaths also need to be skilled in psychology since they recognise that physiological complaints may frequently be caused by psychological problems. Any medicaments they use are virtually confined to those used by herbalists, and naturopaths frequently study herbalism itself. Naturopathy is also closely linked to osteopathy and many naturopaths are qualified osteopaths and use these skills in treating their patients.

Qualifications and Training

Entry requirements are *one* of the following: a minimum of two A levels in biology and chemistry; a science access or foundation course; mature students with other qualifications; equivalent qualifications from European and overseas applicants. Training, which is full-time and lasts four years, is currently only provided by the British College of Naturopathy and Osteopathy. This course leads to a BSc (Hons) degree in naturopathic medicine validated by the University of Westminster.

Personal Qualities

Professional skills must be combined with a sympathetic and caring manner.

£ Salaries vary depending on hours worked, number of patients and fee scales.

i The British College of Naturopathy and Osteopathy, Frazer House, 6 Netherhall Gardens, London NW3 5RR; 020 7435 6464

NAVAL ARCHITECT

Naval architects are engineers who play a key role as project leaders and specialists in the design, building and marketing of all systems which have to move just above, on or under the sea including merchant ships, warships, offshore structures, submarines, hovercraft, yachts and other small craft. They work for ship and repair yards, offshore rig fabricators and operators, government departments, classification societies, consultants, equipment manufacturers, small craft and yacht builders, research organisations, educational establishments and shipping companies.

Qualifications and Training

Fully qualified and informed naval architects may become members of the Royal Institution of Naval Architects if they meet the education, training and experience requirements. They need to have had an aggregate of seven years' engineering education, training and responsible experience, and have passed an exam of the standard of an accredited honours degree in engineering. It is also possible to register with the UK Engineering Council as a Chartered Engineer (CEng), an Incorporated Engineer (IEng) or as an Engineering Technician (EngTech) through the Royal Institution of Naval Architects (RINA).

Personal Qualities

Any young man or woman who has a keen interest in engineering and the sea and who wants to play an important part in society will find a career as a naval architect challenging and satisfying. A naval architect needs precision and attention to detail as well as an interest in and a sound knowledge of the sea. An ability to work as part of a team is essential.

£ £20,000 per year with five years of responsible experience after qualifying.

i The Royal Institution of Naval Architects (RINA), 10 Upper Belgrave Street, London SW1X 8BQ; 020 7235 4622
www.rina.org.uk

NEUROPHYSIOLOGY TECHNOLOGIST

A more familiar name for the neurophysiology technologist is the EEG (electro-encephalography) technologist, who is responsible for setting up and operating electronic equipment which records electrical activity in the brain and nervous system. These tests often include visual or auditory or other types of evoked potentials (EPs), which are the response of the brain to specific stimuli. EEG and EP tests are performed to help in the diagnosis of patients with, for example, epilepsy, cerebral tumours, strokes, dementias, multiple sclerosis.

In many departments, the technologist is also required to assist the clinician with electromyography (EMG) and nerve conduction studies (NCS). These tests look at the way in which nerves and muscles in the body are working, and help in the diagnosis of diseases such as dystrophies and nerve dysfunction. All these procedures are carried out either in the department or in the wards, intensive care units or operating theatres. Both out-patients and in-patients come to the department and the tests are performed on all ages (babies, children, adults). Heart rate and respiration may also be recorded. The neurophysiology technologist works as part of the hospital team in the surgical, neurological or psychiatric department.

Qualifications and Training

Five GCSEs, grade C or above, are normally required, including maths, English and combined science. There are two main ways of entering the profession: as a student technologist employed by a hospital in an EEG clinical neurophysiology department; or as a student supernumerary technologist employed by a regional health authority. Training takes place mostly on the job with day-release facilities to study for an Edexcel (BTEC) qualification/NVQ award, level 3.

Personal Qualities

A medical technologist needs to be willing to take responsibility, able to keep calm under pressure and must be meticulous. In addition, a pleasant manner to put patients at their ease is essential.

£ Trainee £6,693–£8,719; once qualified £9,064–£25,908. This salary scale is only a guide, as many NHS trusts use their individual scales.

i Electrophysiological Technologists' Association, EEG Department, Staffordshire General Hospital, Weston Road, Stafford ST16 3SA (enclose sae)

NOTARY PUBLIC

A Notary Public is an international officer of the law whose duty is to prepare and authenticate legal documents intended to take effect abroad. There are two classes of notaries: General Notaries, who are allowed to practise throughout England and Wales, apart from the area reserved exclusively to Scrivener Notaries; and Scrivener Notaries, who have an exclusive right to practise in the City of London, the City of Westminster, the Borough of Southwark and within a radius of three miles of the boundary of the City of London. Scrivener Notaries may also practise throughout England and Wales.

Qualifications and Training

Entry to the profession is now restricted to graduates. Most General Notaries are also solicitors and, if they are not solicitors, they must have a legal background. They have to take examinations in various subjects in accordance with standards set by the Faculty Office of the Archbishop of Canterbury.

Scrivener Notaries have to work with a practising Scrivener Notary and take two sets of examinations. There are fewer than 30 of these Notaries, but openings are often available to suitable candidates.

Personal Qualities

In addition to having a basic legal knowledge, a Notary must be a person of discretion and integrity. Linguistic skills are desirable for General Notaries and essential in the case of Scrivener Notaries.

£ A General Notary will only receive the remuneration earned as a Notary. This will, of course, be in addition to any income arising from a position as a solicitor. A Scrivener Notary upon admission may expect to earn about £30,000 per annum.

i The Notaries' Society, 23 New Street, Woodbridge, Suffolk IP12 1DN; 01394 384134

The Society of Scrivener Notaries, 10 Philpot Lane, London EC3M 8BR; 020 7623 9477

NURSE

Nurses are employed in a wide variety of situations in hospitals, institutions (such as prisons and colleges), the armed forces, schools, industry and in private organisations. A student nurse may choose to specialise from a number of different fields – adult nursing, children's nursing, mental health, learning disability or in specialities within those fields. Currently, a nurse qualifies (that is, becomes registered) on the Adult, Mental Health, Mental Handicap or Children's Part of the Register. Nurses may work in the NHS, in private hospitals or in the community.

There are increasing opportunities for work in the community for all types of nurses. Community paediatric nurses take nursing care into the homes of children who are seriously ill or who have long-term conditions. Most people with a mental health problem will be allocated a community psychiatric nurse. People with learning disabilities now tend to live a supported life at home rather than in a hospital or home. Community nurses with specialist training support this group. Nurses offer support to the patient and their carers.

Qualifications and Training

Courses are offered at degree and diploma level. Entry to degree courses is through the university entrance system. For the diploma, entry is directly to the Colleges of Nursing and Midwifery in Northern Ireland and Wales and through central clearing houses in England and Scotland. A minimum of five GCSEs or equivalent are required but candidates without such qualifications may sit an education test known as the DC test. The minimum age of entry to programmes is 17 and a half years (17 in Scotland).

Courses are offered in colleges of nursing and midwifery (except for Northern Ireland – *see* Further Information), which may be linked with a university or college of higher education. The 18-month Common Foundation Programme gives a general introduction to nursing, and then 18 months are done in one of four branches, chosen before the course begins: adult nursing, mental health nursing, nursing people with a mental handicap or children's nursing. The focus of the course is equally split between theory and practice. Students spend time in the hospital and the community gaining experience, and have full student status. This means they are not employed as part of the workforce and not included on duty rotas until the later part of training.

Once registered, nurses practise in a wide variety of settings. Some take further courses to gain specialist knowledge in meeting the needs of patients in differing clinical specialties. Others may choose nurse teaching or management within the health services. Whatever the area chosen, the initial nursing qualification will be the first step in a lifetime of professional education.

Personal Qualities

Nursing is always about people: patients, their families, their friends and the team of colleagues working to deliver nursing care. The ability to get on with others and good communication skills are essential. As nursing is physically demanding, candidates need to be fit. Nurses must be committed to constantly developing their knowledge and skills , enhancing their ability to care.

£ Nurses in training do not get a salary but are entitled to a bursary which is currently £4,572 (under 26 years of age) and £5,148 (over 26 years of age). London weighting is an additional £796. The minimum salary for a registered nurse is £14,400–£15,905.

i England: NHS Careers, PO Box 376, Bristol BS99 3EY; 0845 60 60 655

Scotland: CATCH, PO Box 21 Edinburgh EH2 1NT; 0131 247 6622

Northern Ireland: School of Nursing and Midwifery, The Queen's University of Belfast, 1/3 College Park East, Belfast BT7 1LQ; 028 9027 3745

Northern Ireland School of Health Sciences, University of Ulster, Cromore Road, Coleraine BT52 1SA; 028 7032 4316

Wales: Welsh National Board for Nursing, Midwifery and Health Visiting, 2nd Floor, Golate House, 101 St Mary Street, Cardiff CF10 1DX; 029 2026 1400

Careers in Nursing and Related Professions (Kogan Page)

NURSERY NURSE

A nursery nurse works with babies and children under eight in the public, private and voluntary sector. This can include schools, nurseries and hospitals. In schools, nursery nurses work in nursery, reception and infant classes alongside the teacher, providing and supervising educational and play activities. Nursery nurses in hospitals can work in maternity and special care units, and on children's wards. Day nurseries, both private and local authority, employ nursery nurses to care for children under five whose parents are unable to care for them during the day. Nursery nurses can also be employed in clinics, residential homes, the community, family centres and in private homes as nannies.

Qualifications and Training

There is a variety of recognised training courses for nursery nurses; these normally run for two years and lead to a diploma in nursery nursing. The courses are a combination of theory and practical placements in schools, nurseries, etc. The minimum age for entry to a course is usually 16, with individual colleges setting entry qualifications. Private colleges may set a minimum age for entry at 18 years.

Personal Qualities

A genuine love of children is essential, with the ability to work with patience, tolerance, imagination and energy. Good motivation skills and a sense of fun are important.

£ £8,000–£10,000 as a nursery assistant, £10,000–£13,000 as a nursery nurse/officer.

i National Association of Nursery Nurses, 10 Meriden Court, Great Clacton, Essex CO15 4XH (enclose sae)

Council for Awards in Children's Care and Education (CACHE), 8 Chequer Street, St Albans, Hertfordshire AL1 3XZ; 01727 847636

The Scottish Nursery Nurses' Board (SNNB), 6 Kilnford Crescent, Dundonald, Kilmarnock, Ayrshire KA2 9DW; 01563 850440

NURSING AUXILIARY

Auxiliaries work on the wards assisting qualified nursing staff with routine tasks (such as taking temperatures, making beds, sterilising equipment, and so on). They may work full- or part-time but generally have to put in a set number of hours each week. (In psychiatric hospitals, the term nursing assistant is used.)

In time, the title of 'nursing auxiliary' will be changed to that of 'healthcare assistant'. Healthcare assistants will be able to take NVQs and undertake more tasks than nursing auxiliaries do at present.

Qualifications and Training

No special qualifications are demanded. Candidates are interviewed by the hospital concerned and, if found suitable, are sent on an internal training course (generally about two weeks), and then continue training on the job.

Personal Qualities

Like qualified nurses, auxiliaries must have patience, tact, tolerance and an ability to communicate with the patients in their charge. Physical fitness is essential as the job sometimes involves heavy work (such as lifting and turning patients).

£ Grade A £7,171–£9,603; Grade B £9,297–£10,583.

i Local Jobcentres and Careers Offices
Personnel departments of local hospitals

O

OCCUPATIONAL THERAPIST

Occupational therapists are concerned with assessing and treating people with a wide range of physical and psychological problems. The aim of occupational therapy is to enable people to be as independent as possible in their work, leisure and daily living, despite illness, disability or old age. Occupational therapists begin by establishing the reasons why people have difficulty with a particular task and then, together with the patient, devise a programme of activity to solve that problem. People of all age groups with a wide variety of permanent or temporary disability can be helped by occupational therapy.

Occupational therapists work in hospitals, social service departments, schools, in voluntary organisations, in private practice and in people's own homes. As patients now spend less time in hospital and there is an increasing emphasis on caring for people in the community, the skills of occupational therapists are more in demand than ever before.

Qualifications and Training

Candidates must be 18 years of age (17 and a half in Scotland). Five GCE/GCSE/SCE passes (including English language and a science); a minimum of two A levels, or three Highers, are also required. Most schools will now accept alternative entry qualifications, particularly for mature students. Most courses are full-time and last for three years, leading to the award of a BSc degree in occupational therapy. There are accelerated courses for those who already have a degree in a related subject. Although courses vary, all include the principles and practice of occupational therapy, behavioural, biological and medical sciences, and periods of clinical practice in a variety of hospital and community settings.

Personal Qualities

In addition to academic ability, potential occupational therapists require good communication skills, an interest in people and problem-solving ability. Occupational therapy attracts students from a wide variety of backgrounds and men are increasingly choosing to enter the profession.

£ £14,845 for the newly qualified, rising to over £23,000 for occupational therapy managers. Therapists working in London receive London weighting.

i College of Occupational Therapists, 106-114 Borough High Street, Southwark, London SE1 1LB; 020 7357 6480
www.cot.co.uk
Careers in Nursing and Related Professions (Kogan Page)

OCEANOGRAPHER

Oceanography is the study of the seas, the organisms within them and the sea floor and its sediments. Scientific and commercial interest in this field has increased considerably over the past few decades and researchers are investigating the possibilities of deriving energy sources, minerals and food from the sea. Oceanographers are also concerned with the study of pollution and erosion, navigation and underwater work, climate change, submarine geology and satellite remote sensing of the land, air and sea interfaces.

Qualifications and Training

An honours degree in one of the sciences is usually essential. There are only a few universities (Liverpool, Plymouth, Southampton and the University of Wales at Bangor) which run first degree courses in oceanography itself. However, most oceanographers have a first degree in physics, maths, chemistry or biology, with a postgraduate qualification in their specialist area.

Personal Qualities

Candidates should have a scientific aptitude and training together with an enquiring mind. Many jobs involve going to sea in research ships and a few involve diving or the use of submersibles.

£ £15,000 (Scientific Officer level), and £19,000 with a doctorate (PhD).

i The Society for Underwater Technology, 80 Coleman Street, London EC2R 5BJ; 020 7382 2601; fax 020 7382 2684 www.sut.org.uk
Southampton Oceanography Centre, Empress Dock, Southampton SO14 3ZH; 023 8059 6666 www.soc.soto.org.uk
Scottish Association for Marine Science, Dunstaffnage Marine Laboratory, PO Box 3, Oban, Argyll PA34 4AD www.nerc-oban.ac.uk/dml/

OIL/GAS RIG WORK

(see also Diver, Geologist)

There are various openings for personnel working on oil or gas drilling rigs, both onshore (on land) and offshore (such as those in the North Sea). Opportunities in all fields are generally limited to experienced and/or highly qualified applicants. An offshore rig has to be self-sufficient and is virtually a combination of a factory, hotel and heliport. The catering and accommodation are similar to the provision onshore. Many of the routine factory tasks (such as cleaning and maintenance) are carried out by outside contractors and service companies.

Geologist
The oil companies employ certain technical experts, including geologists, geophysicists and drilling and petroleum engineers. Geologists collect and analyse data from a variety of sources in an effort to determine whether drilling might prove successful at a particular site and to optimise production from existing oilfields. There are opportunities at home and overseas.

Geophysicist
Geophysicists use remote sensing to study the composition and structure of the sub-surface. A major element of this is computer-aided analysis of seismic data.

Drilling Crew
The drilling crew are responsible for the drilling of wells, and the operation and maintenance of a variety of heavy machinery. The crew consists of a toolpusher who manages the team and is responsible for the safety and integrity of the operation, and a team of people including a driller, assistant driller, derrickman, roughnecks and roustabouts. A typical drill crew will number around ten people. Progression to the role of driller is hierarchical, with people working through general labouring jobs (roustabouts), working on the drill floor (roughnecks) or at the top of the derrick (derrickman). The work is physical, from the operation of the drilling equipment to the cleaning and maintenance of pumps and equipment. A graduate drilling engineer and a range of other specialists such as logging engineers, directional drilling specialists and mudloggers will also work with the drill crew.

Divers
Divers are employed in exploration and production work, as well as underwater repair work such as welding. (*See* Diver.)

Engineers
Engineers are also employed in the rig work or petroleum, drilling or facilities engineering. Their work is generally split between the office and the production site. The production engineer supervises activities ranging from production and storage, gas compression and injection (to assist in the recovery of the oil), and tanker loading. The reservoir engineer is concerned with the behaviour of the oil accumulation or reservoir, and has to attempt to discover how much oil remains below ground and what are the most effective methods of recovery. Economics plays an important role. The maintenance engineer must ensure that all equipment is functioning properly, selecting and monitoring the companies under contract. (*See also* Engineering.)

Qualifications and Training

Geologist
A good honours degree is the minimum required; some companies prefer postgraduate training. Training courses cover areas not touched on in sufficient detail at university, including essential links to geophysics, and petroleum engineering can be offered.

Geophysicist
An honours degree in geology or geophysics is a standard qualification but companies also employ graduates in other numerate disciplines, such as maths or physics. Postgraduate training may be an advantage. Companies arrange courses to cover specific technical areas, and to build essential links to petroleum geology and engineering.

Drilling Crew
Traditionally, experience and 'rise up the ladder' were the main criteria; however, there are now a variety of courses at all levels. Generally, applicants are sponsored by drilling companies. Roughneck courses last four weeks. Drillers, toolpushers and drilling engineers will receive further training, including statutory well-control and emergency response training.

Divers
All divers must be trained on courses approved by the Health and Safety Executive. Training is expensive and courses are few. Most candidates are sponsored by employers such as service companies.

Engineers
Oil companies recruit graduates for engineering posts, normally with an engineering degree. Specialist postgraduate training may be an advantage. Training courses then supplement the knowledge gained at university and build links to allied areas such as petroleum geology.

Personal Qualities

Geophysicist
Scientific aptitude, numeracy, a good eye for detail and an enquiring mind are essential, as is the ability to work in a team under pressure.

Drilling Crew
All drilling crew must be physically fit, as the work is arduous, and must be prepared to work as part of a team for long periods of time.

Divers
Physical fitness and the ability to stay calm in a crisis are essential.

£ Salaries vary depending on position, but are often relatively high.

i The Engineering Careers Information Service, 41 Clarendon Road, Watford, Hertfordshire WD1 1LB; 01923 238441

The Geological Society, Burlington House, Piccadilly, London W1V 9AG; 020 7434 9944

Aberdeenshire Council, Woodhill House, Westbury Road, Aberdeen AB16 5GB; 01224 664634

Petroleum Exploration Society of Great Britain, 17-18 Dover Street, London W1X 3PB; 020 7495 6800

OPTICIAN

(see also Orthoptist)

Opticians are classified in two categories: ophthalmic and dispensing. Both must be registered in accordance with the Opticians Act in order to practise.

Ophthalmic Optician/Optometrist

They are trained to examine eyes and test sight, to detect and measure defects in healthy eyes and, if necessary, to prescribe spectacles, contact lenses or other appliances to correct or improve vision. They do not treat actual eye diseases; patients with these are referred to medical practitioners. Most Optometrists work in general practice in a variety of arrangements including independent businesses, partnership, as an employee of corporate bodies or as a franchisee. There are also job opportunities in research organisations, academic departments, ophthalmic hospitals and clinics.

Dispensing Optician

A Dispensing Optician does not examine eyes or test sight, being concerned only with supplying and fitting spectacles, lenses and other aids prescribed by the Ophthalmic Optician. They usually work in general practice in a variety of arrangements, including independent businesses, partnership, as an employee of corporate bodies or as a franchisee. There are also job opportunities in ophthalmic hospitals and clinics.

Qualifications and Training

An Optometrist must be registered with The General Optical Council before being permitted to practise in the UK. To obtain registration an Optometrist must pass the professional qualifying exam of the College of Optometrists. The exam is in two parts: for part 1, the candidate must gain a BSc honours degree in optometry after three years of study at an accredited institution (or four years in the case of Glasgow Caledonian University); for part 2, the candidate must complete a pre-registration year of supervised practice and pass part 2 of the professional qualifying exam.

For acceptance on to a university course the student will normally need three A levels, two of which must be maths or science, or four/five Scottish Highers, two of which must be maths or science. GCSE/Scottish Standard grades should include English and physics if not gained at A level or H grade. Average entry grades vary but are usually between 20–22 A level points. The professional qualifying exam combines practical and oral assessment of the candidate's ability to manage patients and practise safely as an independent Optometrist.

A Dispensing Optician needs to be a Fellow of the Association of British Dispensing Opticians and to gain registration with the General Optical Council. Minimum educational standards required for training are five GCSE/SCEs (including English, maths – each at grade A or B only – plus a third science-based subject).

Training can be undertaken at Glasgow Caledonian University (BSc in Ophthalmic Dispensing); Bradford & Ilkley Community College (BSc Hons in ophthalmic dispensing with management) and Anglia Polytechnic University (BSc in optical management). All three degrees include the full syllabus in ophthalmic dispensing leading to the Association's Fellowship Examination. Day-release and distance-learning course are also available. Contact the relevant colleges for more detailed information.

Personal Qualities

Opticians need mathematical and scientific skills to make accurate observations and calculations. They also need an ability to get on with patients of all ages and backgrounds and to be able to put them at their ease.

£ Salaries are from £30,000+ for Ophthalmic Opticians and £18,000+ for Dispensing Opticians.

i Association of British Dispensing Opticians, 6 Hurlingham Business Park, Sulivan Road, London SW6 3DU; 020 7736 0088

College of Optometrists, 10 Knaresborough Place, London SW5 0TG; 020 7373 7765
www.college-optometrists.org.uk
The General Optical Council, 41 Harley Street, London W1N 2DJ; 020 7580 3898
www.optical.org.uk
Scottish Committee of Optometrists, 3 Castleton Crescent, Newton Mearns, Glasgow G77 5JX; 0141 639 6483

ORDNANCE SURVEY WORK

(see also Cartography)

The Ordnance Survey is part of the Civil Service and is responsible for producing all kinds of official maps covering the whole of Britain. For example, large-scale OS maps are used by local authorities, estate agents, solicitors, architects, civil engineers and Government departments, while the 'one-inch' maps are popular with ramblers, riders and cyclists. Other OS maps show historical detail, such as Roman Britain, or statistical data (for example, population density).

There are limited job opportunities within the Ordnance Survey. Field surveyors check out detail and new features such as buildings, hedges, fences and roads, and note any alterations that have occurred since the map was last printed. They input the new features on hand-held computers. Increasingly, OS work involves the use of information technology, ranging from digital atlases and computer games to complex geographical databases.

The Ordnance Survey headquarters are in Southampton and most employees are based there. Field surveyors, however, may be posted virtually anywhere in England, Scotland or Wales.

Qualifications and Training

A good general education and five GCSE passes at grade C or above, including maths, English and geography or information technology.

Personal Qualities

A willingness to work in an outdoor environment, excellent interpersonal skills and an ability to work with all sections of the community, as well as the confidence, initiative and motivation to work alone or as part of a small team.

£ From £11,000.

i The British Cartographic Society, c/o R W Anson, Oxford Centre for Cartography & Geographical Information Services, School of Planning, Oxford Brookes University, Headington, Oxford OX3 0BP; 01865 483346
Ordnance Survey, Romsey Road, Southampton SO16 4GU; 023 8079 2000; fax 023 8079 2452

ORTHOPTIST

(see also Optician)

Orthoptists diagnose and treat various abnormalities and weaknesses in the eye, such as a squint or double vision. Many patients are children and special equipment and exercises are used to help correct any defects while they are still young. Orthoptists work closely with medical eye specialists and, where operations are necessary, with ophthalmic surgeons. Most Orthoptists work within the NHS, in hospitals and clinics (including school clinics). There are also opportunities in private practice and in teaching.

Qualifications and Training

The minimum age limit for training is 17 (although most schools require candidates to be at least 18 years of age). Applicants must have five GCSEs (plus three A levels), to include at least one science, English language and maths. Scottish students must hold SCEs in six subjects, including four at H grade (again, at least one science, English and maths). Qualification is by a degree in orthoptics. Orthoptic degree courses are based at the Universities of Sheffield and Liverpool.

Personal Qualities

Orthoptists have to be able to win the confidence of their patients (who are often very young), and so need a sympathetic manner and a good deal of patience. Some mathematical and scientific ability is also called for.

£ From £14,845 in the NHS, generally slightly more in private practice.

i The British Orthoptic Society, Tavistock House North, Tavistock Square, London WC1H 9HX; 020 7387 7992 (information pack available)

OSTEOPATH

Osteopathy is a system of diagnosis and treatment whose main emphasis is on conditions affecting the musculo-skeletal system. Osteopaths use predominantly gentle manual and manipulative methods of treatment to restore and maintain proper body function.

Osteopaths work in private practice and are increasingly being asked to work as part of mainstream medicine.

Qualifications and Training

Entry requirements are one of the following: a minimum of two A levels in biology and chemistry; a science Access or Foundation course; mature students with other qualifications; equivalent qualifications from European and overseas applicants. Courses include the study of anatomy, physiology and biochemistry, together with a clinical course in the principles, diagnoses and techniques of osteopathy. Extensive hands-on clinical experience with patients is a key feature of any course. Most courses lead to a BSc (Hons) degree in osteopathic medicine or osteopathy.

Personal Qualities

Osteopaths require good manual dexterity and a genuine desire to help and care for people. An ability to get on with and gain the confidence of their patients is also important.

£ Within the first five years of practice new graduates can earn approximately £25,000–£30,000 per annum.

i The British College of Naturopathy and Osteopathy, Frazer House, 6 Netherhall Gardens, London NW3 5RR; 020 7435 6464

The British School of Osteopathy, 1–4 Suffolk Street, London SW1Y 4HS; 020 7930 9655

Working in Complementary and Alternative Medicine (Kogan Page)

P

PACKAGING TECHNOLOGIST

The purpose of packaging is to protect, preserve, contain and present its contents. It may also have a selling function. Opportunities for work exist with manufacturers of raw materials which may be converted into packaging, with companies that carry out the converting, and with companies that have a product to be packed. Many small firms will not have their own packaging adviser/technologist and will hire a consultant when the need arises.

There are work opportunities in actually designing and making the packaging material – sample making, cutting, folding, glueing – and for scientists and technologists.

Qualifications and Training

Many firms insist on formal qualifications. The internationally recognised standard is the Institute of Packaging diploma. There are also opportunities to take packaging as an optional module with some first degrees and for progression to an MSc in packaging technology.

There are various courses (part-time, residential and correspondence) for those wishing to take the Institute of Packaging's membership exam. Candidates should have four GCSEs including English and maths, or, if they are over 25, have an equivalent standard of education and three years' experience.

Personal Qualities

Manufacturing workers must be able to work neatly and with dexterity. Technologists and scientists must be able to look at problems in a practical way and have the ability to communicate their ideas to others both verbally and on paper.

£ Apprentices in manufacturing about £70–£80 a week at 16, technicians £5,000+ a year and graduates £12,500+.

i The Head of Training, Institute of Packaging, Sysonby Lodge, Nottingham Road, Melton Mowbray, Leicestershire LE13 0NU; 01664 250 0055; fax 01664 564164 (for details of available training and careers advice)
www.iop.co.uk

PAINTER AND DECORATOR

(see also Interior Decorator)

Painting and decorating involves much more than just hanging paper and applying paint. Appropriate paint for different surfaces must be chosen, surfaces must be prepared and holes and cracks in walls filled in; scaffolding may have to be erected. Specialist skills include graining – using paint to give the effect of wood; marbling – doing the same for marble; and gilding – the application of gold and silver leaf to wood, glass and other surfaces. Painters and decorators work for large firms, building contractors, local authorities and as self-employed craftsmen.

Qualifications and Training

No formal educational requirements are necessary, but good mathematical ability is useful. Training is on the job by three-year apprenticeship. During this time apprentices may work towards NVQs, awarded jointly by City and Guilds and the Construction Industry Training Board.

Personal Qualities

As well as the necessary practical skills, painters and decorators must have an artistic sense, be neat in their work, able to get on with people and be prepared to work out of doors, standing most of the time.

£ Recommended weekly rates are: £73.90 at 16; £103.46 at 17; £147.81 at 18; and, when qualified, the craftsman rate is £178.62.

i Construction Industry Training Board, Bircham Newton, King's Lynn, Norfolk PE31 6RH; 01553 776677 (ext 2466)

PATENT AGENT/PATENT EXAMINER

Patent Agents advise individual clients and companies on matters relating to patent law and act on their behalf if they wish to patent an invention, or to register a trademark or a design in the UK or abroad. First, records are searched to gauge the likelihood of a patent being granted. The Patent Agent then draws up the particulars of the client's invention in as clear and concise a way as possible and ensures that it neither infringes another patent nor is liable to be copied without infringing the patent. In cases where a client's patent has been infringed, the Agent advises as to the best course of action.

Patent Agents are employed by private practice firms of patent agencies, industrial companies with a patent department and the Government.

Patent Examiner
They are Civil Servants and examine the applications for patents submitted by Patent Agents and others. The principal task is to establish the originality or otherwise of the invention, and whether or not the applicant is entitled to the protection claimed. There is some opportunity to work abroad in the European Patent Office.

Patent Officer
Civil Servants employed in protecting Crown rights in new inventions and developments, compensating the owners of patents used by the Crown and generally advising Government departments on matters relating to patents.

Qualifications and Training

The minimum educational requirements for an Agent are five GCSEs/Standard grade passes and two A levels/three H grades including either physics or chemistry, but in practice a degree in a science or technology subject is required. Training is on the job and involves passing the exams of the Chartered Institute of Patent Agents. Nowadays it is becoming more important to hold a degree in a science subject as it is usually necessary to register as a Patent Agent in the European Patent Office. This involves taking the European qualifying exams for which a degree is necessary.

Patent Examiners and Officers need a first or second class honours degree in engineering, physics, chemistry, maths or an equivalent professional qualification.

Personal Qualities

Necessary qualities are curiosity, the ability to assimilate new ideas, good analytical and critical skills, clear and concise thinking and the capacity for logical and clear expression both in speech and writing.

£ About £13,000 for trainee Patent Agents; newly registered Agents earn about £20,000; Examiners begin at £13,651 and progress to about £43,000. These are approximate.

i Chartered Institute of Patent Agents, Staple Inn Buildings, High Holborn, London WC1V 7PZ; 020 7405 9450
www.cipa.org.uk

The Patent Office, Cardiff Road, Newport, Gwent NP9 1RH; 01633 814544 (Patent Examiners)
www.patent.gov.uk

Pattern Cutter,* see *Clothing Industry, Fashion

PERSONAL ASSISTANT

(see also Secretary)

A Senior Secretary or Personal Assistant (PA) may work with one or more senior executives. Accurate skills in shorthand or audio typewriting, word processing and information management, and a knowledge of office-based software, are desirable. The PA may also act as administrator, information centre, organiser of the manager's day, progress chaser, arranger of travel and meetings, receptionist, and communicator (oral and written) internally and externally. A Senior Secretary or PA assumes responsibility without direct supervision and takes decisions within the scope of assigned authority.

Qualifications and Training

GCSEs (including English), A levels or a degree are all acceptable qualifications. (Numeracy and a second language are very useful.) NVQs in Administration (Secretarial) are available. A secretary usually gains experience as a member of a management team, although some find jobs at a senior level following a postgraduate secretarial or secretarial/linguist course. Some secretaries progress to management through further study in personnel, administration, public relations, marketing, information technology, and so on.

Personal Qualities

Good secretaries are judged by what they do, but qualities such as self-motivation, discretion, tact, loyalty, personality, flexibility, communication skills and smart appearance are expected.

£ £12,000–£20,000, or more in London.

i Institute of Qualified Private Secretaries Ltd (IQPS), First Floor, 6 Bridge Avenue, Maidenhead SL6 1RR; 01628 625007; fax 01628 624990
www.iqps.org.uk
Careers in Secretarial and Office Work (Kogan Page)

PERSONNEL OFFICER

Personnel management is all about the effective use and development of people's skills, knowledge and experience to achieve the goals of an organisation – in other words, getting the best out of people at work. A major part of personnel work is concerned with the staffing of businesses and ensuring that jobs are filled by people with the required abilities, and that people are employed where their abilities can best be used. To do this, the Personnel Officer undertakes job analysis, observing the work done and asking questions. The information enables a job specification to be completed, detailing the skills, knowledge and qualifications the job requires. The Personnel Officer may then undertake recruitment and follow this with a programme of training.

The Personnel Officer in a big firm also ensures that young qualified staff gain experience in a wide range of departments. The officer may also deal with grievances, industrial relations, training and development, salary structure, as well as hygiene, safety and welfare. In some organisations, house magazines and sports and social activities all come under the personnel department's responsibility.

Qualifications and Training
Applicants for membership of the Institute of Personnel and Development through the Institute's Professional Education Scheme should normally have three GCSEs or equivalent and two A levels or equivalent, or have two years' experience in a responsible personnel management position.

Personal Qualities
Personnel Officers should have good administrative and organisational skills, be fair, logical and possess excellent interpersonal skills.

£ A graduate's salary is between £12,000 and £15,000. An average salary is £18,000.

i The Institute of Personnel and Development, IPD House, 35 Camp Road, London SW19 4UX; 020 8971 9000
www.ipd.co.uk

PEST CONTROLLER

Pest controllers control not only mice, rats, cockroaches and ants that may be damaging foodstuffs in a factory or hotel, or present in private homes, but also rabbits, moles, birds and foxes that attack farmers' crops. They work for local authorities and private firms. Service staff are employed to lay traps, set poison, and so on. There are also opportunities for graduates in research and management.

Qualifications and Training
Service staff should have GCSEs to include science subjects and English. Training is on the job and, in local government, there are courses available. Graduates should have a biology degree or a relevant science degree.

Personal Qualities
This is not a job for the squeamish but also not for the vicious. The work demands a mature outlook, and an ability to get on with many kinds of people, to work in varying conditions, and to work alone. The ability to drive is useful.

£ Salaries range from about £8,000+ to £13,000+, the higher figure being for graduate entrants.

i Local authorities

Petrol Pump Attendant*, see *Garage Work

PHARMACIST

The main work of the Pharmacist is the dispensing of doctors' prescriptions. There are three branches of the profession: Community Pharmacists, Hospital Pharmacists, and Industrial and Research Pharmacists.

Community Pharmacist
Working in a shop, dispensing prescriptions – either those they have made up themselves or ready-made ones – they also explain the use of the drug to customers, keep a poisons register, and act as a link between the doctor and the pharmaceutical manufacturer, being prepared to discuss developments with both. In addition, they sell a wide range of non-pharmaceutical articles.

Hospital Pharmacist
They dispense drugs for hospital in- and out-patients. In addition, in some hospitals, Pharmacists manufacture their own products, take part in research work, and come into direct contact with in-patients by accompanying medical staff on their ward rounds.

Industrial and Research Pharmacist
They research diseases, develop new drugs and carry out clinical trials. Industrial Pharmacists are also recruited to work in the areas of manufacturing, regulatory and medical affairs, sales and marketing, computer science/information technology, and others.

Qualifications and Training

Minimum qualifications are five GCSEs or equivalent to include English language and maths, and three A levels, in chemistry plus two subjects from a biological science, maths and physics. They lead to a three- or four-year degree course in pharmacy, plus one year's paid practical training before registration.

Personal Qualities

Meticulous attention to detail, a sense of responsibility and an ability to get on with people are required.

£ Pre-registration year £7,000–£9,000 in London, £6,000–£7,500 elsewhere; qualified £15,000 (Community), £12,350 (Hospital), £15,500 (Industry).

i The Association of the British Pharmaceutical Industry, 12 Whitehall, London SW1A 2DY; 020 7930 3477 (free booklet offering guide to careers for graduates)

Guild of Hospital Pharmacists, 50 Southwark Street, London SE1 1UN; 020 7378 7255

The National Pharmaceutical Association, Mallinson House, 36–42 St Peter's Street, St Albans, Hertfordshire AL1 3NP; 01727 832161

Pharmaceutical Society of Northern Ireland, 73 University Street, Belfast BT7 1HL; 028 9032 6927

Royal Pharmaceutical Society of Great Britain, 1 Lambeth High Street, London SE1 7JN; 020 7735 9141 www.rpsgb.org.uk

Royal Pharmaceutical Society of Great Britain, Scottish Department, 36 York Place, Edinburgh EH1 3HU

'Entrance Requirements to Schools of Pharmacy' (The Royal Pharmaceutical Society of Great Britain)

'Pharmacy' (HMSO)

'Pharmacy: Effective Caring' (The Royal Pharmaceutical Society of Great Britain)

PHARMACY TECHNICIAN

Pharmacy technicians work as part of the pharmacy team and are supervised by a Pharmacist. Their duties can include the dispensing of medicines from prescriptions, preparing sterile medicines, assessing stocks of drugs, patient counselling, advising on health promotion issues and collecting and collating information on drugs from a variety of sources. Pharmacy technicians can work in chemists, hospitals, in the armed forces or the prison service, or within the pharmaceutical industry.

Qualifications and Training

A nationally recognised qualification is the S/NVQ Pharmacy Services (level 3) which is available from approved centres. Entry requirements for this are generally four GCSEs at Grade C or above. Mature applicants are welcome, and previous education and work experience are considered.

Personal Qualities

Pharmacy technicians should be accurate in their work, reliable, careful and have high standards of hygiene. They should also enjoy working with other people and in teams.

£ A trainee technician could expect £7,233–£8,839. Once qualified, the starting salary for a Pharmacy Technician is around £9,796.

i Education Officer, Association of Pharmacy Technicians UK, The Pharmacy Department, Wrexham Maelor Hospital NHS Trust, Croesnewydd Road, Wrexham, North Wales LL13 7TD

The National Pharmaceutical Association, Mallinson House, 36–42 St Peter's Street, St Albans, Hertfordshire, AL1 3NP; 01727 832161

Royal Pharmaceutical Society of Great Britain, 1 Lambeth High Street, London SE1 7JN; 020 7735 9141 www.rpsgb.org.uk

PHOTOGRAPHER

(see also Medical Illustrator)

Photography is an international means of communication. Its great advantage over the written word is that it does not need to be translated for use in a different country. The uses of photography range from commercial and press to medicine and crime detection. With the advent of microfilming, the storage and retrieval of information have been made much more convenient and involve the use of far less space.

Photography is also a popular hobby, providing jobs for many in the photographic manufacturing, retailing, servicing and photo-finishing trades (*see also* Photographic Work).

Commercial Photographer

This work includes advertising, fashion, industrial and general practice photography. Photographers in advertising, editorial and fashion are nearly always freelance, employed for a particular campaign or job. Industrial photographers may be freelance or employed by large organisations where they take photographs for brochures, catalogues, instruction manuals and in-house magazines. General practice photographers are mainly involved in portraiture and taking wedding photographs, and so on.

Photojournalism and Press Photographer

Press photographers work for newspapers, magazines, periodicals and technical journals. All these media, particularly the last three, employ freelance as well as in-house staff. Photojournalists are photographers who are able to tell a story with pictures. They are almost always freelance and the main market for their work is Sunday colour supplements.

Institutional and Specialist Photography

Scientific photographers are used to provide information essential for research in a scientific or engineering field. This work may include aerial photography as well as the use of techniques such as holography, photomicrography and macrophotography. The main employers are the Civil Service, private industries and universities. The main uses for photography in hospitals are to satisfy clinical, research, publication and teaching requirements. Clinical photography in particular demands the use of specialist techniques: photomicroscopy, macrophotography, endoscopic photography and the use of infra-red and ultraviolet light sources.

Institutions that require photographers include museums, trade associations, national parks departments, charities, advisory councils, education authorities, libraries, auction houses and national galleries.

Photographers are also employed to teach photography in colleges and in schools run by manufacturers and major retailers. There are opportunities to teach part-time photographic courses in many schools and some colleges.

There are also opportunities to be a photographer in the Army, Royal Navy and Royal Air Force but no one can join the Army or Royal Navy solely to be a photographer. The RAF does recruit directly into ground photography. As regards the police force, other than the City of London force, most photographers are civilian employees.

Qualifications and Training

Formal educational qualifications are not always required but, for a place on a course, four to five GCSEs or equivalent are usually necessary. (*See* Medical Illustrator for the requirements for medical photography.) To be a trainee press photographer, five GCSEs at grades A, B or C are necessary, or four GCSEs and one A level, or two GCSEs and two A levels. English language is necessary.

The Royal Navy requires a good general education to GCSE level with particular attention to maths and English. In the police force requirements vary; some ask for City and Guilds qualifications and some three GCSEs including English, maths and a science.

There are a number of HND and degree courses available and for entry to these five GCSEs plus two A levels or equivalent are necessary. Some establishments will accept individuals with a good portfolio of work.

Training is often on the job in photography, in a junior position; for example, a messenger or general assistant in an advertising studio or as a trainee assistant photographer in the police force. Some employers provide courses and others allow time off for attendance at outside courses. NVQs in Photography at levels 3 and 4 are available.

Personal Qualities

Photographers generally require a blend of artistic and technical skills, the ability to deal with people and to put them at their ease, and good eyesight and colour vision. Medical and police photographers must have the ability to remain 'outside' their work and not be too squeamish.

£ Salaries vary enormously but the following are intended to give some indication: assistant photographers can earn £40-100 per day; established photographers in the areas of advertising, fashion and editorial can earn anything from £150 to £1,000 per day; photographers working in advertising generally earn more than those working in editorial. Social and wedding photographers with experience could expect an annual salary of about £10,000; newspaper trainees start at £7,000, rising to £10,000 after a year. In London, the rates are £18,000 with experience for a weekly publication, and higher for a national newspaper. Medical photographers begin at £6,210; £8,408 when trained.

i Association of Photographers Ltd (AFAEP), 81 Leonard Street, London EC2A 4QS; 020 7739 6669

British Institute of Professional Photography, Fox Talbot House, Amwell End, Ware, Hertfordshire SG12 9HN; 01920 464011

The National Council for the Training of Journalists, Latton Bush Centre, Southern Way, Harlow, Essex CM18 7BL; 01279 430009

www.itecharlow.co.uk/nctj/

Local Army, Royal Navy, Royal Air Force and Police Careers Offices

Great Careers in Video, Film and Photography (Kogan Page)

PHOTOGRAPHIC WORK

There are many varied activities of interest associated with the production of photographs and images.

Wholesale Photofinishing Laboratories

Catering for the amateur photographic markets, these laboratories are handling large film volumes amounting to many thousands per day. Highly sophisticated state-of-the-art printing, processing, finishing, pricing and hands-free dispatch equipment are used to ensure that very exacting service times are maintained. Most laboratories operate over a 24-hour cycle; skilled technicians and operators are a requirement of this sector of the industry.

Professional Laboratories/Imaging Centres

The professional laboratory/imaging centre can be divided into two major segments: social and commercial. The social laboratories harness all the skills of photographic processing technicians, covering a diversity of requirements from printing (hand and machine), processing (paper and film), colour negative/colour transparency, black and white, small prints to works of art adorning many stately homes. Weddings and portraiture are the life blood of a social laboratory. With the rapid advance of digital imaging, the commercial laboratories are having to face the challenge of a rapidly changing environment; a new breed of 'technocrats' is appearing – people with advanced computer skills and a creative talent to match. From dye-sublimation to ink-jet, from thumbnail images to giant murals, exhibitions, corporate organisations, PR agencies, a whole gamut of new and exciting markets awaits this sector of the business.

Manufacturing, Retailing and Service Trades

In the past the UK supported a host of camera manufacturers. Today, only highly specialised cameras are produced. However, large quantities of film, photographic and non-photographic papers and chemicals continue to be manufactured. Opportunities exist for technicians to research and develop new products; all aspects of the industry need support technicians, engineers and a whole plethora of sales personnel.

Qualifications and Training

The industry has its own training organisation, the Photography and Photographic Processing National Training Organisation (PPPNTO). NVQ and apprenticeship schemes are already well established for all aspects of the photographic, digital and allied services. There is an increasing requirement for personnel with degrees in the sciences. A new emerging workforce is beginning to appear with all the challenges associated with learning new skills and marrying them to the knowledge that has kept the industry to the forefront of new technology.

Personal Qualities

Staff are handling other people's memories, which are often unique and carry commercial or sentimental value. All personnel must have a caring and responsible attitude to their work. Good colour vision is essential, especially for personnel engaged in colour coordination, equipment integration, and so on. Photo scientists must have an interest in discovering environmental improvements, technological advancements, product improvements and increased efficiency.

£ Laboratory technicians in photofinishing and pro-labs have a commencing salary of £5,000–£8,000. A technician would start at about the same as a non-graduate entry, rising to £12,500–£21,000, London rates being higher. Graduates in manufacturing and senior technical roles start at £12,000–£15,000 rising to £25,000–£30,000+ per annum.

i Professional Photographic Laboratories Association (PPLA), 29 Hempfield Road, Littleport Ely, Cambridgeshire CB6 1NW; 01353 863255; fax 01353 863522

PHYSICIST

Physics deals with the interrelation of matter and energy. Physicists are needed wherever the physical properties of materials have to be studied. They are employed in the fields of electronics, nuclear power, computing, aerospace, optics, telecommunications, engineering and instrument manufacture. In addition, hospitals employ medical physicists whose work includes support for medical use of radiation and design and implementation of new equipment for diagnosis and treatment of disease. Some physicists lecture in universities or teach in schools. Physics technicians assist fully qualified physicists.

Qualifications and Training

A qualified professional physicist needs a degree in physics. It is envisaged that this might be equivalent to NVQ level 4 in three subjects. College and university requirements are two A levels or three H grade passes to include physics, or a subject including physics, and a maths subject.

Junior technicians need a good education to GCSE level with particular attention to maths, a science and a subject showing the use of English in order to take an Edexcel (BTEC) national certificate. There are special certificate courses for medical junior physics technicians. For senior technicians an Edexcel (BTEC) HND award is available; the requirements are an A level (two H grades) in physics and GCSE maths, chemistry and English. An Edexcel (BTEC) NC or ND award is acceptable in place of A level/H grade. Training for technicians is generally on the job with time off to attend courses.

Personal Qualities

Physicists must be able to recognise a problem and plan an experiment or set of experiments to solve it. They should be imaginative, persevering, have good powers of concentration and adopt a sound, logical approach. Technicians should have the practical skills necessary to carry out experiments, be responsible, accurate and caring in their attitude to work.

£ Trainee technicians start at £6,500+, the majority of senior technicians earn from £12,000–£18,000+ and qualified physicists' earnings are in the region of £13,000–£26,000+.

i The Institute of Physics and Engineering in Medicine, Fairmount House, 230 Tadcaster Road, York YO24 1ES; 01904 610821; fax 01904 612279
www.ipem.org.uk
The Institute of Physics, 47 Belgrave Square, London SW1X 8QX; 020 7235 6111

PHYSIOTHERAPIST

A Chartered Physiotherapist treats patients suffering from a wide variety of diseases, conditions or injuries by physical means. They help people who have had strokes to regain the use of lost functions, treat sports injuries and people with arthritis, and help children with cerebral palsy to learn to walk. The techniques used include massage and manipulation, exercise, electrotherapy and hydrotherapy. Most physiotherapists work in the health service but there are many opportunities now for employment in industry, sports clinics, schools and private practice.

Qualifications and Training

A minimum of five GCSEs and three A levels are normally required for a place on a three- or four-year course, leading to a degree. Many candidates offer three A levels but there are other routes such as Edexcel (BTEC) science (health studies). Subjects at GCSE should ideally include English and two sciences and A levels should include a biological science.

Personal Qualities

Physiotherapists must be caring, patient, reasonably fit, good communicators and have the ability to inspire confidence in their patients.

£ From £15,405, to £29,720 for senior staff.

i The Chartered Society of Physiotherapy, 14 Bedford Row, London WC1R 4ED; 020 7306 6666 (enclose A5 sae)

Careers in Nursing and Related Professions (Kogan Page)
'Physiotherapist' (DH Leaflets Unit, PO Box 21, Stanmore, Middlesex HA7 1AY)

PIANO TUNER

Piano tuners or technicians are able both to tune a piano evenly throughout the scale and to discover and put right any fault. They work with a kit of specialised tools, and are employed in piano factories and by piano dealers. Some also work for themselves.

Qualifications and Training

Courses are available at five institutions: City of Leeds College of Music, London Guildhall University, Newark and Sherwood College, The Royal National College for the Blind, Hereford, and Stevenson College of Further Education, Edinburgh. Entry requirements are usually four GCSEs at grade C or above. The Piano Tuners' Association will accept a candidate for membership after five years from the start of training – at least two years' training and at least two years' working as a piano tuner.

Personal Qualities

Musical ability, while not essential, is an advantage. Patience and deftness are required, together with an aptitude to be able to use woodworking, home-improvement, DIY and/or car-maintenance tools. As tuners are mostly self-employed, the ability to work alone, competence in managing a small business and self-motivation are also important.

£ Salaries vary: £150–£170 a week when trained, lower without experience. Many piano tuners are self-employed and may earn up to £400 a week when established.

i Pianoforte Tuners' Association, c/o 10 Reculver Road, Herne Bay, Kent CT6 6LD; 01227 368808 (send sae)
www.pianotuner.org.uk

Pilot*, see *Civil Aviation

PLASTERER

Plasterers are among the most skilled of the building craftsmen. They not only wet-plaster large wall areas but also may construct plaster fittings in a workshop and then fix them into place on a building site. Intricate details such as ceiling mouldings are also made wet by the plasterer or constructed in a workshop from fibrous plaster. Plasterers may also lay cement floors and carry out external finishes on houses. There are opportunities for work with building contractors and local authorities, and also for being self-employed.

Qualifications and Training

No formal educational requirements are necessary. Training is on the job as plasterer's mate, and by a three-year apprenticeship during which time it is possible to work towards NVQs awarded jointly by City and Guilds and the Construction Industry Training Board.

Personal Qualities

Plasterers must be physically strong and have the ability to work very quickly. Defects in a wall or ceiling surface are often very obvious so high standards and a responsible attitude to work are important.

£ Recommended weekly rates are: £73.90 at 16; £103.46 at 17; £147.81 at 18; and, when qualified, the craftsman rate is £178.62.

i Construction Industry Training Board, Bircham Newton, King's Lynn, Norfolk PE31 6RH; 01553 776677 (ext 2466)

PLUMBER

Plumbers fit and repair pipes connecting the cold and hot water supply, central heating or some domestic appliance such as a washing machine, and remove rain water and sewage. Plumbers work on roofs fitting flashings and are also responsible for putting up rainwater pipes and gutters. They may work on building sites employed by building contractors, property companies or local authorities and, also, many plumbers are self-employed, working mainly in private houses.

Qualifications and Training

No formal educational requirements are necessary. Training is on the job, and by a four-year apprenticeship during which time it is possible to work towards NVQs levels 2 and 3. NVQs levels 4 and 5 will be available in the future.

Personal Qualities

Plumbers must be agile, deft and able to work neatly, carefully and accurately. They must also be prepared to work outside and have a head for heights.

£ Recommended weekly rates are: £73.90 at 16; £103.46 at 17; £147.81 at 18; and, when qualified, the craftsman rate is £178.62.

i Construction Industry Training Board, Bircham Newton, King's Lynn, Norfolk PE31 6RH; 01553 776677 (ext 2466)
Institute of Plumbing, 64 Station Lane, Hornchurch, Essex RM12 6NB; 01708 472791

Podiatrist* see *Chiropodist

POLICE OFFICER

The purpose of the police is to uphold the law, fairly and firmly, to prevent crime, to pursue and bring to justice those who break the law, and to be seen to do all this with integrity, common sense and sound judgement.

There are many different specialities within the police service, although everyone joins as a constable. These include the Criminal Investigation Department (CID); traffic police; dog handlers; mounted police; river police; and crime prevention officers.

There are also special police forces in existence – the British Transport Police, the Ministry of Defence Police and (in London) the Parks Police. These special forces are separate from the other 43 forces in England and Wales, which are the general responsibility of the Home Secretary.

Qualifications and Training

There are no minimum formal educational requirements although applicants should have achieved a good all-round standard of education. All candidates sit an entrance test, made up of five separate tests to measure the following abilities: to spell and construct sentences; to check information quickly and correctly; to solve numerical problems accurately; to reason logically; and to observe scenes carefully and to recall the details accurately. Normal entry is at 18 and a half. Apart from learning about police life and experiencing police work, cadets have the opportunity to further their academic qualifications and to work in the community. Cadetship does not guarantee entry into the regular force. Many forces operate a voluntary cadet scheme, and YT schemes may also be in operation in many forces.

All recruits, whether they have been a cadet or not, serve a two-year probation period as police constables with training on residential courses included. After the two-year period there are opportunities for specialisation.

Graduates may apply to join the Accelerated Promotion Scheme for Graduates (APSG). After the initial two-year probationary period and after passing the sergeant's exam, these graduates will enter the Accelerated Promotion Course (APC). Officers who have joined the force under standard entry will have the opportunity to gain entry on to the APC if they have passed the sergeant's exam.

The 43 forces in England and Wales, the eight Scottish forces and the one in Northern Ireland each have their own entrance requirements and it is advisable to check these before applying.

Personal Qualities

Being a Police Officer is a varied job demanding many different qualities, but all officers must have self-discipline, be independent yet able to work in a team, adaptable, have a genuine concern for people, be completely fair and honest, with good powers of observation. In addition, Police Officers must be prepared to work unsocial hours, which may disturb their family life, and to be witness to the seamy side of life.

£ Constables begin on £16,056 and increase to £17,944 after initial training. Constables in London receive London weighting and a London allowance in addition.

i Local police forces
Metropolitan Police Service, Recruitment and Selection Centre, 26 Aybrook Street, London W1M 3JL; 0345 272212
England and Wales: Police Recruiting Department, Room 514 (graduate entry: Room 548), Home Office, Queen Anne's Gate, London SW1H 9AT
www.homeoffice.gov.uk/police-rec/recruit
Scotland: Police Division, Scottish Office Home Department, Room E1-7, Saughton House, Broomhouse Drive, Edinburgh EH11 3XD
Careers in the Police Service (Kogan Page)
'Police Officer' (Home Office)

POLITICS

Politics is a career for relatively few; there are approximately 659 Members of Parliament and over 80 British Members of the European parliament. MPs work long hours, often sitting in the House until the small hours. In addition, they spend at least one day a week in their constituency and often specialise in a particular subject, such as health or education. Ministerial responsibilities impose many extra duties of national importance. All MPs must have another career to support them while they are seeking election and to fall back on if they lose their seats. Many also have spouses who have successful careers.

Another job in politics is that of Constituency Agent, working for local branches of the party, organising the party and its publicity, and acting as a link between the MP and the party. Since early 1999, there have been separate parliaments established in Scotland and Wales. These have limited powers at present and it is not yet known exactly how they will develop.

There are also opportunities for administrative and office staff in the central party offices. These central office staff, as well as carrying out general office duties, are responsible for writing speech material for party spokesmen and providing information to the national press.

Qualifications and Training

No formal educational requirements are necessary for political jobs, although most politicians have a good academic background. MPs are adopted by a constituency party because they are already well known to the party through their active voluntary work or, sometimes, because they have made a name for themselves in some other field.

Agents have an excellent knowledge of electoral law and party organisation, and are given training on courses increasingly useful as a background in Public Relations and the skill to build good working relationships with all aspects of the media. Head office staff are usually recruited from Constituency Agents and assistants.

Personal Qualities

It is necessary in politics to be hard working, persevering, resilient and, for Agents and administrative staff, to have excellent organisational skills. MPs should also have a certain personal charisma and be able to put their ideas across clearly and persuasively.

£ MPs' salaries are £43,000. Cabinet Ministers receive £87,851, Ministers £74,985 and Under-secretaries £67,483. The Prime Minister is entitled to £102,417 but the highest paid is the Lord Chancellor at £140,665.

i Local constituency parties
www.conservative-party.org.uk
www.labour.org.uk
www.libdems.org.uk
For a list of all UK political parties, visit: www.club.demon.co.uk/politics/parties.html

POLYMER SCIENCE AND TECHNOLOGY

Polymers is the name given to materials that are made up of large molecules of identical or similar units and united by chemical bonds. The main polymers are natural and synthetic rubbers, plastics and natural and synthetic fibres. The plastics industry makes products both for industrial and domestic use and is also involved in moulding, laminating and finishing products. The rubber industry produces tyres, hoses and footwear as well as numerous other products. Scientific staff work in research and development, and there are also opportunities for salespeople and technical advisers.

Qualifications and Training

NVQs are available for all the polymer processes, for example: injection moulding, blow moulding, extrusion, tyre manufacture, general rubber goods and retreading tyres. Technicians who wish to take the Edexcel (BTEC) certificate in polymer technology need GCSE passes in English, maths and a science.

The Edexcel (BTEC) certificate course is available full- and part-time. On completion of the certificate it is possible to take the higher certificate on a part-time course. Professional qualifications are available through the Plastics and Rubber Institute at both technician and degree level (Engineering Technician, Incorporated Engineer, Chartered Engineer). In addition, the Edexcel (BTEC) certificate can contribute as evidence towards the attainment of NVQ level 3 and both the NVQ and Edexcel (BTEC) form part of the Modern Apprenticeship scheme (for further information contact the BPTA).

To take a degree in polymer science and technology, five GCSE passes or equivalent vocational qualifications are necessary in chemistry, physics and maths, two A levels or three H grades. There are also higher degrees offered for students who have less applicable first degrees.

Personal Qualities

An interest in solving practical problems, the ability to work as one of a team and high standards of professionalism are required. Technical staff also need practical skills necessary to carry out experiments.

£ A trainee technician at 16 would earn about £8,000, £9,775–£11,000 when qualified, graduates £11,500–£14,000.

i The British Plastics Federation, Bath Place, Rivington Street, London EC2A 3JE; 020 7457 5000

British Polymer Training Association, Coppice House, Halesfield 7, Telford, Shropshire TF7 4NA; 01952 587020.

The British Rubber Manufacturers' Association, 90 Tottenham Court Road, London W1P 0PH; 020 7580 2794

The Institute of Materials, 1 Carlton House Terrace, London SW1Y 5DB; 020 7839 4071

POST OFFICE

The Post Office has changed out of all recognition. It now consists of three independent businesses. The Royal Mail delivers 60 million letters a day in an enormously complex distribution operation. Royal Mail Parcelforce is at the forefront of the UK's fiercely competitive parcel services market. Post Office Counters is Britain's largest retail network.

Opportunities for school leavers include postal cadet, administration, secretarial, postman, postwoman, counter clerk, retail assistant, apprentice engineer. There are generally opportunities for graduates in marketing, personnel, finance, operations, planning, information technology and operational research.

Qualifications and Training

No formal educational qualifications are necessary for the jobs listed above for school leavers but they must take an aptitude test. In the future NVQs will be available for a number of different tasks at a number of levels. Apprentice engineer entrants must have studied maths and science subjects to GCSE level. Graduate entrants should have studied a relevant degree. Useful subjects are business studies, computing, maths, geography, transport and planning, mechanical and electrical engineering.

Personal Qualities

All employees who meet the public need to be able to communicate with people, and counter clerks and retail assistants, in particular, should be patient and prepared to help. Counter clerks also need numerical skills. Graduates should be numerate and possess good interpersonal and organisational skills.

£ School leavers £5,620–£8,830; graduates from £14,800, plus London and south-east allowances where appropriate.

i School leavers: The Personnel Officer at the local Royal Mail, Royal Mail Parcelforce or Post Office Counters office (addresses and telephone numbers in local telephone directory)

Graduates: The Assessment Consultancy, Freepost, Coton House, Rugby CV23 0BR
www.postoffice.co.uk

POTTER

Employees in the pottery industry make ordinary domestic china, earthenware, vases and ornaments, fine bone china, ceramic tiles, sanitary ware, industrial and electrical porcelain and huge insulators used in generating electricity. Although the industry is mechanised, there is still a predominant demand for skilled workers: hand painters, fettlers and spongers, casting, lithographing, binding and lining, to name a few. Some potters work individually, hand throwing or casting their own pieces and selling them personally or through a shop or gallery.

Qualifications and Training

No formal educational requirements are needed for the industry, and training is mainly on the job. Craftsmen potters sometimes become apprenticed to master potters but more commonly they take foundation courses followed by vocational or degree courses at an art school.

Personal Qualities

Potters need a good eye for shape and design, a steady hand and a delicate touch. Potters working for themselves must also be inventive and have business skills and marketing ability.

£ Industry employees at 16, about £80 a week. Craftsmen set their own rates and, if they are selling their work through a gallery, must pay the owner a percentage.

i Crafts Council, 44a Pentonville Road, London N1 9BY; 020 7278 7700 (send sae)

The Craft Potters' Association, William Blake House, Marshall Street, London W1V 1FD; 020 7437 7605

PRE-SCHOOL WORKERS

Pre-school workers (also known as playleaders and pre-school leaders) work in pre-schools and playgroups where they provide an appropriate service for children (usually from two and a half years upwards) by means of a range of educational play activities. Groups operate from a fixed time each day – some are morning or afternoon only, some are all day. Pre-school workers are assisted by paid assistants and one or more adults, including parents, on a voluntary basis. The majority of groups are registered charities, managed by parents and volunteers from the local community. Groups may also be funded by local authorities or private concerns.

Qualifications and Training

The Qualifications and Curriculum Authority (QCA) is currently working towards creating a framework of qualifications for the whole childcare and education sector. Current qualifications include the diploma in pre-school practice, which is available at further education colleges and via the Pre-School Learning Alliance.

In Scotland, a self-study pack called 'Basic Training in Playwork' provides the basic knowledge and skills needed to work with young children in a play setting. The contents of the pack are matched against the underpinning competencies and knowledge required in SVQs Early Years Care and Education. Approved statement status is awarded in respect of some of the elements associated with this vocational qualification.

Personal Qualities

Playworkers should have a genuine interest in pre-school children. They should have excellent knowledge of how children learn and child development in order to develop a coherent curriculum for the children. They also need to have the ability to work well in a team, liaise with parents, other adults and other professionals. In addition to the above, pre-school leaders need to have the skills necessary to lead a team.

£ Salaries vary for pre-school workers from one area of the country to another.

i Pre-School Learning Alliance, 69 Kings Cross Road, London WC1X 9LL; 020 7833 0991; fax 020 7837 4942

Scottish Pre-School Play Association (SPPA), 14 Elliot Place, Glasgow G3 8EP; 0141 221 4148; fax 0141 221 6043

Wales PPA, 2A Chester Street, Wrexham, Clwyd LL13 8BD

Northern Ireland PPA, Information Centre, 6C Wildflower Way, Apollo Road, Belfast BT12 6TA

PRINTING

The purpose of printing is communication, whether the printed matter be books, magazines, newspapers, security documents or bank cards. Printers are also involved in other products, from wallpaper and floor coverings to advertising slogans on milk bottles. The printing industry covers a wide range of jobs in both factory and office.

Pre-Press

Most setting is via floppy disk or CD. The pre-press operator is responsible for a keyboard, similar to that of a typewriter, which transfers typematter for output to paper or film.

Proofreader

Proofreaders check customers' proofs for spelling mistakes and incorrect typefaces before returning them. When setting to disk, proofreading is done automatically.

Camera Operator/Scanner Operator

Camera operators photograph the original of a drawing or photograph and from this produce a negative or positive as required. In colour work a separate piece of film for each colour has to be produced. The operator requires considerable skill and judgement to do this accurately. Now the reproduction of colour photographs is largely done by electronic scanners and not so much skill is needed on the part of the operator.

Planner/Platemaker

If the process is not completed electronically, make-up planning operators take the film and place the type and illustrations in the right place in the correct pages.

Machine Minder

The machine minder sets up and controls the quality of the printed materials, and ensures that the quality of the printing is consistent.

Binding and Finishing

This involves trimming the paper, assembling sections into book form and binding or stitching these together. In the case of hardback books, the hard cover is attached at this stage.

Office Jobs
Order clerks/account executives look after individual printing jobs; they write instructions for each department and check the product's arrival into and departure from each section.

Estimators work out how much a job will cost. Cost clerks go through the costs item by item and discover where and why the money was spent. Sales staff find customers, and design staff are also needed.

Qualifications and Training

Academic qualifications are not mandatory for craftworkers but the following subjects studied to GCSE level are preferred: English, maths, computer studies and science. Training is to NVQ levels 2 and 3, with time off to attend courses.

Office staff have qualifications ranging from GCSEs to a degree. GCSEs are preferred for junior clerks and there are opportunities to gain further qualifications through Edexcel (BTEC) or City and Guilds awards. To take the higher diploma in printing on a two- or three-year basis, four GCSEs to include English, maths and a science plus one A level are necessary, or an Edexcel (BTEC) or NC/ND in printing. There are in addition three print-related degree courses, for which two A levels are necessary.

NVQs at levels 2 and 3 are available in Print Production and Print Administration, and Modern Apprenticeships and National Traineeships are available for production and office trainees.

Personal Qualities

The printing industry is changing rapidly; employees must be prepared to move with the times and re-train if necessary. A responsible attitude and a pride in what is being produced are necessary. Production workers need good colour vision and manual dexterity.

£ Salaries vary but at 18 all workers should earn £170+ a week.

i British Printing Industries Federation (BPIF), 11 Bedford Row, London WC1R 4DX; 020 7242 6904
Institute of Printing, The Mews, Hill House, Tunbridge Wells, Kent TN1 1PJ; 01892 538118
www.globalprint.com/uk/iop

Scottish Print Employers Federation, 48 Palmerston Place, Edinburgh EH12 5DE; 0131 220 4353

Print and Graphic Communication NTO, 926 Alum Rock Road, Ward End, Birmingham B8 2NS; 0121 789 7345

PRISON OFFICER

Prison officers are employed in prisons, detention centres, young-offender institutions and remand centres. The work involves supervising prisoners inside the place of detention, escorting them to courts and other prisons and, if relevant, teaching a skill or trade. Some specialist prison officers are employed as hospital officers, dog handlers, security experts and caterers.

Qualifications and Training

Five GCSEs including maths and English are required and applicants must pass an aptitude test and an interview. Training lasts for two weeks at a local prison then nine weeks at an officers' training school. In Scotland, the training period is initially for one month followed by a six-week course. There is special training for caterers, dog handlers, physical education instructors and medical staff.

Personal Qualities

Officers must be good listeners, assertive and have excellent communication skills. They need to be good team players and have the ability to mix with a wide range of people.

£ £15,264-£21,831; officers in London are also paid a London weighting allowance.

i Prison Officers' Association, 245 Church Street, London N9 9HW; 020 8803 0255

Prison Service HQ, Home Office, Cleland House, Page Street, London SW1P 4LN; 020 7217 3000 www.hmprisonservice.gov.uk

Scottish Prison Service, Carlton House, 5 Redheughs Rigg, Edinburgh EH12 9HW; 0131 556 8400

'HM Prison Service in England and Wales' (Home Office, Freepost, London SW1V 1YZ)

'HM Prisons in Scotland' (Scottish Prison Service)

PROBATION OFFICER

(see also Social Work and Social Care)

Probation Officers are attached to particular courts and may be asked by a court to provide a report on an offender. Offenders who are given probation by a court are placed under the care of a Probation Officer who sees them regularly and tries to help with any problems. Some officers are based in prisons and give advice to inmates. Others become involved with separation and divorce proceedings and give advice to the courts when they are concerned with the custody of children. In Scotland, the functions of the Probation Officer are performed by social work departments in local authorities.

Qualifications and Training

The main professional qualification is the Diploma in Social Work (DipSW), which can be studied part-time while working or full-time via a college course. Entry requirements are five GCSEs plus two A levels or five SCEs including three at H grade. Mature entrants may be accepted without these qualifications.

Personal Qualities

Probation Officers should be strong characters, well balanced, have a flexible approach yet be able to work within the court system, and have a genuine interest in people of all types and a desire to help them.

£ Students studying full-time receive a grant of £3,220 in London, £2,525 elsewhere. Qualified staff under 30 start at £14,268 and those over 30 at £14,835.

i C6 Division, Home Office, Room 442, 50 Queen Anne's Gate, London SW1H 9AT; 020 7273 3000

Careers in Social Work (Kogan Page)

PSYCHOLOGIST

Psychologists study the processes, motives, reactions and nature of the human mind. The profession has many different specialities, from clinical psychology, concerned with human behavioural problems, to market research where psychologists may research why and how consumers prefer one product to another. Psychologists work in the NHS, private hospitals, industry, for government and local authorities, in schools and privately as consultants and practitioners.

Since 1987, the British Psychological Society has maintained the Register of Chartered Psychologists, which has stringent entry requirements. Anyone who wishes to become a Chartered Psychologist should ensure that their degree is accredited by the society as conferring the Graduate Basis for Registration (GBR). This is required for all BPS-accredited postgraduate training courses in applied psychology.

Clinical Psychology

Clinical psychologists use their knowledge of psychology when working with people with health problems or severe learning difficulties. They work alongside professionals such as doctors, nurses, social workers and counselling psychologists within NHS Trusts, hospitals, clinics, children's homes, and other community or related settings. They also work in private practice or research and academic institutions.

Counselling Psychologists

Counselling psychologists work with individuals, couples, families and groups such as people with disabilities or those who are discriminated against. They work to improve their client's sense of well-being, reduce stress and to help them resolve crises. They help people understand their problems and develop coping strategies and solutions. Counselling psychologists work in GP surgeries, NHS Trusts and hospitals, business institutions or specialist agencies.

Educational Psychologists

Educational psychologists work primarily in schools and colleges with teachers and lecturers, and with parents. They can work directly with a child or young person (up to the age of 19) or indirectly via parents and teachers. Educational psychologists are often involved in policy planning within the education departments of local authorities.

Occupational Psychologists

Occupational psychologists focus on the performance of people at work and in training, how organisations function and how individuals and groups behave in the work environment. The services of occupational psychologists are increasingly in demand and this area of psychology is broader in scope and less formalised than others. The work of an occupational psychologist can include work with individuals, organisational consultancy, assessment and training, vocational guidance and counselling, ergonomics and health and safety.

Teaching and Research
There are no formal qualifications that are preparation for teaching at university, although most universities encourage newly appointed staff to take a postgraduate certificate in higher education. All university lecturers are expected to be involved in developing their subject via research projects. For example, an educational psychologist may research on how to teach concepts to blind children and an occupational psychologist may research the relationship of stress to work conditions.

Qualifications and Training

Clinical Psychology
Applicants must have a good accredited psychology degree and some work or research experience, which should have clinical relevance. To register as a Chartered Clinical Psychologist candidates must obtain GBR and complete an accredited postgraduate training course in clinical psychology.

Counselling Psychologists
A degree in psychology and postgraduate professional training in counselling psychology is necessary for Chartered Counselling Psychologist status.

Educational Psychologists
An appropriate qualification in psychology, a teacher training qualification, teaching experience and a postgraduate qualification are all necessary to become registered as a Chartered Educational Psychologist in England, Wales and Northern Ireland. Teachers can re-train by undertaking an accredited qualification in psychology, postgraduate training and supervised experience. In Scotland, there is no requirement to become a fully qualified teacher.

Occupational Psychologists
To register as a Chartered Occupational Psychologist it is necessary to obtain GBR, gain an accredited postgraduate course in occupational psychology and complete 2–3 years' supervised practice.

Teaching and Research
A degree in psychology is acceptable for teaching in Further Education but most individuals involved in teaching and research in Higher Education will have a PhD or have held a research post. A teaching qualification such as the Postgraduate Certificate in Education (PGCE) is also increasingly required.

Personal Qualities

All psychologists should have a genuine interest in people, their behaviour and have an empathy for their problems. They also need to be excellent communicators and have the skills to work with people from different backgrounds and social groupings.

£

For newly graduated psychologists approximately £14,386. For experienced psychologists with management responsibilities, salaries range from £24,910 to £29,143. Senior psychologists managing departments or specialist sections can earn from £30,308 to £50,468.

Counselling Psychologists
This is based upon nationally agreed scales and should range between £14,386 and £50,468, depending on experience and level of responsibility
.

Educational Psychologists
Educational psychologists in Britain are usually employed by LEAs as part of the psychological service. In Northern Ireland they are appointed by the Education and Library Boards. Main grade educational psychologists earn between £21,642 and £32,274. Senior Principal Educational Psychologists earn £29,241 to £39,270.

Occupational Psychologists
Salaries vary enormously. The range for those employed in Government service is as follows: graduates £12,369–£13,651, Higher Psychologists earn between £14,909–£18,185, Senior Psychologist £18,911–£23,009 and Principal Psychologists earn between £24,239–£37,539. Private-sector and industry salaries can vary from £12,000–£50,000, depending on experience and expertise.

Teaching and Research
Salaries at FE and HE institutions range from £11,067–£20,052 for Lecturers, to £24,198–£32,000 for Senior Lecturers and Professors.

i The British Psychological Society, St Andrews House, 48 Princess Road East, Leicester LE1 7DR; 0116 254 9568 (free information leaflets and a range of books)
www.bps.org.uk

Association of Educational Psychologists, 26 The Avenue, Durham DH1 4ED; 0191 384 9512

PSYCHOTHERAPIST

Psychotherapy involves treatment and preventive care for psychological disturbances of emotions, thought and behaviour. It concentrates on the whole individual, viewing symptoms as representing only a part of the whole being. Both adults and children are treated by psychotherapists, for such problems as over-shyness, over-aggression, sleeping disorders, separation difficulties, behavioural problems, eating difficulties, self-harm and depression. Adults' problems may be less easy to perceive, but may be emotional, interfering with a person's work and home life.

Psychotherapists work in hospitals, in- and out-patient clinics, child and family consultation centres, GPs' surgeries, special schools for disturbed children and in private practice.

Qualifications and Training

A psychology or related degree is required, followed by a postgraduate degree or diploma in clinical or educational psychology plus relevant experience. After completing the latter requirement, training then takes a further four years and involves academic study, workshops and supervised therapeutic treatment.

Personal Qualities

Psychotherapists must have a genuine interest in the problems of children and adults, and a desire to help. They must themselves be emotionally well balanced.

£ £16,000–£20,000.

i The Association of Child Psychotherapists, 120 West Heath Road, London NW3 4S8; 020 7458 1609
The British Psychological Society, St Andrew's House, 48 Princess Road East, Leicester LE1 7DR; 0116 254 9568

PUBLICAN

The licensee of a pub may be a manager who is paid a salary, or a lessee or tenant who rents the property from a brewer, a pub company, or a free trader who owns the premises. As well as the ever-popular traditional town and country pubs there is now a wide variety of pubs ranging from theme pubs, cafe bars and steak bars to pubs with gourmet restaurants and full entertainment facilities. Nearly all pubs serve food and an increasing number also offer accommodation.

Qualifications and Training

Increasingly, those with NVQs (offered by the Hospitality Training Foundation), diploma or degree qualifications, especially in hotel, catering and licensed retail management, are sought.

Brewery companies will put their managers through a comprehensive training programme. Licensees could well be running businesses grossing more than half a million pounds a year. They must know how to market their services and devise new ideas to attract customers. They must also have a good knowledge of subjects such as bookkeeping, licensing laws, hygiene, staff motivation, customer care and cellar management. Other training courses are available from centres approved by the BII.

Personal Qualities

Publicans should be ambitious and able to take responsibility. They should enjoy working with people, have a customer-care focus and good interpersonal skills.

£ Managers who are single earn from £18,312 with participation in bonus schemes, up to a maximum of £35,500 in London. Accommodation, lighting and heating are normally provided.

i Retail Department, Brewers and Licensed Retailers Association, 42 Portman Square, London W1H 0BB; 020 7486 4831

British Institute of Innkeeping, Wessex House, 80 Park Street, Camberley, Surrey GU15 3PT; 01276 684449
Hospitality Training Foundation, International House, 3 High Street, London W5 5DB; 020 8579 2400
Hotel and Catering International Management Association (HCIMA), 191 Trinity Road, London SW17 7HN; 020 7672 4251
Springboard UK, 1 Denmark Street, London WC2H 8LP; 020 7497 8654
Working in Hospitality (Kogan Page)
The Publican's Handbook (Kogan Page)

PUBLIC RELATIONS OFFICER

The chief aim of the public relations officer/executive is to ensure that the correct information about their employer or client is made known to the right people. This is done by a variety of means, including media relations, internal and external communication, company literature, exhibitions and events. Corporate PR work is concerned with putting across an organisation's policy and activities to a variety of people, including Government departments, employees and stakeholders. Consumer PR is giving information about a product; it is closely allied with marketing and advertising. Other areas of PR include community relations, sponsorship and financial PR. PR executives are employed by organisations, PR consultancies or work as freelance consultants.

Qualifications and Training

Qualifications vary from a certificate/diploma in public relations to a masters degree. Fifteen courses in public relations are approved by the Institute of Public Relations as qualifications for membership. Entry requirements for a certificate course are five GCSEs plus one year's experience or five GCSEs plus two A levels/Edexcel (BTEC)/NC/ND equivalents. Entry requirements for a degree course vary according to the institution, but most require five GCSEs and A levels or equivalents. The IPR runs its own diploma courses and postgraduate foundation course.

Personal Qualities

Public relations officers must understand people and what motivates them and have the ability to get on well with people from different backgrounds. They must be imaginative, creative, reliable and have good managerial skills. Excellent writing skills are essential.

£ Trainees in PR earn around £10,000. Salaries vary across the business sectors.

i The Institute of Public Relations, The Old Trading House, 15 Northburgh Street, London EC1V 0PR; 020 7253 5151
Communications, Advertising and Marketing Foundation Ltd, Abford House, 15 Wilton Road, London SW1V 1NJ; 020 7828 7506
www.camfoundation.com
Careers in Marketing, Advertising and Public Relations (Kogan Page)

PUBLISHING

Publishing is concerned with choosing, planning, editing, designing and producing hardback or paperback, fiction or non-fiction or specialist books, periodicals and newspapers. School or university textbooks may be published for sale to schools or libraries or to parents. Books, journals or magazines may be aimed at a specific trade or profession, for example, the legal profession. Periodicals include weekly magazines, learned journals, trade publications and in-house staff magazines.

Book publishing is divided into three main functions: editorial, production and design, and marketing (including sales and publicity). Some may argue that it is all 'marketing', and that all the functions work towards satisfying the needs of the customer.

Editorial

Editors tend to separate into commissioning editors who are responsible for initiating new ideas, finding authors and assessing and sponsoring unsolicited manuscripts, and desk editors who prepare manuscripts and put them into house style, rewriting parts if necessary, and correcting proofs. In a small publishing house these functions are often combined. Editors in small houses are also sometimes concerned with selling rights to a foreign publishing house and taking in books from abroad.

Production and Design

The production department is responsible for buying paper, dealing with typesetters, printers and binders and seeing that schedules are kept. The design or art department is responsible for the overall appearance of the book including choosing the typeface and designing the jacket. In a small house these functions may be combined, with freelance designers engaged for book cover/jacket design.

Marketing

The sales and marketing department must ensure that the book is ordered by bookshops and that information reaches potential buyers both in the UK and overseas. Over 30 per cent of all books published are exported. In some companies, representatives are employed to visit bookshops, library suppliers and educational establishments. Adverts are placed in relevant daily and trade publications, mailings are sent to specific groups of people, review copies of new books are dispatched and publicity executives try to obtain interviews for authors in the press and on radio and television.

Magazine Publishing

The functions of the above departments are similar, with the following variations. commissioning editors tend to commission articles rather than books. The design of the magazine once established must be followed. Often much more colour work is involved in magazine than in book production. The advertising for the sale of popular magazines is more aggressive than for the sale of books.

Picture Research

This may be a separate department in a large house or one dealing with highly illustrated books, a function performed as necessary by the editorial department, or by a freelance. Picture researchers are responsible for finding pictures to illustrate a book or magazine. Sometimes they may search for very specific material to illustrate certain subject matter, while sometimes pictures generally pertaining to a topic are required.

Packagers

A book packaging company sells complete books to publishers, often supplying publishers at home and abroad simultaneously. The publishers are then responsible for marketing and selling the book.

Designers

Design skills are needed in all areas of publishing from jacket covers to creating the image of a magazine. Designers have excellent IT skills and are able to use a number of software packages with expertise.

Qualifications and Training

There are no formal educational requirements necessary but most publishers expect applicants to have a degree. This is particularly necessary in a house dealing with a very small, specialised area only. Oxford Brookes University, West Herts College, the Robert Gordon University, and Napier University offer first and second degree courses and diplomas in publishing. Computer literacy is also in demand by publishers.

Production staff generally first take a printing course, or a degree as above. The London College of Printing and Distributive Trades offers a BA in publishing, and a diploma course in publishing production, entry requirements being three GCSEs or two years' appropriate experience. Various diploma courses are available and training centres run a variety of short courses. Women in Publishing and the Society of Freelance Editors and Proofreaders also run training programmes.

Most artists and designers have taken appropriate courses. The LCPDT course in graphic origination and reproduction requires five GCSEs or two years' experience. Sales and marketing staff do not always have academic qualifications but it is usual and many have degrees. Sales representatives need a good standard of general education.

NVQs are available for periodicals publishers, details of which can be obtained from the Periodicals Training Council.

Personal Qualities

Attributes vary depending on department, but all staff should have a feeling for books or language combined with a keen business sense. In addition, commissioning editors need imagination and creativity and desk editors a eye for detail. Design staff must have good colour vision. Picture researchers must have an excellent visual memory.

£ Editorial Assistant £9,000–£15,000; Commissioning Editor £16,000–£26,000; Picture Researcher £10,900–£14,100; production staff salaries from £10,500–£14,400 for qualified workers; art department salaries from £9,000–£11,000; sales, marketing and publicity from £10,000–£14,000; and sales representatives £13,000–£18,000.

i The Publishing Training Centre, 45 East Hill, London SW18 2QZ; 020 8874 2718

Periodicals Training Council, Queens House, 55–56 Lincoln's Inn Fields, London WC2A 3LJ 020 7404 4168 www.ppa.co.uk/ptc

Publishers Association, 1 Kingsway, London WC2 6XF; 020 7565 7474

Society of Freelance Editors and Proofreaders, Mermaid House, 1 Mermaid Court, London SE1 1HR, 0207 403 5141

Women in Publishing, c/o J Whitaker & Sons Ltd, 12 Dyott Street, London WC1A 1DF; 020 7836 8911

The Kogan Page Guide to Working in the Media, Allan Shepherd; *Careers in Publishing and Bookselling*; and *Careers Using English* (all Kogan Page)

PURCHASING OFFICER

(see also Buyer)

Purchasing officers are responsible for the buying in of raw materials needed for manufacture, ready-made components and finished goods and services. They must be aware of price, quantities to be supplied and delivery dates. In addition they must be familiar with new developments in their purchasing field and any new technology. Purchasing officers may or may not be involved in drawing up specifications. When a product is decided upon, the purchasing officer must approach a number of suppliers for quotations, select one and negotiate terms.

Qualifications and Training

Entry is possible at various stages: with five GCSEs, with A levels or Edexcel (BTEC) NC/ND in business studies, and with a degree. Training is largely on the job and some employers have special training schemes. Qualifications are also offered by the Chartered Institute of Purchasing and Supply (CIPS).

To take the CIPS examinations five GCSE passes plus an A level are necessary. Edexcel (BTEC) qualifications are also acceptable. Applicants without these qualifications may be accepted provided they are 23, have suitable experience and have their employer's support.

At supervisory level, the Institute offers an open-access certificate programme.

Personal Qualities

Officers must be prepared to take responsibility, be able to get on with people easily, be firm and persuasive. They must be prepared to undertake a lot of travel and work under considerable stress.

£ £13,500–£15,000.

i The Chartered Institute of Purchasing and Supply, Easton House, Easton-on-the-Hill, Stamford, Lincolnshire PE9 3NZ; 01780 56777

Q

Quantity Surveying, see *Surveyor/Surveying Technician*

QUARRYING

The quarrying industry is concerned with extracting from the ground of materials such as limestone, granite, slate, chalk, gravel, clay and sandstone. Some quarries also produce materials, for example, making lime, ready-mixed concrete and coating stone needed for road building. The industry employs people at operative, craft, technician and management levels.

Qualifications and Training

Operatives need no formal qualifications although NVQs are available in mobile plant and process operations and will soon be available in drilling and shotfiring operations. Applicants can also enter an apprenticeship scheme to qualify for an NVQ in Engineering Maintenance. Those entering the industry with A levels or an Edexcel (BTEC) national diploma certificate may enter the three-year sandwich degree course in quarrying and road surfacing at Doncaster College. Technicians, supervisors and management trainees with other qualifications can prepare for the HNC-level Institute of Quarrying professional exam by way of the Doncaster-assisted private-study course. Passes in the degree or the professional examination, with appropriate experience, lead to corporate membership of the Institute of Quarrying.

Personal Qualities

Operative and craft employees must have good physical ability and possess the necessary mechanical skills to operate quarrying machinery such as loaders and dumptrucks. Supervisors must have the usual organisational skills combined with a knowledge of the technology and of the materials involved.

£ Operator (basic) £150–£200 per week; skilled operator/supervisor £200–£250 per week; management trainee £10,000–£12,000 pa.

i Institute of Quarrying, 7 Regent Street, Nottingham NG1 5BS; 0115 9411315
www.inst-of-quarrying.org/iq/
EPIC (NTO), 36-38 London Road, St Albans, Herts AL1 1NG; 01727 869008

R

Radio, see *Broadcasting*

RADIOGRAPHER

Radiography is a caring profession which calls for considerable technological expertise. There are two branches: diagnostic radiography and therapeutic radiography.

Diagnostic radiographers are responsible for producing high-quality images on film and other recording materials which help doctors to diagnose disease and the extent of injuries. Therapeutic radiographers help to treat patients, many of whom have cancer, using X-rays, ionising radiation and sometimes drugs.

Qualifications and Training

All radiography qualifying courses are now at degree level, and most are honours degrees. It normally takes three years to qualify (except in Northern Ireland, where the course is a four-year honours degree course). Even though the course will normally be in a university or higher education institution affiliated to a university, half the course will be spent on clinical education with hospital departments associated with the university.

On graduation, entrants are eligible for State Registration by the Radiographers Board of the Council for Professions Supplementary to Medicine, which is an essential requirement for employment in the NHS. The requirements for entry to radiography courses are two A levels and three GCSEs at grade C or above although other combinations of A and AS levels and GCSEs are acceptable.

Edexcel (BTEC) national certificates and diplomas in relevant studies are also acceptable.

Entry is also possible through validated access courses and applications from mature candidates are especially welcomed by many radiography education centres.

These are the minimum entry requirements and radiography education centres may ask for additional or more specific qualifications than the minimum.

Personal Qualities

As well as having an interest in science, you should be a caring and compassionate person, sufficiently level-headed not to get upset when dealing with sick people. You should be patient and calm when faced with people who may be frightened or difficult. Your health must be good and you have to be reasonably strong, because you may have to help lift people and move heavy equipment. In addition, radiographers should be good-humoured, and able to work well in a team and assume responsibility.

£ £12,634.

i College of Radiographers, 2 Carriage Row, 183 Eversholt Street, London NW1 1BU; 020 7391 4500; fax 020 7391 4504

Careers in Nursing and Related Professions (Kogan Page)

Radiotherapist*, see *Radiographer

RAILWAY WORK

British Rail/Railtrack employs a vast number of people: drivers, guards, signalmen, general railmen, clerical workers, technicians, craftsmen and managers. The latter are responsible for the day-to-day running of the railways or in charge of departments such as planning, engineering, marketing and accounts.

Qualifications and Training

Train drivers do not require formal educational qualifications but are expected to have studied English, maths and a science. Training is on the job. Guards, signalmen and general railmen are also trained on the job and do not need academic qualifications. Clerical staff should hold four GCSEs or else pass an entrance exam. Technicians need four GCSEs including maths, English and a science. They undertake four years' training involving attendance at day and block release courses leading to an Edexcel (BTEC) qualification. Technician trainees without suitable GCSEs who have studied the relevant subjects may also be accepted but will follow City and Guilds rather than Edexcel (BTEC) courses. City and Guilds courses are also taken by craft trainees who are recruited to take care of track repair and maintenance rather than civil, mechanical and electrical engineering tasks performed by technicians. NVQs levels 1 to 4 are being developed.

Managers are recruited with five GCSEs and two A levels, or with a degree. Trainees with A levels may be sponsored for a degree course on a sandwich basis; or they may be trained on the job with some time spent in colleges of further education. Training for graduate trainees varies depending on the nature of their work and lasts two years.

Personal Qualities

All rail staff must have a strong interest in providing an efficient service and in promoting and caring for passengers' needs. In addition, drivers need perfect vision without glasses. Managers need qualities appropriate to their departments plus managerial and administrative skills.

£ Operatives' salaries range from £160 a week to £225+, with drivers commanding the higher amounts. Senior technical officers earn £11,000+ to £14,500, signal and telecommunications staff £9000–£24,000, clerical officers £10,000+ to £13,500.

i The National Training Organisation for the Rail Industry, RITC Ltd, B118 Macmillan House, Paddington Station, London W2 1FT; 020 7313 1035; fax 020 7313 1074

RECEPTIONIST

(see also Hotel Work)

Receptionists work in hotels, large organisations and private firms, sometimes combining the job with the duties of telephonist. In hotels, they welcome the guests, make bookings and prepare the final account. They also deal with reservation correspondence and act as a general information office. In small hotels this can be handled by one person but in most, and especially the larger hotels, they work in a team headed by the Reception Manager.

In large official organisations, such as a town hall, or in firms with many staff, receptionists direct visitors to the correct department. In small firms the job is often combined with answering the phone, typing and franking the mail.

Medical receptionists fulfil a very important role in a wide variety of working environments. They need, in addition to the standard skills of a receptionist, a full understanding of the principles of medical ethics and confidentiality, knowledge of the NHS and social services, medical terminology and clinical procedures.

Qualifications and Training

Formal educational qualifications are not necessary, but proficiency in English and simple maths is, and languages are an advantage. Training is mostly on the job and there are local authority courses available leading to RSA examinations. Receptionists in catering may work towards NVQs levels 1, 2 and 3.

The AMSPAR diploma in health service reception is a nationally recognised professional qualification. It can be achieved by an examination and a competency route and is available from a wide network of approved centres throughout the UK.

Personal Qualities

Receptionists should be friendly and pleasant and have a neat appearance. They also need stamina, as they are expected to work on shifts and during evenings and weekends. They should have a real liking for people and a good memory for faces. It helps to have a methodical approach and an aptitude for accounting machines/computers.

£ From £7,000–£12,500+, more in London.

i Hotel and Catering Training Company, Careers Information Services, International House, High Street, London W5 5DB; 020 8672 4251; fax 020 8682 1707; Hospitality Training Helpline 020 7497 8654
www.hcima.org.uk

Hotel and Catering International Management Association (HCIMA), 191 Trinity Road, London SW17 7HN; 020 8672 4251

Springboard UK, 1 Denmark Street, London WC2H 8LP; 020 7497 8654
Association of Medical Secretaries, Practice Managers, Administrators and Receptionists (AMSPAR), Tavistock House North, Tavistock Square, London WC1H 9LN; 020 7387 6005

Recording Engineer, **see** *Broadcasting, Engineering*

Recreational Manager, **see** *Leisure and Amenity Management, Sport and Recreation Facility Management*

RECRUITMENT CONSULTANT

The aim of recruitment/employment consultants is to fit people to jobs. Agencies deal with all types of staff, from office and secretarial to highly complex and specialist technical roles. The work involves interviewing prospective job candidates, keeping records of their details and matching them to employers' requirements. Much of the work involves selling to potential users.

Qualifications and Training

Many recruitment consultants have come into the industry after some experience of another job, for example, sales, personnel or office work. They are trained either in-house or on courses run by the Institute of Employment Consultants. The IEC offers two levels of qualification: the foundation award, suitable for those in their first year in the industry, and the certificate in recruitment practice, for those with more than one year's experience in the industry. Both qualifications can be studied for by distance learning, in addition to which the certificate can be studied at evening class.

Personal Qualities

Recruitment consultants must be able to get on with all kinds of people, have good communication skills, work quickly and calmly under pressure and be organised.

£ Varies greatly for trainees, but with experience consultants can earn a salary of £25,000+ with commission.

i Institute of Employment Consultants, 6 Guildford Road, Woking, Surrey GU22 7PX; 01483 766442

Refrigeration Engineer, **see** *Engineering*

REGISTRAR

Registrars are involved in registering births, deaths and marriages. They also supply copy certificates to members of the public. Registrars of Marriage officiate at Registry Office marriages, and also marriages at churches where the incumbent is only able to perform the spiritual functions but not to legalise a marriage. Registrars must be knowledgeable in all aspects of the law relating to birth, death and marriage.

Qualifications and Training

No formal educational requirements other than a good general education are necessary. Training is on the job.

Personal Qualities

Registrars must be able to get on with people, giving advice calmly and sympathetically and be even-tempered. They should be able to do their job well in situations of excitement, emotion and distress. Good handwriting is important, and the ability to drive is an advantage. Entrants must be prepared for Saturday work.

£ £10,500+.

i Office of Population Censuses and Surveys, St Catherine's House, 10 Kingsway, London WC2B 6JP; 020 7242 0262
Local authorities

REMOVALS

Removals is an industry in which people matter. In a modern society the remover plays a key role in the chain of events leading up to a family's departure from one home and arrival in another – which can be around the corner or on the other side of the world. It is the remover's job to see that all the customer's belongings are professionally packed and transported to their destination. The jobs available will depend very much on the employer company, which could range from a small firm with up to a dozen or so vans, to a huge multinational. Each will offer particular benefits, which should be considered.

A removals career may be started with work on a van as a porter and finish as Managing Director of a large company, or running a privately owned removals business. Throughout a career there are ample opportunities for training at all grades, including training to gain an LGV driving licence.

Removals Estimator

Estimators are the technical salespeople in a removals company. They visit customers' homes and estimate the amount of packing space needed, the time it will take and the price. They should have a good standard of education with good passes preferably in English, maths, geography and modern languages, hold a full car driving licence and be able to express themselves clearly and persuasively. Training is on the job and some estimators attend a qualification course.

Qualifications and Training

No formal education requirements for operatives, but management entrants should be at least 18 years old and have a minimum of six GCSE grades, preferably including English, maths and geography. Training is provided by BARTS, the training company of the British Association of Removers, and ranges from packing to a certificate recognised by the Department of Transport, which will allow the holder to operate a transport company.

Personal Qualities

Removers should be fit and strong. They must be honest and have a sense of responsibility towards other people's possessions.

£ £150–£230 a week; young entrants about £70.

i British Association of Removers (Training Services) Limited, 3 Churchill Court, 58 Station Road, North Harrow, Middlesex HA2 7SA; 020 8861 3796
www.removers.org.uk

The Movers Institute (address as above)
Local Jobcentres and Careers Offices

Reporter, **see** *Broadcasting, Journalist*

REPRESENTATIVE – SELLING

A sales representative usually works for a manufacturer, wholesale distributor or service industry, persuading potential customers to buy the firm's products and also looking after the needs of existing customers. The representative is usually assigned an area to cover and travels regularly around it on the firm's behalf. It is possible to be a representative for any number of products from soap powder and double glazing to books, machine tools and beauty products.

Qualifications and Training

Requirements for potential trainees vary, but most firms would look for two or three GCSEs grades A, B, C or equivalent. Training periods vary from one firm to another. Representatives may study for examinations set by such bodies as the Chartered Institute of Marketing, the Institute of Sales and Marketing Management which offer joint ISMM/City and Guilds courses in local colleges of further education and correspondence courses, or the Managing and Marketing Sales Association. Diplomas and certificates are also issued by various trade associations representing particular types of product. Technical sales representatives usually have a degree or equivalent in the relevant subject.

Personal Qualities

An outgoing, friendly personality, a manner that inspires confidence and the ability to speak forcefully and persuasively, plus persistence and stamina, are all important.

£ £13,000–£18,000 plus car.

i The Institute of Sales and Marketing Management (ISMM), Romland House, Romland Hill, St Albans, Herts AL3 4ET; 01727 812500

RETAILING

The retailing industry covers a range of businesses: department stores, supermarkets, cash-and-carry and discount warehouses, mail order firms, local shops, and some manufacturing companies which sell direct to the public. Work opportunities include shop assistants, warehousemen, cashiers, managers – store or department – and buyers. Larger concerns will also have administrators, personnel officers and transport departments. In some shops – in a profession such as pharmacy, or in a trade such as butchery – the owner or Manager must have special training. Most people in the retail trade have to work on Saturdays and, increasingly, at least one late night a week, but there is often a rota system to make the working week more flexible. Sunday trading is becoming more common, and stores need full staffing. In large stores, bank holiday working is often recompensed by time off plus extra payment.

Qualifications and Training

Sales staff generally do not need academic qualifications and training is on the job. Entrants may work towards NVQs levels 1 to 4. However, to be taken on as a junior trainee or trainee supervisor, three to four GCSEs or equivalent are required. Trainee managers and buyers need two A levels and some have degrees. Junior and management trainees are trained by their firms and there are also vocational courses available involving day and evening study and correspondence options. Trainees without A levels may qualify for management traineeship after gaining experience and studying further.

Personal Qualities

Employees in retailing should enjoy meeting and helping people and have a pleasant manner. Those involved with handling money and checking stock should be numerate and methodical. The majority of applicants in retailing must be prepared to spend a great part of the day on their feet, and at times to have little to do.

£ On average, sales assistants earn £8,300–£8,500.

i Local Careers Offices
Department stores/supermarkets, personnel departments

RIDING INSTRUCTOR

Riding instructors teach people, individuals or groups, how to ride. They may also accompany riders who hire horses by the hour and be required to help train horses and look after them, cleaning tack and stables. The work includes teaching in riding schools and clubs and in summer camps, training competition riders and, occasionally, sitting as a judge or examiner.

Qualifications and Training

To take the British Horse Society's Assistant Instructor certificate, candidates must be members of the society and, if under 18, have four GCSEs, one of which should be in English. On completion of stages 1, 2 and 3, the preliminary teaching test, a full first aid at work certificate and 500 hours of teaching experience, they are awarded the Assistant Instructor's certificate.

There are two methods of training: at a school, paying fees for instruction, board and lodging – the courses can be as short as three months or as long as a year, depending on the type of course; or as a working pupil at a riding school, doing stable work while receiving some instruction. This takes one year, the last three months being a concentrated course of instruction. Pupils pay for their keep, and the instruction is given in return for their work.

After being awarded the Assistant Instructor's certificate, candidates may take the Intermediate Instructor's exams after reaching 20. At 22, Intermediate Instructors may go on to take the British Horse Society Instructor's certificate. The Fellowship may be taken from 25 years.

Personal Qualities

Patience and authority, but above all a love of horses, are indispensable for this work. A riding instructor must enjoy being out of doors and get on well with people, especially children.

£ £6,000–£8,000 for an Assistant Instructor as a rough guide; the amount will vary depending on whether instruction is being provided, accommodation and stabling for the instructor's own horse, and the instructor's age and experience.

i The British Horse Society, British Equestrian Centre, Stoneleigh, Kenilworth, Warwickshire CV8 2LR; 01203 696697

Rivers Authority, National see *The Environment Agency*

ROAD HAULAGE

(see also Freight Forwarding, Lorry Driver, Road Transport, Vehicle Technician)

Moving goods internationally can be very complicated, so a company with goods to dispatch can employ the services of a freight forwarding firm to make the arrangements for them. They will select the means of transport most suited to their requirement of cost, date of delivery and nature of the goods. Freight forwarders will be responsible for the documentation, for legal and insurance requirements and for the clearance of cargo through customs.

Qualifications and Training

For driving, no formal educational qualifications are required, but drivers are tested for road sense by the licensing authorities. A theory test, followed by practical driving tests, is required, depending upon the class of the vehicle to be driven. A variety of training schemes are available; length of training varies according to type of vehicle driven.

Mechanics are usually expected to have GSCEs or equivalent in maths and a science and their apprenticeship averages four years.

Trainee managers need to show a good basic educational background and will train for a varying period depending on their type of work.

To take the Institute of Logistics and Transport's qualifying examinations for chartered membership, five GCSEs and one or two A levels or equivalents are necessary.

Personal Qualities

Drivers need to have a robust physique, stamina, initiative, practical intelligence, and a liking for an active, roving life. They must be responsible, safety-conscious, able to keep to schedules and understand something of vehicle mechanics.

Mechanical staff need the usual technical abilities, plus physical fitness, a sense of responsibility and an affinity for motor vehicles.

For managerial and clerical staff the qualifications are more general, but an interest in road transport is obviously paramount. Possession of the Royal Society of Arts Certificate of Professional

Competence (CPC) is necessary for many transport management positions.

£ Drivers earn from £200–£400 a week; mechanics £65–£70 at 16, £150–£400 when qualified. Managers' salaries are variable and negotiable.

i The Institute of Logistics and Transport, 80 Portland Place, London W1N 4DP; 020 7467 9400

Freight Transport Association, Hermes House, St John's Road, Tunbridge Wells, Kent TN4 9UZ; 01892 526171

Institute of Road Transport Engineers, 22 Greencoat Place, London SW1P 1PR; 020 7630 1111

Institute of Transport Administration, 32 Palmerston Road, Southampton SO1 1LL; 023 8063 1380

Road Haulage and Distribution Training Council, Warren Farm Office Village, Stratford Road, Wolverton Mill, Milton Keynes MK12 5NW

Road Haulage Association, Roadway House, 35 Monument Hill, Weybridge, Surrey KT13 8RN; 01932 841515

RTITB Services Centre, York House, Empire Way, Wembley, Middlesex HA9 0RT; 020 8902 8880

ROAD TRANSPORT

(see also Bus and Coach Companies, Road Haulage)

This industry includes road haulage, plus passenger transport and commercial companies that have their own transport and delivery facilities. Passenger transport covers bus and coach services. Commercial companies need to plan the flow of materials or parts for manufacturing and the subsequent delivery of their products to their customers. Similarly, retail organisations need transport to bring merchandise to their outlets. The work divides into loading, moving and unloading, involving a wide range of operative and administrative staff: drivers, warehousemen, depot managers, mechanics, clerical staff, transport planners and many others. There is a variety of public-sector and private-sector employers.

Qualifications and Training

Jobs range from those that demand formal qualifications to those that require a degree. Training varies similarly. However, there are a number of relevant courses: NVQs in Road Passenger and Road Freight Transport for operative staff; the Edexcel (BTEC) national certificate (entry requirements four GCSEs or equivalent to include English and maths); the Chartered Institute of Transport qualifying examination course (entry requirements five GCSEs and one or two A levels, or equivalents). A degree in transport or business subjects may lead to full or partial exemption from the qualifying exam.

Personal Qualities

Similar to those that apply to road haulage: a robust physique, stamina, initiative, practical intelligence, and a liking for an active, roving life. A responsible, safety-conscious approach, an ability to keep to schedules and an understanding of vehicle mechanics.

£ Drivers earn from £150–£250 a week, mechanics £65–£70 at 16 to around £150–£230 when qualified; clerks £6,000–£7,000 a year at 16, £10,000+ with experience; warehousemen £8,000+, transport managers £12,000–£16,000+.

i *See* contact names and addresses under Road Haulage

ROOFER

This title covers a variety of jobs concerned with erecting a roof: laying down roofing felt, nailing down wooden battens to support tiles, tiling and slating. Other specialities include built-up felt roofing, when layers of felt are alternated with tar, then finished off with slabs of concrete or other materials; and roof sheeting, when large sheets of waterproof material are attached to roof frames. Some roof work includes working from scaffolding.

Qualifications and Training

Formal educational requirements are not necessary. Apprenticeship lasts for three years; training is on the job and at training centres, leading to NVQs levels 2 and 3, awarded jointly by City and Guilds and the Construction Industry Training Board.

Personal Qualities

A head for heights is essential, plus an ability to work out of doors in all weather conditions.

£ Recommended weekly rates are: £73.90 at 16; £103.46 at 17; £147.81 at 18; and, when qualified, the craftsman rate is £178.62.

i Construction Industry Training Board, Bircham Newton, King's Lynn, Norfolk PE31 6RH; 01553 776677 (ext 2466)

ROYAL AIR FORCE

The RAF consists of a small flying force (almost exclusively Officers) supported by a large number of ground workers including engineers, mechanics, caterers, air traffic controllers, medical personnel and many more categories. Altogether it embraces over 18 officer branches and 40 different non-commissioned trades. It integrated with the Women's Royal Air Force in 1994.

Qualifications and Training

Officers

Candidates for permanent commissions must be aged between 17 and a half and 39 (24 for a pilot) and have at least five GCSEs/Standard grades at grade C/level 3 or above including English and maths, and two A levels at grade C or three Highers. Training for a pilot lasts about three years. Other Officers train for varying periods depending on the job. The RAF offers students sponsorship while still qualifying – ranging from a bursary at £1,500 per year to a salary paid up to £26,000 for a three-year degree.

Non-Commissioned Personnel

Candidates must be between 16 and a half and 39. Entry at the lowest level requires no formal qualification. Other levels vary in their requirements – for example, technician candidates need GCSEs/SCEs at grade C/level 3 or above in maths and physics or their equivalent. Length of training varies with trade.

Personal Qualities

Air Force personnel must enjoy teamwork and a disciplined regime. They need physical fitness, dedication, commitment, initiative and a sense of responsibility.

£ The following are intended to give an indication of salary: Officer Cadet £10,165, Pilot Officer £14,486, Flying Officer £19,147. Those who are under 16 on entry receive £5,653, £6,862 at 17. Those over 17 receive £9,077. In addition to basic salaries, there are many extra allowances, including travel, accommodation and overseas service.

i Local RAF Careers Information Offices; www.raf.mod.uk

ROYAL MARINES

The Royal Marines is an arm of the Royal Navy. Its personnel are trained for amphibious assaults and for commando operations on land. It has a well-deserved reputation for toughness, and training is arduous.

Qualifications and Training

Officers

Full career entry is between 17 and a half and 22, and at least two A levels are required. Graduates can enter up to the age of 25. Basic training varies from 15 months to three years depending on the intended length of service and level of entry. Undergraduates may be recruited on a university cadetship scheme whereby they are sponsored throughout their time at university.

Other Ranks

Entry for most categories is between 17 and a half and 28. Recruits are given 14 weeks' initial training, plus a period of more advanced training, depending on category for length.

Personal Qualities

The same basic qualities are needed as for the other services: discipline, dedication, fitness, initiative and an ability to work with others, plus an appetite for operating in tough conditions.

£ Officers' salaries start from £9,774–£13,932; ratings' salaries start from £717 a month. Extra allowances are made for such items as education and family separation.

i Local Royal Navy Careers Information Offices
Directorate of Naval Recruiting, Victory Building, HM Naval Base, Portsmouth PO1 3LS; 01705 727 340
Officers Enquiry Section (address above)
www.royal-navy.mod.uk

ROYAL NAVY

(see also ROV Pilot Technician)

Navy personnel work in the nation's combat fleet and at its land bases. Like the other services, the Navy uses many trades and skills. It is the smallest of the three armed forces.

Qualifications and Training

Officers
Entry is at various levels, each of which has different age limits and requirements. For the Naval College, entrants must be between 17 and 23 and have five acceptable GCSE grades including English language and maths, and two A levels. Length of training varies likewise according to level of entry, intended length of service and other factors. Undergraduates may take advantage of the cadetship scheme whereby the Navy sponsors them throughout their time at university.

Ratings
For most categories the age of entry is 16–33 and most candidates do not have to possess formal qualifications but only pass a selection test. The majority have six weeks of initial training, followed by specialised training, varying in length according to category.

Personal Qualities

For most Navy personnel a liking for the sea is important. Other requirements are the same as for the other services: discipline, dedication, fitness, initiative and an ability to work with others.

£ Officers' salaries start from £9,774–£13,932; ratings' salaries from £717 a month at 18. Extra allowances are payable for such items as accommodation and removal.

i *See* contact names and addresses under Royal Marines

ROV PILOT TECHNICIAN

Remotely operated vehicles (ROVs) were introduced into the military and offshore fields in the late 1970s and early 80s and now offer a career path for well-educated technical staff. ROVs are operated by the Royal Navy, offshore companies, environmental agencies, police and salvage companies. These underwater robots carry out the work of a diver at depths where diving is impossible.

Qualifications and Training

In 1999, the International Marine Contractors Association introduced a competency scheme for all marine safety-critical positions include divers and ROV pilot technicians. Entry into the scheme requires two years' post-academic experience in a related field such as electrical, electronic, hydraulic or mechanical engineering or NVQ or HN or degree level academic education in one of those fields. An introductory course is available under the scheme at training centres around the world. However, direct recruitment by the subsea contractors is also possible. Some of the schools also offer training to NVQ or HN level in the appropriate fields.

Personal Qualities

Initiative and ability to work in small close-knit teams, willingness to work outside the UK for reasonable periods of up to 60 days. Medically and physically fit.

£ Starting salaries are around £18,000 and after three years can reach £28,000. After five years, for the lucky few who become supervisors, up to £40,000 is practical.

i The International Marine Contractors' Association, 177A High Street, Beckenham, Kent BR3 IAH; 020 8663 3859

Health and Safety Executive, Rose Court, 2 Southwark Bridge, London SE1 9HS; 020 7717 6000

Fort Bovis and Underwater Centre, Plymouth, Devon PL9 0AB
Society for Underwater Technology, 80 Coleman Street, London EC2R 5BJ; 020 7382 2601; fax 020 7382 2684
The Underwater Centre, Fort William, Highlands PH33 6LZ; 01379 703786
Local police forces
Local Royal Navy Careers Information Offices

RSPCA INSPECTOR

Inspectors for the Royal Society for the Prevention of Cruelty to Animals (RSPCA) deal with complaints from the general public about the alleged ill-treatment of animals, and also perform more routine tasks. Inspectors have no power to take an animal from its owner unless the owner legally signs it over. They may caution people and, in some circumstances, the organisation will ensure that cases go before the courts. Inspectors also visit boarding kennels, pet shops and riding schools. They can be involved in physical rescues, often working unsociable hours and driving considerable distances.

Qualifications and Training

A good general education is necessary, personal attributes being more important than formal qualifications. However, GCSEs or equivalent in English and a science are an advantage. Training is by a six-month training course at the RSPCA Training School. Candidates must have the academic capability to deal with the study of animal law in depth and dexterity to deal with ropes, boats and ladders in rescue situations.

Personal Qualities

As well as having compassion for animals, inspectors must be firm, authoritative, tactful, persuasive and have good communication skills.

£ In the region of £9,800, plus an accommodation allowance.

i Chief Superintendent, Training School, RSPCA Headquarters, Causeway, Horsham, West Sussex RH12 1HG; 01403 264181
Careers Working with Animals (Kogan Page)

S

SADDLER

Saddles are still made by hand, by craftsmen of considerable experience. They usually work in one of the many small companies which specialise in saddlery, and making harnesses, and other leather goods such as satchels and wallets. Saddlers' shops stock all these items and may also stock suitcases and sports goods, and offer a repair service.

Qualifications and Training

The Society of Master Saddlers administers a four-year apprenticeship indenture scheme leading to certification by the Worshipful Company of Saddlers. Saddlery courses of varying lengths are available at the Cordwainers College in Hackney and the Walsall College of Arts and Technology. Cordwainers College offers two courses in saddlery: a diploma in saddlery studies and an HND in saddlery technology. Both courses cover many aspects of running a small business, and both last for two years.

The Society of Master Saddlers runs a National Saddlery Skills Assessment Scheme by which those making saddles, bridles and harnesses may have their skills assessed and gain qualifications at levels 1, 2 and 3. These qualifications are recognised by other members of the trade.

Personal Qualities

Painstaking attention to detail and pride in craftsmanship are needed. Owners of saddlers' shops often have a strong interest in horses too.

£ £70–£200+ with experience.

i Cordwainers College, Mare Street, London E8 3RE; 020 8985 0273

Worshipful Company of Saddlers, Saddlers Hall, 40 Gutter Lane, London EC2V 6BR; 020 7726 8661

Walsall College of Arts and Technology, Leather Department, Shelley Campus, Scarborough Road, Walsall; 01922 720889

The Society of Master Saddlers, Kettles Farm, Michfield, Stowmarket, Suffolk IP14 6BY; 01449 711642

Salesperson,* see *Representative – Selling, Retailing

Sales Representative,* see *Representative – Selling

Sawyer,* see *Furniture and Furnishing

SECRETARY

(see also Personal Assistant)

A secretary probably works for several people and is a member of a management team, or may be employed by an agency as a temporary (working at a different organisation every few weeks). The work is extremely varied, but secretaries must have accurate skills (shorthand or audio typewriting, word processing and computer skills), and may act as administrator, information centre, organiser of the manager's day, progress chaser, arranger of travel and meetings, receptionist and communicator (verbal and written) internally and externally. A secretary may be asked to assume responsibility without direct supervision and take decisions within the scope of assigned authority.

Bilingual Secretary

A bilingual secretary is fluent in a second or third language and may work in commerce, overseas or as an EU employee.

Farm Secretary
In addition to accurate skills (including the use of computers), the work involves helping the employer to complete forms, keep records and accounts and calculate farm employees' wages. A farm secretary may work for one employer, be freelance or be sent out by an agency to smaller farms.

Legal Secretary
Accurate skills have always been paramount for legal paperwork, but word processors have made the job much easier. Legal secretaries are employed by barristers and solicitors (in professional practice and in large commercial organisations).

Medical Secretary
Medical secretaries are good administrators, keep records, handle correspondence and filing. They work in hospitals, for individual doctors/consultants and in health centres. Accuracy and confidentiality are essential, as is a thorough knowledge of medical terminology.

Qualifications and Training

NVQs in Administration are available at levels 2 and 3. GCSEs are usually required to obtain a place on a full-time secretarial course. A good working knowledge of the English language is essential. Additional qualifications are needed to specialise as a legal, medical or farm secretary. The Institute of Linguists (IOL) offers a Diploma in Translation.

Personal Qualities

Good secretaries are judged by what they do, but qualities such as self-motivation, discretion, tact, loyalty, personality, flexibility, communication skills and smart appearance are expected.

£ About £10,000 without experience in London, senior secretaries in London earn from £14,000–£23,000.

i The Institute of Para-Legal Training, The Mill, Clymping Street, Clymping, Littlehampton, West Sussex BN17 5RN; 01903 714276

Association of Medical Secretaries, Practice Managers, Administrators and Receptionists (AMSPAR), Tavistock House North, Tavistock Square, London WC1H 9LN; 020 7387 6005

Institute of Linguists, Saxon House, 48 Southwark Street, London SE1 1UN; 020 7940 3100; fax 020 7940 3101 www.iol.org.uk

Institute of Qualified Private Secretaries, First Floor, 6 Bridge Avenue, Maidenhead SL6 1RR; 01628 625007; fax 01628 624990

SECURITY WORK

There are many aspects of security work, including patrolling, guarding, operating delivery services for documents and valuables, advising on burglary prevention and installing security systems. There is also work in other areas such as preventing industrial espionage, the personal protection of public figures and the supplying of store detectives. The industry has two main sections: in-house, where organisations have their own security force dealing with the protection of their property and assets; and contract guarding, in which guards, patrolmen, drivers of 'cash-in-transit' vans and so on, are supplied by another company.

Qualifications and Training

Experience and skills such as those acquired in the armed forces or the police are useful. Otherwise, there are no specific entry requirements. Training varies, but the relevant British Standard requires at least two days' induction training and larger companies often provide additional training in areas such as the equipment used, legal responsibilities and relations between the company, the police and the public. With the introduction of NVQs (level 2), recognised training standards provide an effective career structure for employees.

Personal Qualities

It is essential to have an impeccable background for security work plus a fair amount of strength and common sense, initiative and reliability. Entrants must also be prepared for night work. Good communication skills are now increasingly required in security officer roles, because of the greater public interface now involved.

£ There is a great variety in payment; Security Officers earn £5 to £5.50 per hour.

i British Security Industry Association Limited, Security House, Barbourne Road, Worcester WR1 1RS; 01905 21464 www.bsia.co.uk

Inspectorate of the Security Industry, Unit 3, Roman Way Business Centre, Droitwich, Worcestershire WR9 9AJ; 01905 773131

International Institute of Security, Suite 8, The Business Centre, 57 Torquay Road, Paignton, Devon TQ3 3DT; 01803 663275

International Professional Security Association, IPSA House, 3 Dendy Road, Paignton, Devon TQ4 5DB; 01803 554849

Security Industry Training Organisation, Security House, Barbourne Road, Worcester WR1 1RS; 01905 20004

Service Engineer, **see** *Electrician*

SERVICE MECHANIC

Mechanics are needed to service and repair a range of business machines such as typewriters and photocopiers, as well as domestic machines such as washing machines and televisions. Service mechanics are employed by machine manufacturers. Although some work may be done in the company's workshop, more frequently the mechanic will visit offices or private homes.

It is also necessary to service office information technology equipment and systems. This work is not done by 'mechanics' as there is no mechanical element involved in the equipment.

Qualifications and Training

These vary, but formal academic qualifications are not necessary. Some employers require City and Guilds certificates in mechanical, electrical or electronic engineering. Training is then given in the company workshop. Some employers (for example, sewing machine manufacturers) train completely on the job without requiring prior qualifications.

Personal Qualities

Service mechanics spend a great deal of their time in other people's homes, so a polite and friendly manner plus the ability to work quickly and neatly are useful. A driving licence is an advantage.

£ £65–£70 a week at 16, and £160+ when trained.

i Local Jobcentres and Careers Offices

SHEET-METAL WORKER/PLATER

Sheet-metal workers/platers are engaged in shaping, cutting and joining together pieces of metal. Sheet-metal workers work with thin metal sheet up to 3mm thick, using a wide range of hand and power tools to manipulate it. They make such items as aircraft sections and car prototypes. Platers work with metal plates from 3mm thick upwards. As well as hand and power tools, heavy presses are needed to bend the plate. Products include ship and submarine parts and industrial boilers.

Qualifications and Training

No formal educational qualifications are required but mathematical ability is necessary. It is possible to work without a formal apprenticeship. Training with an apprenticeship takes up to four years, during which time courses are available leading to NVQs.

Personal Qualities

Sheet-metal workers/platers must be strong, good at working with their hands, able to read technical drawings, and to work as one of a team in a noisy atmosphere.

£ About £85 a week at 16, £230 when trained.

i Engineering Careers Information Service, 41 Clarendon Road, Watford, Hertfordshire WD1 1HS; 01923 238441; Freephone 0800 282167

Local Jobcentres and Careers Offices

SHIPBROKER

Shipbrokers act as go-betweens for shipowners, looking for cargo to fill their vessels, and charterers, seeking to ship their dry cargo and tanker requirements. Sale and purchase of vessels is also an important service offered to clients. Brokers are paid commission on the contracts arranged. The Baltic Exchange in London is the centre of the chartering market, covering the whole world and keeping a register of those seeking employment in this field. Additionally, shipbrokers/ship's agents in ports make arrangements when a ship calls for customs clearance – loading and discharging cargoes, meeting crew requirements, and so on. Port agents who attend to cargo liners may also be involved in marketing and documenting cargo. In order to maintain contact with the international scene, shipbrokers tend to work long hours and to travel abroad frequently.

Qualifications and Training

There are no specific academic qualifications needed for shipbroking beyond a good general educational background. However, members of a firm who wish to make a career in the shipping business usually study for the examination leading to membership of the Institute of Chartered Shipbrokers. Such study can be part-time or by correspondence course and covers not only shipping practice but more general studies in law, economics and international trade. The Institute also offers a foundation diploma in shipping for those just beginning in the business.

Personal Qualities

A good business sense, the ability to learn through practical experience, willingness to work long and irregular hours and to travel are all necessary.

£ Earnings vary greatly.

i The Baltic Exchange, 14–20 St Mary Axe, London EC3A 8BH; 020 7623 5501

The Institute of Chartered Shipbrokers, 3 St Helen's Place, London EC3A 6EJ; 020 7628 5559; fax 020 7628 5445 www.ics.org.uk

SIGNWRITER

Signwriters design and hand paint company names and logos on to shop fronts and the sides of vans and lorries; they may also paint estate agents' signboards and a wide variety of other temporary signs and notices. Some signwriters are in business on their own, while others work for commercial signwriting companies.

Qualifications and Training

Some commercial signwriting firms may take on trainees who also take an evening course such as that run by City and Guilds. An art school course in graphic design will normally include some typography and signwriting in the syllabus and will provide a wider training. Academic qualifications are not always necessary for entry to art school for those with exceptional talent.

Personal Qualities

Artistic talent combined with an interest in lettering is a prerequisite for this job.

£ Low initially; £160+ a week when trained.

i Local Jobcentres and Careers Offices

SOCIAL WORK – HEALTH CARE SETTINGS

Health care settings are managed by any branch of the health service, such as hospitals, GP practices, clinics, accident and emergency units and psychiatric hospitals. The list can also include hospices, clinics for the treatment of substance abuse, and so on. Social workers work in these areas and offer a range of services.

Mental Health Social Work

Social workers can also specialise in working with people with mental health problems. Anyone with two years' experience can train further to become an Approved Social Worker (ASW) and a Mental Health Officer (MHO). The role of the ASW or MHO is to try to ensure that people with mental health problems can be supported and treated in the community, or can go to hospital on a voluntary basis, if they need treatment.

Qualifications and Training

Social Work – Health Care Settings
The Diploma in Social Work (DipSW) is the recognised qualification for all social workers in the UK and for probation officers in Northern Ireland. The DipSW is designed and delivered by partnerships between colleges and social care agencies. It takes two to three years to complete. Approximately half the time is spent in the university or college and the remainder is spent in the workplace under the supervision of a qualified and experienced social worker.

Mental Health Social Work
DipSW – as above – plus ASW/MHO training.

Personal Qualities

All individuals working in the area of social work need patience and a warm, sympathetic personality. They need to have excellent communication skills, be good listeners and trustworthy, and have compassion for others.

£ *Social Work – Health Care Settings*

£14,000–£25,000.

Mental Health Social Work

£18,000–£25,000.

i England: Central Council for Education and Training in Social Work (CCETSW) England Information Service, Caledonia House, 223–231 Pentonville Road, London LS1 5QB; 020 7833 8090

Northern Ireland: CCETSW, 6 Malone Road, Belfast BT9 5BN; 028 9066 5390

Scotland: CCETSW, Information Services, 5th Floor, 78/80 George Street, Edinburgh EH2 3BU; 0131 220 0093

Wales: CCETSW, South Gate House, Wood Street, Cardiff CF1 1EW; 029 2022 6257

CCETSW provides an information service on all aspects of social work and social care training. It is available from any of the above addresses.
www.topss.org.uk

SOCIAL WORK AND SOCIAL CARE – ADULT SERVICES

Home Carer

Home carers provide emotional and practical support for the elderly, people with physical disabilities, people with HIV or AIDS, people with mental health problems and sick or disabled single people.

The role of the home carer has changed over the years and now includes housework, shopping, dressing, bathing, toileting and supervising medication. They are offered training and support by a Home Care Organiser, who also provides team supervision. Most home carers work via local authorities or private agencies.

Home Care Organiser

The Home Care Organiser undertakes assessment of a person's needs and their financial circumstances, and decide whether or not the person is eligible for support, and exactly what financial support they need. They then arrange for home care provision. They work in teams alongside social workers and care managers, mainly in local authorities, the voluntary sector or for private agencies.

Qualifications and Training

For home carers, NVQs in Care are available. For a Home Care Organiser, some relevant experience and NVQs in Care or Management, a diploma in domicillary care management, a certificate/diploma in management studies are all qualifications that are increasingly required.

Personal Qualities

All individuals working in the area of social work need patience and a warm, sympathetic personality. They need to have excellent communication skills, be good listeners and trustworthy, and have compassion for others.

£ For home carers, salaries vary locally. A Home Care Organiser may earn £13,000–£19,000, depending on qualifications and experience.

i *See* Social Work – Health Care Settings

SOCIAL WORK AND SOCIAL CARE – CHILDREN AND YOUNG PEOPLE

Childminding
Childminders provide a service for parents who need to leave their children in a safe environment while they go to work. All childminders have to be registered by the local authority and social workers from the authority visit the premises of the childminder to ensure that they are of an adequate standard and meet health and safety regulations. Most childminders are paid directly by the parents although some are paid by the local authority.

Youth and Community Work
Youth and community workers work in youth clubs or on projects for young people. Some youth workers work on 'outreach' projects, whereby they seek out young people who may be homeless or at risk of drugs or prostitution and help to rehabilitate them with their families or in a safer environment. Youth workers are employed by local authorities and the voluntary sector in England, education and library boards and the voluntary sector in Northern Ireland, and by the education department in Scotland.

Social Worker with Children and Families
Since 1995, social service departments have been required by law to identify and support children in need in their area and to protect children who may be at risk from harm. The workers in this area are qualified social workers, who can be employed by local authorities in children and families teams or in specialist agencies such as the NSPCC (National Society for the Prevention of Cruelty to Children) in England. The NSPCC is commissioned by the local authority to do this work.

Social workers work with children and their families to ensure that the child is in the most appropriate environment. They give advice and support on a range of issues, including housing, mental health, drugs, alcohol, abuse or neglect of children and relationship problems.

Qualifications and Training

Childminding
Childminders do not need any specific qualifications although many do complete NVQs in Child Care or the diploma in nursery

nursing. All childminders must have a Registered Childminder's certificate.

Youth and Community Work
Relevant experience is essential and recognised qualifications include the diploma in youth and community work, NVQs in Community Work or the DipSW.

Social Worker with Children and Families
The DipSW is an essential qualification for those wishing to work in this area.

Personal Qualities

All individuals working in the area of social work need patience and a warm, sympathetic personality. They need to have excellent communication skills, be good listeners, trustworthy and have compassion for others. Those who work with children and young people also need to communicate effectively with other adults who are involved with the child or young person.

£ *Childminding*

From £70 to £80 per week, per child.

Youth and Community Work

£13,000–£20,000.

Social Worker with Children and Families

£16,000–£25,000.

i England: National Youth Agency, 17-23 Albion Street, Leicester LE1 6GD; 0116 285 6789

Northern Ireland: Youth Action NI, Hampton, Glenmachan Park, Belfast BT4 2PJ; 028 9076 0067

Scotland: Scottish Community Education Council, Rosebery House, 89 Haymarket Terrace, Edinburgh EH1 5EZ; 0131 313 2488

Wales: Wales Youth Agency, Leslie Court, Lon-y-Lyn, Caerphilly CF83 1BQ; 01222 880088

CCETSW (*see* Social Work – Health Care Settings, for contact details) provides an information service on all aspects of social work and social care training; it is available from any of the above addresses.

The youth organisations listed above also have career information leaflets that are available from them directly.

SOLICITOR

The role of the solicitor is to provide clients with skilled legal representation and advice. The clients can be individual people or companies, or any type of organisation or group. A solicitor may work on all kinds of legal matters, from house purchases to defence of people accused of crimes; from selling a corporation to drafting a complicated will or trust. Solicitors may also represent clients in all courts but will often brief a Barrister (*see* Barrister) to represent the client, and then act as liaison between them.

Scottish solicitors can appear in all courts and tribunals in Scotland up to and including the Sheriff Court. They can also gain rights of audience enabling them to appear in the higher courts by becoming a Solicitor-Advocate, or may brief an Advocate to represent their clients.

While some solicitors may deal with a variety of legal problems, others specialise in a particular area such as shipping, planning and construction, financial services or social security. Specialisation within the profession is increasing.

The majority of solicitors work in private practice with firms made up of several partners. Many others work as employed solicitors in commerce, industry, local and central government, and other organisations.

Qualifications and Training

England: The Law Society governs the training of solicitors in England and Wales, which takes place in two stages – the academic and the professional. Most, but not all, entrants to the profession are graduates. Training begins for non-law graduates by taking the Law Society's common professional examination (CPE); those with the qualifying law degrees are exempt from this. The next stage, the vocational stage, is taken via the legal practice course, available at a number of colleges or universities. It is a one-year full-time or two-year part-time course. The trainee solicitor then has to undertake a two-year training contract with an authorised firm or organisation. During the course of this, a 20-day professional skills course is undertaken, usually on a modular basis.

Scotland: The Law Society of Scotland governs the training of solicitors in Scotland. It is possible to study for a Bachelor of Laws Degree at five Scottish universities: Aberdeen, Dundee, Edinburgh, Glasgow and Strathclyde. Alternatively, it is possible to take the Law Society's own examinations by finding employment as a pre-diploma trainee.

After completion of the LLB degree of professional examinations, all graduates who would like to become solicitors must take the diploma in legal practice – a postgraduate course. The new diploma in legal practice, which offers increased training in office and business skills, has been on offer since October 1999.

After successful completion of the degree and the diploma, those who wish to become solicitors then serve a two-year training contract with a Scottish solicitor. From May 2000 it will be a provision that trainees must undertake a further four-week course of university study during their traineeship. From the same date onwards, trainees will also keep training records, which will be examined and monitored by the Society. All trainees who begin their training after May 2000 will take a test of professional competence. The trainees can then apply to the Law Society of Scotland for a practising certificate. All Scottish solicitors must hold a Law Society of Scotland practising certificate.

Personal Qualities

A high level of academic achievement, integrity, good communication skills, patience, discretion, a good command of language, and problem-solving skills are all required.

£ Salaries vary but trainees can receive up to about £20,000 in the City of London and newly qualified solicitors can earn considerably more than this. Those working for provincial solicitors and for small firms may find the salaries slightly lower. The Law Society lays down minimum salaries below which trainees cannot be paid. On average, qualified solicitors earn £28,000–£30,000.

In Scotland, the Law Society does not lay down salaries, but recommends minimum salary rates for trainees, which are currently £8,840 for trainees in their first year and £11,960 for trainees in their second year.

i The Law Society, Regulation and Information Services, Ipsley Court, Redditch, Worcestershire B98 0TD; 0870 606 2555 www.lawsociety.org.uk

The Law Society of Scotland, 26 Drumsheugh Gardens, Edinburgh EH3 7YR; 0131 226 7411; fax 0131 225 2934; e-mail *lawscot@ lawscot.org.uk*
www.lawscot.org.uk

Directorate of Army Legal Services (ALS 1), Ministry of Defence, AGC Centre, Worthy Down, Winchester SO21 2RG

Careers in the Law (Kogan Page)

SPEECH AND LANGUAGE THERAPIST

Speech and language therapists (SLTs) identify, assess and treat people who have communication disorders. A large proportion of these will be children but SLTs also help adults who may have speech problems caused by disease, accident or psychological trauma. Some SLTs may specialise in a particular patient group, for example, in the areas of severe learning difficulties, hearing impairment or neurological disorders, while others choose more general, broad-based practice. The NHS is the largest employer of SLTs, using them in community clinics, hospitals, special schools and homes for the mentally or physically disabled. Some of the larger voluntary organisations also employ SLTs. Often, the SLT works closely in a team which may include members of the medical, teaching, therapeutic, psychological and other caring professions.

Qualifications and Training

Speech and language therapy is a degree-entry profession. Courses leading to professional qualifications are offered at 15 universities and colleges of higher education throughout the UK, with three- and four-year courses providing both honours and ordinary degree qualifications. In addition, there are a number of two-year postgraduate diploma and masters courses available to candidates with relevant degrees.

Entry qualifications for courses vary from one institution to another, but the minimum is five GCSEs and two A levels or seven SCE passes with three at Higher grade. A good balance of language and science is expected. Other equivalent qualifications are considered on merit. All courses will consider applications from mature students (over 21), who are encouraged to apply in the normal way.

Students who successfully pass all academic and clinical components of an accredited course are eligible to obtain a certificate to practise and to enter the professional register of the Royal College of Speech and Language Therapists as full professional members.

Opportunities also exist to work as a Speech Therapist's Assistant. An NVQ in Care at level 3 is available.

Personal Qualities

It is essential that speech therapists themselves should have clear speech, with a good ear. In addition, they must have a real interest in people as individuals, as well as an enquiring mind, initiative, patience, imagination and a willingness to take responsibility.

£ Around £13,800.

i Royal College of Speech and Language Therapists, 7 Bath Place, Rivington Street, London EC2A 3SU; 020 7613 3855

'Speech and Language Therapist' (Health Service Careers, PO Box 204, London SE99 7UW)

SPORT AND RECREATION FACILITY MANAGEMENT

(see also Leisure and Amenity Management)

Sport and recreation facility managers are responsible for the efficient running of leisure centres, swimming pools, sports halls and associated facilities. Managers usually start their careers as Recreation Assistants and progress through supervisory and Assistant Manager positions and via on-the-job training and professional development.

Qualifications and Training

The Institute of Sport and Recreation Management (ISRM) offers a comprehensive programme of training and qualifications designed to cover all aspects of sport and recreation facility management and operation ranging from Recreation Assistant, NVQ level 2 and Supervisor, NVQ level 3, to Management, NVQ levels 4 and 5.

Personal Qualities

A liking for people, a strong interest in sport, and organising skills are essential. Swimming and lifesaving ability are essential for swimming pool work.

£ Recreation Assistants at 18 years old, around £155 a week; managers' salaries are variable depending upon level of responsibilities, type of facility, location, qualifications and experience.

i Institute of Sport and Recreation Management, Giffard House, 36–38 Sherrard Street, Melton Mowbray, Leicestershire LE13 1XJ; 01664 565531; fax 01664 501155

SPORTSPERSON

(see also Coach, Jockey, Leisure and Amenity Management, Sport and Recreation Facility Management)

There are opportunities in sport for professional sportspeople, and for careers in coaching.

Not all sports allow players to be professionals, and there are others, such as snooker, where there is room for only a very few professionals. Sports attracting professionals in relatively large numbers are football, cricket, golf, horse racing, rugby league and tennis.

Sportspeople's careers are generally short but if, during their careers, they have made a name for themselves, there may be opportunities in journalism, broadcasting or consultancy work.

Qualifications and Training

Professional sportspeople naturally need to be very good at their sport. Those in team games generally begin by playing for their school, town or county side. In this context, a young player may be noticed by professional selectors. In the case of football, it is not necessary to join a local football league club; apprentices are taken on from all over the country. Because a club apprentice has no guarantee that he will ever play for the first side, some clubs encourage apprentices and allow them time off to obtain academic qualifications.

Coaches must gain recognised coaching qualifications, which are awarded by the governing bodies of the various sports and acquired either at evening class or weekend school.

Personal Qualities

As well as talent, professional sportspeople must possess dedication, perseverance, commitment and a degree of ruthlessness. Coaches and teachers also need perseverance, as well as patience, tact and the ability to inspire children or adults of very different abilities, often in less than ideal situations.

£ Salaries for professionals are often low initially, but the rewards for top performers may be very high. The amount of money earned varies enormously depending upon the sport. Coaches' salaries vary according to whether the work is full- or part-time, what type of work they are doing and the number of hours.

i Institute of Professional Sport, Francis House, Francis Street, London SW1P 1DE; 020 7630 7486

Sport England, 16 Upper Woburn Place, London WC1H 0QP; 020 7273 1500
www.english.sports.gov.uk

The Scottish Sports Council, Caledonia House, South Gyle, Edinburgh EH12 9DQ; 0131 317 7200

The Sports Council for Wales, Sophia Gardens, Cardiff CF1 9SW; 029 2039 7571

Careers in Sport (Kogan Page)

Great Careers for People Interested in Sports and Fitness (Kogan Page)

Stage Manager,* see *Theatre

STATISTICIAN

Statisticians are concerned with the collection, analysis and interpretation of numerical data. They work in both central and local government, commerce and industry, universities and other research and teaching institutions.

Qualifications and Training

Most statisticians begin their careers by gaining a degree in statistics, or a maths degree with a specialisation in statistics, or a postgraduate degree in statistics. Examinations up to graduate Diploma level are also administered by the Royal Statistical Society. These are available on a part-time and distance-learning basis.

Personal Qualities

Skill at maths, a logical mind and the ability to select and interpret essential facts and figures are required, and also the ability to analyse problems and communicate the results.

£ £12,000+.

i The Professional Affairs Officer, Royal Statistical Society, 12 Errol Street, London EC1Y 8LX; 020 7638 8998
'Careers in Statistics' (The Royal Statistical Society)

Steel Erector, **see** ***Building***

STEEPLEJACK

Steeplejacks are the mavericks of the building industry, able to tackle any job at any height in any trade. While working high up, safety chairs and harnesses are used and, sometimes, safety nets and rescue lines. Steeplejacks are mostly employed on repair and maintenance work, perhaps painting, pointing brickwork and masonry. Basic electrical skills are needed on some jobs.

Some firms of steeplejacks specialise, for example, in power-station chimneys, demolition work, restoration work, and the erection and maintenance of lightning conductors.

Qualifications and Training

The Construction Industry Training Board offers a course for those aged 16 and over. The course provides some work experience and is an entry to the industry's own apprenticeship scheme. NVQs are available at levels 1, 2 and 3.

Personal Qualities

A head for heights is most important, plus the ability to work quickly, neatly and carefully, and being prepared to work on one's own for longish periods.

£ Recommended weekly rates are: £73.90 at 16; £103.46 at 17; £147.81 at 18; and, when qualified, the craftsman rate is £178.62.

i Construction Industry Training Board, Bircham Newton, King's Lynn, Norfolk PE31 6RH; 01553 776677 (ext 2466)
National Federation of Master Steeplejacks and Lightning Conductor Engineers, 4D St Mary's Place, The Lace Market, Nottingham NG1 1PH; 0115 955 8818

STOCKBROKER

A stockbroker works for one of the broking companies which is a member of the Stock Exchange. Stockbrokers buy and sell securities on the Stock Exchange on behalf of investors, who may be individuals but are increasingly institutions, such as banks, insurance companies, pension funds or unit trusts.

Traditionally, securities were traded face to face on a market floor, but this ended in 1987, and now all trade is carried out by stockbrokers from their own dealing rooms.

Qualifications and Training

A degree is desirable, but good A levels may be accepted. Before being allowed to trade, all staff must pass the Securities and Futures Authority Registered Persons exam, administered by the Securities Institute, and must be registered with the regulator. Stockbrokers are eligible for Securities Institute membership provided they have at least three years' experience and have passed the Securities Institute diploma examinations.

Personal Qualities

Entrants should be confident, numerate and able to express ideas clearly and concisely. Good interpersonal skills are essential, in order to ensure effective client relationships, as is the ability to work as part of a team.

£ Depending on location, starting salaries vary from £12,000 to £20,000. Brokers' salaries depend on the amount of business carried out, and £45,000 is average, while top brokers can earn in excess of £250,000.

i The Securities Institute, Centurion House, 24 Monument Street, London EC3R 8AJ; 020 7645 0600 www.securities-institute.org.uk

STONEMASON

Stonemasons repair and restore stonework on old buildings and also provide stonework for new buildings, from walls, cladding and paving, to arches, staircases and fireplaces. The two kinds of masonry work are banking and fixing. Banker masons prepare the rough stone ready for use in a building and fixers assemble the stone where needed. In large firms the jobs are separate, but in smaller firms a mason may do both.

There are many different jobs for stonemasons: some specialise in monumental work – making and carving gravestones; others specialise in particular types of stone – for example, granite, marble, limestone.

Qualifications and Training

Formal academic qualifications are not required. Training is by a three-year apprenticeship supplemented by study through day or block release leading to NVQs, levels 2 and 3, awarded jointly by City and Guilds and the Construction Industry Training Board. The Building Crafts College also offers a one-year full-time City and Guilds course in advanced stonemasonry, covering basic traditional stonemasonry up to City and Guilds craft level (NVQ 3) and, additionally, stone carving, letter cutting and conservation and restoration techniques.

Personal Qualities

Manual skills are all-important in stonemasonry. Candidates must also be strong, prepared to work out of doors and possess great patience and accuracy.

£ Recommended weekly rates are: £73.90 at 16; £103.46 at 17; £147.81 at 18; and, when qualified, the craftsman rate is £178.62.

i Building Crafts College, 153 Great Titchfield Street, London W1P 7FR; 020 7636 0480

College of Masons (General Secretary: R Francis), 42 Magdalen Road, London SW18 3NP; 020 8874 8363
Construction Industry Training Board, Bircham Newton, King's Lynn, Norfolk PE31 6RH; 01553 776677 (ext 2466)

Stores Supervisor*, see *Purchasing Officer

Structural Engineering*, see *Engineering

Studio Manager*, see *Broadcasting

Sub-Editor*, see *Journalist

SURVEYOR/SURVEYING TECHNICIAN

(see also Estate Agent, Land Agent)

Surveying covers a wide variety of work within one profession, and a number of professional bodies offer qualifications in the different areas (*see* below). There are also technician qualifications. Surveying technicians work in all the same fields as surveyors but without being professionally qualified.

General Practice
This includes auctioneering, estate agency, valuation and estate management. People working in this area are responsible for the selling or letting, surveying, valuation and management of both urban and rural property. Qualifications in general practice are offered by the Royal Institution of Chartered Surveyors (RICS), the Professional Society of Valuers and Auctioneers (ISVA), the Association of Building Engineers (ABE) and the Architects' and Surveyors' Institute. Technician qualifications are also offered by the Society of Surveying Technicians (SST).

Aerial Surveying
A specialisation of land surveying (*see* below), aerial surveying involves photogrammetry – the use of aerial photographs as a basis for calculations.

Rural Practice
This is often combined with land agency and concerns the use and development of agricultural land. The qualifying bodies in this area are RICS, ISVA, the Architects' and Surveyors' Institute (ASI) and the SST.

Archaeological Surveying
This relatively new specialisation involves working on an archaeological dig, making plans, maps and cross-sections of the excavations. It thus involves the skill of a cartographer as well as that of a land surveyor. The Architects' and Surveyors' Institute has members in this discipline.

Building Surveying
The structural surveying of properties and reporting on their condition and valuation is carried out by building surveyors/building engineers. They advise on necessary repairs and maintenance and prepare plans and specifications for alterations and improvements. Local and central government employ a large proportion of qualified building surveyors, although many are in private practice. Qualifications in this area are available from RICS, ISVA, ABE, ASI and the SST.

Hydrographic Surveying
The hydrographer surveys and charts underwater areas, such as ports and harbours and offshore areas where drilling for oil takes place. Hydrographic surveying qualifications are offered by RICS, ASI and the SST.

Land Surveying
The land surveyor measures and charts the earth's physical features so that maps can be drawn. The scale of the work can range from a one-house building site to a whole region of Africa and there are opportunities in public services (the Ordnance Survey and the Ministry of Defence, for example), as well as in private practice or large commercial organisations. The RICS, ASI and the SST all offer qualifications in land surveying.

Minerals Surveying
Minerals surveyors assist in the design, development and surveying of quarries and underground mines, ensuring safety for the workers as well as optimum profitability for the company extracting the minerals. They also value mineral workings for rating and

taxation and therefore need to be all-rounders with a knowledge of geology, the management of mineral workings, taxation and planning legislation. This area of surveying is unique in having its qualifications and duties laid down by law. Minerals surveyors must hold the surveyor's certificate granted on behalf of the Secretary of State for Industry by the Mining Qualifications Board. They must be at least 21 and have at least four years' practical experience (including 2,000 hours underground) in order to sit the exam for this certificate. Further qualifications are provided by the RICS, ASI and the SST.

Quantity Surveying
In private practice, quantity surveyors work with an architect to draw up design specifications in line with the client's budget. When the finished design is agreed, the quantity surveyor draws up a bill of quantities, detailing the materials and labour that will be needed. Building contractors work on this bill of quantities in preparing their tender for the job; they will use their own quantity surveyors to estimate their costs. Quantity surveyors also monitor costs as the work progresses and is completed. If they train for this work while employed by construction contractors, they usually take the qualification of the RICS. Professional qualifications are also offered by the IAAS and ASI. Technician qualifications are offered by SST.

Qualifications and Training

There are several professional bodies offering a range of qualifications in the many different areas of surveying. Minimum entry requirements are generally five GCSE or equivalent passes plus two A levels or three H grades. English and maths passes are required. For graduates there are two components to qualifying as a Chartered Surveyor. First, an RICS-accredited degree or diploma must be successfully completed, followed by a period of practical training known as the Assessment of Professional Competence (APC). Postgraduate conversion courses are also available: full-time one year and part-time two years.

Four GCSEs grade A to C or equivalent including English and maths are the entry to Technician qualification. Surveying technicians begin by working as trainees in a professional Surveyor's office, taking Edexcel (BTEC) or higher certificates which are being replaced gradually by NVQs and GNVQs. A number of NVQs at levels 3 and 4 are currently available from the University of Central England.

Personal Qualities

Logical and orderly thinking, ability in figure work and detailed drawings are called for in this precision work. Communication skills and business acumen are essential. Good oral and written English is an asset and some areas may require specialised mathematical ability.

£ Trainees at 18, £8,000–£9,000; graduates with relevant degrees, £11,000–£13,800, with the higher amounts being paid in London; newly qualified, £13,000–£19,000.

i Architects and Surveyors Institute (ASI), St Mary's House, 15 St Mary Street, Chippenham, Wiltshire SN15 3WD; 01249 444505

The Association of Building Engineers (ABE), Jubilee House, Billing Brook Road, Weston Favell, Northampton NN3 8NW; 01604 404121

ISVA (Incorporated Society of Valuers and Auctioneers), 3 Cadogan Gate, London SW1X 0AS; 020 7235 2282

The Royal Institution of Chartered Surveyors (RICS), 12 Great George Street, London SW1P 3AD; 020 7222 7000

The Royal Institution of Chartered Surveyors in Scotland, 9 Manor Place, Edinburgh EH3 7DN; 0131 225 7078

Society of Surveying Technicians, Surveyor Court, Westwood Way, Coventry, West Midlands CV4 8JE

Built Environment Education Development Services (BEEDS), Faculty of Built Environment, University of Central England, Perry Barr, Birmingham B42 2SU; 0121 331 5174

T

TAX ADVISER/TECHNICIAN

Tax advisers/technicians work for private firms or independently, offering assistance to other firms/individuals who need guidance through the complications of the tax laws. A tax adviser would be able to advise clients on how to plan and present their taxable income so that they legally pay the least tax possible.

Tax technicians work for firms of accountants or solicitors, in clearing banks and for consultancy firms which offer a complete tax service to their clients. However, the largest area of work involves corporate tax in organisations that have their own tax department to prepare corporate tax and VAT returns on behalf of the company.

Qualifications and Training

Many tax advisers qualify first as accountants, but a growing number begin with A levels as tax trainees. The Chartered Institute of Taxation offers a qualifying exam for candidates already qualified as accountants or lawyers. The Association of Taxation Technicians is a starting point for all other tax trainees and offers an exam. This may be sufficient in itself for those candidates who do not expect to give detailed planning advice in their careers, or provide a stepping stone to the Institute's exam.

The ATII qualification denotes Associateship-level membership of the Institute and members may use the practising title of Chartered Tax Adviser.

Personal Qualities

Tax advisers/technicians must be prepared to keep on learning, be able to keep up to date with numerous tax changes each Budget, have an analytical mind, be able to apply lateral thinking and have good communication skills.

£ The starting salary is similar to others in finance and the eventual rewards are high.

i Association of Taxation Technicians, 12 Upper Belgrave Street, London SW1X 8BB; 020 7235 2544; fax 020 7235 4571
The Chartered Institute of Taxation (address as above); 020 7235 9381; fax 020 7235 2562
www.tax.org.uk

TAX INSPECTOR

Tax Inspectors work for the Tax Inspectorate of the Inland Revenue, the branch of the Civil Service concerned with assessing income tax, corporation tax and capital gains tax. Inspectors are responsible for particular tax districts (there are about 750 of these) and are often in charge of a substantial number of junior staff (known as Revenue Officers). They assess the tax liability of individuals and companies, examine appeals against such assessments and (if there is cause) examine possible cases of tax evasion or fraud.

Qualifications and Training

Many Tax Inspectors work their way up by internal promotion from the lower grades. It is possible to enter as a Revenue Officer with five GCSEs or equivalent. Training on the job may then lead to internal examinations and promotion to Revenue Executive, and thence to Inspector. Inspectors must qualify in tax law, accountancy and management by means of courses, which generally last some three years (and include part-time and private study). Honours graduates with degrees of sufficiently good standard may apply to join via the direct-entry scheme and shorten the training time.

Personal Qualities

Tax Inspectors must be highly responsible and very discreet. They are required to sign a declaration under the Official Secrets Act saying that they will not discuss their work. A mathematical mind and an ability to communicate clearly and pleasantly (face to face and on the telephone) are also necessary.

£ A newly qualified graduate Tax Inspector earns from about £12,000–£24,000 outside London; salaries in London are higher.

i Inland Revenue, Somerset House, Strand, London WC2R 1LB; 020 7438 6622

TAXI DRIVER

(see also Minicab Driver)

A 'taxi' is a traditional hackney carriage (like the famous black London taxis). The hackney carriage driver is allowed to 'ply for hire' – drive around the streets looking for passengers – and can be flagged down by a 'fare' (passenger). They may also operate from taxi ranks (known as 'standing for hire') in the streets. A private hire vehicle, on the other hand, has to be booked over the telephone or in person at the office from which it operates. Drivers therefore spend a good proportion of their time waiting around for passengers. Hours for both types of driver are generally long and anti-social (since there is a good deal of evening or night work, as well as weekend and public holiday work). Drivers may be owner-drivers (owning their own vehicles and working as and when they please), or may work for a company.

Qualifications and Training

Taxi drivers must be at least 21 years of age to be granted a licence, although in practice, because of insurance requirements, most are over 25. A valid Group A driving licence and relevant driving experience are also necessary. Hackney carriage drivers are legally bound to take the shortest or quickest route to a passenger's destination. Trainee drivers usually have to pass special tests, known as 'Knowledge Tests' to prove that they know their way about sufficiently well. These tests are generally oral, the most demanding being the Knowledge of London Test, which is required before drivers may operate in the capital. This usually takes some 18 months to two years to complete. There are specialised training schools available, and there are also special training schemes for the disabled and for people who have been in the forces. In London, too, an additional driving test must be passed before a licence is granted.

Personal Qualities

Driving in traffic demands a calm, unflappable personality, with lots of patience. Drivers also need to have a good memory. In addition, a taxi driver must be 'of good character', as a licence will not be granted to anyone who has committed certain offences.

£ Almost all taxi drivers are self-employed and have to pay tax and national insurance out of their earnings. Owner-drivers generally earn more than drivers employed by a company (who are often on a fixed rate), although they must also finance the repairs and servicing costs incurred by their own vehicles.

i Local taxi companies

Licensed Taxi Drivers Association, 9–11 Woodfield Road, London W9 2BA; 020 7286 1046

TEACHER

Teaching offers a wide variety of openings working with children and young people of all ages and backgrounds. Teachers do not merely stand in front of a chalkboard and teach facts to their particular class, nor does a teacher's day end when the final bell rings. They are expected to take a full and active part in their pupils' development as well as covering the relevant academic courses for routine examinations. They will also have the opportunity to devise projects, extra-curricular activities, special outings, and so on. A good deal of time out of school hours is spent marking work and preparing lessons, and keeping up with new developments in specific subjects or in education as a whole (and this applies to the relatively long holidays, too).

Teachers' work, naturally, varies with the age group being taught. Nursery teachers take the under-fives, infant teachers the five- to seven-year-olds. Secondary education starts at 11 and continues (in some cases) to 18 or 19. In addition, teachers are needed in sixth-form colleges and the numerous further and higher education establishments. Teachers at primary and junior (8 to 11) level generally teach a variety of basic subjects and specialist-subject teachers are not introduced until secondary level, although specialist music or sports teachers may be brought in at an earlier age.

Teaching has undergone radical changes in recent years and a large part of secondary education in comprehensive schools is now directed at mixed-ability classes, which makes great demands on teachers. The majority of pupils attend state schools (maintained schools), although there are also a limited number of openings in private education. There are also opportunities for teachers in special schools: for the handicapped (either boarding or day establishments), for disturbed children (in community homes or approved schools), for those with learning difficulties (such as deafness, or dyslexia) and in children's hospitals, where long-term patients are expected to take lessons. Such schools often make even greater emotional demands on their staff than normal.

Anyone wishing to teach in a state-maintained school in England and Wales must normally hold Qualified Teacher Status (QTS), obtained by completing an approved course of initial teacher training (ITT). The two main routes to achieving QTS are: the Bachelor of Education (BEd) degree (some institutions offer a BA or BSc degree with QTS) – usually four years; *or* a subject degree appropriate for the national curriculum subject to be taught, followed by a postgraduate certificate in education (PGCE) – three years plus one year. Most BEd courses are for primary teaching, and most PGCE courses for secondary teaching.

All applications for either route regardless of subject or teaching level must have attained the standard equivalent to at least grade C in both GCSE English language and maths. (GCSE science is also required from those born after 1 September 1979 entering teacher training courses after 1 September 1998.)

Entry requirements for BEd courses are five different subjects at GCSE grades A to C, two of which must be at A level or equivalent. For those training as primary school teachers, a GCSE in science is necessary.

Other types of course have been developed with the more mature entrant in mind: the two-year BEd, designed for those who already have appropriate technical and professional qualifications (for example, HND); the two-year part-time PGCE for those with other commitments; *and* the two-year full-time conversion PGCE for those wishing to teach a subject which is not the main subject of their first degree. These courses are not available for all subjects or at all locations.

Other developments include the introduction of postgraduate school-centred courses and the Open University distance-learning PGCE. Both these routes require an appropriate degree.

In Scotland, would-be teachers may obtain a teaching qualification (in primary education) via *either* a university degree course followed by a one-year course at a teacher education institution (TEI); *or* a four-year course at a TEI leading to the award of a BEd. The teaching qualification in secondary education may be obtained by means of one of the following: a relevant university degree followed by a one-year TEI course; a four-year BEd degree in music, technology or physical education; *or* a combined degree including subject study and teacher education.

Personal Qualities

Teachers do not merely need good academic ability; they must also be able to communicate their knowledge clearly and in an interesting fashion. They must also be able to establish a good relationship with their pupils and be prepared to take on considerable responsibility. Infinite patience and a sense of humour are great assets. It is important to have some experience of working with children before training.

£ Salary is determined by an 18-point pay scale ranging from £13,830–£37,041. Starting salary for an honours graduate is £15,537. This will rise automatically by annual increments to £23,193 after seven years. There is further enhancement if extra responsibilities are taken. A pay spine for Advanced Skills Teachers is being introduced with a ceiling of £41,607. The salary range for deputy headteachers is £27,258–£44,841 and for headteachers £28,155–£61,665. Both are determined by the size of the school.

i England and Wales: Teacher Training Agency, Communication Centre, PO Box 3210, Chelmsford, Essex CM1 3WA; 01245 454454
www.teach-tta.gov.uk

Northern Ireland: Department of Education, Rathgael House, Balloo Road, Bangor, Co Down BT19 7PR; 01247 279000
www.deni.gov.uk

Scotland: General Teaching Council for Scotland, Clerwood House, 96 Clermiston Road, Edinburgh EH12 6UT; 0131 314 6000; fax 0131 314 6001
www.gtcs.org.uk

Careers in Teaching (Kogan Page)

TECHNICAL ILLUSTRATOR

The job involves the drawing of technical subjects, freehand and in accurate detail. The subjects illustrated include car engines, the insides of machinery and other scientific, mechanical and technical equipment.

Qualifications and Training

Four GCSEs are preferred. Art is not essential but some artistic ability is necessary. Training is on the job and by attendance at courses. Many courses require the student to have completed a foundation course in art and design. Some firms may offer apprenticeships. City and Guilds qualifications are relevant. There is an Edexcel (BTEC) HND course in design (technical illustration), two years full-time, and an Edexcel (BTEC) HND course (also two years full-time) in design (illustration).

Personal Qualities

Accuracy, neatness, good concentration and the ability to work alone are required.

£ Low to begin with, but with experience a salary of £14,500 upwards may be earned.

i Local Jobcentres and Careers Offices

Technical Writer, **see** ***Writer***

TELECOMMUNICATIONS

The telecommunications industry has changed rapidly over the past ten years and has altered the way we live and work. Communications means much more than using the phone – it also includes technologies such as multi-media, mobile communications and the Internet. Most telecommunications companies have their own career structures. It is best to decide which company you would like to work for and approach them directly for suitable vacancies.

Qualifications and Training

Telephonists need a good general education as most companies provide in-house training. Administrative assistants need to have good GCSE passes, NVQs at levels 2/3 or GNVQs at levels 2/3. Good English language ability is essential. Most of the companies also have their own graduate entry programme, whilst their Web sites often display job vacancies and career advice.

Personal Qualities

All staff who deal with the public either in person or on the telephone must have very good communication skills and a pleasant, helpful manner. Other staff need skills which are specific to their job roles but the generic skills of effective interpersonal skills, organisational skills and time management are always valued.

£ Salaries vary considerably and are dependent on the experience and level at which you enter.

i British Telecom, 81 Newgate Street, British Telecom Centre, London EC1A 7AJ; 0207 356 5000
www.bt.com
Cable and Wireless. Recruitment line: 0800 096 0253
www.cwcom.co.uk
AT&T. Head Office: 0207 925 8000
www.att.co.uk
Mercury Communications Ltd, Head Office: New Mercury House, 26 Red Lion Square, London WC1R 4HQ; 020 7528 2000
The personnel departments of local telephone area offices

TELEPHONIST

(see also Receptionist, Telecommunications)

Telephonists are needed in virtually every commercial organisation. Duties may range from taking calls on a small switchboard with only a few extensions, to working in a large organisation with literally hundreds of telephones in constant use. In addition, there are telephonists who work for British Telecom, routeing the operator calls, the enquiries, the complaints and so on, as well as coping with the emergency 999 calls received daily.

In the business world the telephonist plays an important role, as the first person in the firm to whom a prospective client may speak, and providing the crucial first impression of how a business is run.

The telephonist may frequently be asked to put through overseas calls for busy managerial staff and may be responsible for making sure that the telephone books and relevant number lists (including those needed in an emergency) are available when needed. In some firms, the telephonist manages a switchboard and also acts as a receptionist in the front office.

Qualifications and Training

Some telephonists employed in commerce have been British Telecom-trained. No rigid academic qualifications are demanded; candidates must pass specific aptitude tests before they are accepted. Other telephonists may be trained on the job by their firms.

Personal Qualities

Good hearing and a clear speaking voice are important. Patience and an even temper are essential to cope with difficult or confused callers.

£ BT salaries range from £5,000+ at 16 to about £10,000.

i The personnel department of local telephone area offices
Local Jobcentres and Careers Offices

Television, see *Broadcasting*

THATCHER

Thatchers are self-employed craftsmen who thatch houses, pubs, barns and summerhouses with long straw, combed wheat straw or Norfolk reed. A thatched roof gives good insulation against heat and cold and lasts 20 to 50 years. A roof is thatched by taking off the old thatch and then pegging down layers of new straw or reed. A four-bedroom house, for example, would take a master thatcher and two apprentices about eight weeks to complete.

Qualifications and Training

Academic qualifications are not essential. Thatching can be learnt on the job as an apprentice to a Master Thatcher. Training takes four to five years and may be supervised by a local government training officer or by the Countryside Agency, which also provides a series of short courses to supplement training.

Personal Qualities

Thatchers need to be robust, good with their hands and not mind bad weather or heights. They also need common sense, and the ability to take decisions and deal with customers.

£ About £100 a week as an apprentice, thereafter depending on amount of work and individual charges.

i Thatching Information Service, Thatcher's Rest, Levens Green, Great Munden, Nr Ware, Hertfordshire SG11 1HD; 01920 438710

National Society of Master Thatchers, 20 The Laurels, Tetsworth, Thame, Oxfordshire OX9 7BH; 01844 281568

Countryside Agency, Craft Training Section, Rural Development Commission, 141 Castle Street, Salisbury, Wiltshire SP1 3TP; 01722 336255

The Thatcher's Craft (Rural Development Commission)

THEATRE

(see also Actor)

Theatre comprises much more than the actors and directors who receive the publicity. Many other people are involved in a theatrical production. Lighting and sound effects are created and handled by electricians; scenery and props are built, arranged and moved by technicians; the practical aspects of the production are organised and run by the Stage Manager and his or her assistants. The designer creates the sets; the wardrobe mistress makes the costumes and the director or producer is responsible for the production as a whole. Other staff include the publicity officer, house manager and box office staff.

Producer
The producer chooses the play, rents the theatre, engages the director and actors and is responsible for paying the bills. The producer is responsible for raising the money for the production.

Director
The Director is in charge of the actors, dancers, designers, singers and technicians, working within the managerial brief and, in consultation with producer and playwright, be responsible for casting. The Director's main work is in taking rehearsals and in turning the play into a theatrical production. The Casting Director auditions actors and arranges financial details with the actors and their agents.

Designer
Responsible for sets and costumes, working closely with the Director, and producing drawings of sets and costumes. The scenery and costume departments will work from these drawings, and also from scale models of the sets.

Stage Manager
The Stage Manager is responsible for the smooth running of rehearsals and productions, ensuring that properties and costumes are ready when required, that actors know when they are needed, to supervise lighting, scene-making and scene changes and to be responsible for effects, music, curtain calls and prompting. A Stage Manager will often have an assistant (ASM) and will also be helped by scene shifters. A Stage Manager may sometimes become a Producer or Director.

Lighting Designer
The theatre electrician may be in sole charge of the lighting or, in a large company with sophisticated equipment, be part of a team headed by an expert who will design a lighting plan. Appropriate electrician qualifications are needed.

Production Staff
A large theatre may have a series of production workshops; smaller theatres may combine several jobs in one:

Armoury: the armoury is responsible for making armour or weapons, for special effects like gunfire and shells, and for decorative metalwork. The members of the team are experts, eg gunsmith.

Metal workshop: here the heavy metalwork is designed and manufactured, eg for steel supports and complex trees. A welding qualification is useful.

Carpenters' workshop: technical drawing and carpentry skills come in useful for building sets. RADA offers a course for theatre carpentry.

Paint workshop: this is where the sets are painted. Knowing how to create the right textures and effects is part of the scene painter's skill.

Property-making shop: properties are often bought but in many productions, some props – for example, a throne or special upholstery – have to be specially made. An enthusiasm for research and an eye for detail are needed.

Wardrobe and wigs: although costumes and wigs may be hired, many are made by the wardrobe department. A good knowledge of period fashion and skills in dressmaking and tailoring are needed. Casual help is also needed when there is much sewing for a new production. Special hats are usually produced by a freelance milliner. Accessory making is another specialist job, as is wig- and beard-making, for which a City and Guilds certificate is a useful qualification. The wardrobe department is also responsible for looking after costumes and repairing and cleaning them.

Box Office

The box office is in charge of ticket sales. The manager is responsible for promotion and marketing, for hiring his or her staff and for checking the takings. Experience of accounts or general management is useful. This office makes a good starting place for anyone interested in arts administration.

Press Office

This department deals with all publicity for the theatre. It liaises with the press, arranges for photo sessions and interviews, produces posters, advertisements and mails leaflets and programmes. An arts graduate with secretarial training may find work here. Tact, self-confidence and a pleasant voice are useful qualities.

Theatrical Agent

Agents try to find work for the actors and actresses on their books. Experience and good contacts are essential. Payment is usually 10 to 15 per cent of the client's fee.

Qualifications and Training

Director
A thorough grounding in dramatic arts is essential. A degree in drama is useful. There are a few Trainee Director posts, mostly under the auspices of The Arts Council. A Director will have had extensive experience of the theatre, probably as a Stage Manager or acting. Some Directors come to the theatre from film or television, which also offer training.

Designer
Most designers will have completed a full-time art and design course.

Stage Manager
A full-time stage management course is provided at drama school for one to two years.

Production
NVQs are available at levels 1, 2 and 3 for theatre technicians.

Personal Qualities

Producer
Tact, persuasiveness, sound business sense, flair for organisation and knowledge of what 'sells' in the theatre are all necessary.

Director
Directors need creativity, strong character, the ability to direct and weld together a team of people and a strong sense of the theatre. The Casting Director needs tact and the ability to cope with crises.

Designer
A Theatre Designer needs a thorough knowledge of period settings and costumes, and what looks effective on stage, as well as a sense of style, and an ability to work within a budget and adapt to a variety of stage shapes.

Stage Manager
Managers need organising ability, tact, calmness in a crisis, a good memory, an eye for detail, a practical approach and an interest in the literary and technical aspects of theatrical production.

£ Salaries in the theatre are not high. Design staff, when qualified, should receive £10,000+, production staff too when trained. Office staff receive £130+ a week.

i Royal Academy of Dramatic Art (RADA), 62 Gower Street, London WC1E 6ED; 020 7636 7076
Careers in the Theatre (Kogan Page)

Theatrical Agent, **see** ***Theatre***

Therapist, **see** ***Art Therapist, Dental Therapist (Dentistry), Drama Therapist, Music Therapist, Occupational Therapist, Physiotherapist, Speech and Language Therapist***

TOOLMAKER

Toolmakers work in engineering making a wide range of jigs, used to guide cutting tools and to hold the work in position; fixtures, to hold metal for bending or welding or to hold parts together; press tools in different shapes and sizes for cutting parts; mould tools to make items such as fridge interiors; and measuring gauges. Toolmaker machinists make the tools, often specialising in just one kind. Toolmaker fitters work on large structures that are constructed from many parts. They check all the parts, number them and then fit them together.

Qualifications and Training

Formal educational requirements are not essential but GCSE grade B (or equivalent) in English, maths and a science are recommended, particularly for those who want to take the Edexcel (BTEC) certificate course. Edexcel (BTEC) higher certificate courses are available for those with a certificate or with education to A level standard in maths and a science. Training is on the job by three-year apprenticeship; time off is allowed for course attendance leading to City and Guilds or Edexcel (BTEC) qualifications.

Personal Qualities

Toolmakers must be deft and accurate in their work. Toolmaker fitters must be capable of reading technical drawings.

£ About £75–£80 a week at 16, and over £200 when trained.

i Engineering Careers Information Service, 41 Clarendon Road, Watford, Hertfordshire WD1 1LB; 01923 238441
Local Jobcentres and Careers Offices

TOURIST INFORMATION OFFICER

Tourist Information Officers work for national or regional tourist boards with the aim of attracting visitors to Britain or to a particular region. They provide information, often in the form of brochures, and are responsible for placing advertisements. They keep a watchful eye on standards and visit hotels, tourist attractions, transport and travel organisations. They are also involved in research work, assessing future trends and needs.

Qualifications and Training

Qualifications vary; some entrants begin as clerks and work their way up to higher positions. Assistants should have a good general education, preferably with GCSEs or equivalent. NVQ qualifications are available, awarded by the Association of British Travel Agents (ABTA), National Training Board (NTB) and RSA. GNVQs in Leisure and Tourism are also available at further education colleges nationally. Degrees in travel and tourism are available, and also one-year full-time postgraduate courses leading to an MSc or diploma in tourism.

Personal Qualities

Tourist Information Officers must enjoy working with the general public, and adopt a responsible and helpful attitude in the giving of information. A friendly personality and good administrative skills are useful.

£ £5,000+ at 16 with GCSEs, managers' salaries from £10,000 upwards.

i Institute of Travel and Tourism, 113 Victoria Street, St Albans, Hertfordshire AL1 3TJ; 01727 854395
www.tttc.co.uk

The Travel and Tourism and Events Sector National Training Organisation, The Cornerstone, The Broadway, Woking, Surrey GU21 5AR; 01483 740854
National and local tourist boards
Careers in the Travel Industry (Kogan Page)

TOUR OPERATOR

Tour operators arrange holidays for travellers in the UK and abroad. Some operators deal mainly with traditional package holidays based at one or two resorts, while others are involved with specialist holidays such as trekking or adventure. Holidays are sold to the public directly or via a travel agent. Operators may provide couriers and representatives to look after holidaymakers and deal with any problems. Many of the staff are office-based, dealing with bookings, accounts and administration, but there are opportunities for some employees to go abroad. They may check areas where new holidays are proposed or visit hotels and resorts already in use.

Qualifications and Training

NVQs are available, awarded by the Association of British Travel Agents' National Training Board (ABTA–NTB) and City and Guilds. GNVQs in Leisure and Tourism are also available at further education colleges nationally.

Personal Qualities

Tour operators must be good at dealing with people, and have imagination, administrative and organisational skills. Foreign languages are an asset.

£ Salaries vary according to job and position; a junior clerk would begin at £5,000+ and a graduate at £10,000+.

i Institute of Travel and Tourism, 113 Victoria Street, St Albans, Hertfordshire AL1 3TJ; 01727 854395
The Travel and Tourism and Events Sector National Training Organisation, The Cornerstone, The Broadway, Woking, Surrey GU21 5AR; 01483 740854
Careers in the Travel Industry (Kogan Page)

TOWN AND COUNTRY PLANNER

Planners are concerned with reconciling the needs of the population for buildings, shopping centres, schools, leisure centres, and so on, with the necessity of preserving and enhancing the natural and built environment. They collect information about the present use of land, the position of roads and other features, as well as drawing up plans for new schemes. Planners in development control ensure that buildings or developments intended for a particular area are suitable and do not conflict with existing buildings or the surrounding environment. Planners work for local and central government, environmental agencies and, to an increasing extent, in private practice. There are also varied opportunities for planning support staff.

Qualifications and Training

To enter a degree or diploma course in town planning, five GCSE passes and two A levels are desirable. Useful subjects are maths, English language, geography and history or a foreign language. Those with RTPI-accredited degrees or diplomas in town planning are exempt from the exams of the Royal Town Planning Institute. Planning courses are available at undergraduate and postgraduate levels, full-time and part-time and on a distance-learning basis.

Technicians need four GCSEs or equivalent to include maths, English and preferably the subjects mentioned above. A number of colleges offer courses for technicians on a part-time or block release basis. Qualifications gained are the Edexcel (BTEC) certificate, higher certificate or higher diploma in administration or the higher certificate in planning. An NVQ at level 3 is available for support staff.

Personal Qualities

Town planners and support staff need to have a knowledge of many subjects: economics, sociology, architecture and geography. Planners must be able to work in a team and cooperate with experts in other subjects. They must be good communicators and have imagination and an interest in and understanding of both people and the environment.

£ Qualified planners about £11,000–£16,000, support staff £7,000–£9,000 upwards depending upon qualifications.

i The Royal Town Planning Institute, 26 Portland Place, London W1N 4BE; 020 7636 9107
www.rtpi.org.uk
Society of Town Planning Technicians (address as above)

TRADING STANDARDS OFFICER

Trading Standards Officers are employed within local government with the responsibility to enforce a wide range of legislation aimed at protecting the consumer and honest trader. Laws relate to such diverse subjects as metrology, food and consumer product safety, credit, descriptions of goods and services, prices, animal health and welfare. While most operations are carried out by random inspectional work, officers are also required to investigate complaints and, where appropriate, it may be necessary to pursue matters to court.

Qualifications and Training

The principal qualification is the diploma in trading standards (DTS), which may be obtained via a block-release course or, with an additional exam, to specified honours degree courses in consumer protection. Entrants to the former course will require five GCSE/SCE passes (two at A level or three at H grade), to include English, maths and physics (with certain alternatives). Training will take three years and will include on-the-job experience. A further qualification which pays specific attention to specialised working practices is the diploma in consumer affairs (DCA). This exam demands an entrance of five GCSEs, to include English, and the normal training programme takes two years.

Personal Qualities

Officers will need to be able to apply their training and knowledge in a fair, open and common-sense manner. An ability to communicate clearly, to appreciate the demands of business, and to ensure consumers are not deprived of their legal rights, are all component parts of the duties. The wide variety of interests provided by the job is frequently quoted as a main attraction.

£ Trainees may expect to earn up to £9,000 per annum and on full qualification this can rise to £14,000.

[i] Institute of Trading Standards Administration, 3–5 Hadleigh Business Centre, 351 London Road, Hadleigh, Essex SS7 2BT; 01702 559922

Local Government Opportunities, The LGMB, Layden House, 76–86 Turnmill Street, London EC1M 5QU; 020 7296 6600 (for exam details and careers information)

Local Government Careers Explorer Web site: www.lgnto.gov.uk/igo

TRAFFIC WARDEN

Traffic wardens are civilians who work in conjunction with local police forces. They check parking meters and penalise drivers parking on double yellow lines or in other illegal places. They may also be required to do school crossing patrols or traffic control duty, as well as receiving vehicles towed into the police pound, and looking out for out-of-date car licences.

Qualifications and Training

No formal educational requirements are necessary; training is on the job.

Personal Qualities

Traffic wardens must be responsible, self-confident, good communicators and must possess good health and eyesight.

[£] This varies according to area, ranging from about £10,500; wardens in inner London receive more.

[i] Local police forces

Metropolitan Police Service, Recruitment & Selection Centre, 26 Aybrook Street, London W1M 3JL; 020 7224 7232

TRAINING OFFICER/MANAGER

Training officers work in medium-sized firms and organisations, national and local government, emergency services and countless voluntary organisations. They are responsible for identifying training requirements, designing training programmes, delivering training to individuals or groups and evaluating the success of training.

Qualifications and Training

There are a number of short courses for those interested in training but, for those interested in making training a career, a professional qualification is advisable. The Institute of Personnel and Development (IPD) offers a certificate in training practice for those new to or with limited experience in training and gives associate membership (AssocIPD) of the IPD. The IPD also offers higher-level qualifications at licentiate and graduate membership levels. NVQs in training and development at levels 3, 4 and a level 5 are available. Candidates who successfully complete an NVQ level 3 in Training and Development can apply for associate membership with the IPD and those who complete level 4 can apply for licentiate membership. Those who complete level 5 can apply for graduate membership.

Personal Qualities

Training officers should have good communication, presentation, diagnostic, organisational and negotiation skills. They need to be able to set realistic targets, meet deadlines and plan ahead.

£ Trainees about £13,500; when qualified over £21,000.

i The Institute of Personnel and Development, IPD House, Camp Road, London SW19 4UX; 020 8971 9000; fax 020 8971 3333 (IPD qualifications and membership information, and career pack; course information from the Professional Education Department 020 8263 3313; www.ipd.co.uk)

TRANSLATOR

Translators work freelance from home or as staff translators, within a commercial organisation whose main business is not translation, or within a translation agency. Normally, they only translate from another language into their mother tongue. The work translated varies from whole books to business letters and documents. Translators, especially those who specialise in work for publication, must be able to express themselves very well. In areas where the subject matter of the text is specialised, for example, computing, maths or mountaineering, expert knowledge is required of the translator. A broad-based general knowledge is always an advantage. Translators may be responsible for finding their own work but may also be registered with a translation company or agency.

Qualifications and Training

Proficiency in a foreign language is necessary, as is the ability to write well in the target language. An understanding of the culture of the relevant countries is important. Increasingly, there is a need to be computer-literate. There is a growth in the use of computer-assisted translation tools in some areas of the work. Most translators have a postgraduate qualification or a diploma in translation.

Personal Qualities

Translators must be meticulous, conscientious, creative and persistent. The ability to carry out research as and when necessary and good interpersonal skills are also required.

£ Freelance translators sometimes own the copyright in their work and strictly the payment they receive is for granting others the right to use their translation. Published translators may also receive royalties. Translators are usually paid per 1,000 words. The ITI's Rates and Salaries Survey is a useful source of salary details (*see* below).

i The Institute of Linguists, 48 Southwark Street, London SE11 1UN; 020 7940 3100; fax 020 7940 3101

Institute of Translation and Interpreting (ITI), 377 City Road, London, EC1V 1NA; 020 7713 7600; fax 020 7713 7650 www.iti.org.uk

The Translators Association, 84 Drayton Gardens, London SW10 9SB; 020 7373 6642 (for published translators)

Careers Using Languages (Kogan Page)

ITI pack – send an A4 sae (39p stamp) to the address above, requesting ref 'T/I training and careers pack'

1998 ITI Rates and Salaries Survey, available from ITI, address above

Transport Engineering,* see *Engineering

TRAVEL AGENT

Travel agents sell tickets for travel by air, land and sea on behalf of transport organisations. They make hotel bookings for individual travellers, business people or holidaymakers. Some travel companies deal only with business travel and are also involved in arranging conferences and trade fairs. However, the area in which the travel agent is largely known is the selling of package holidays on behalf of tour operators. Many travel agents will also advise travellers on matters such as visas, foreign currency and necessary injections.

Qualifications and Training

NVQ qualifications are available, awarded by City and Guilds and the Travel Training Company.

Personal Qualities

Travel agents must enjoy dealing with the general public, have a responsible attitude regarding the accuracy of information given and good administrative skills.

£ Varies according to job; assistants earn £7,000+, managers £10,000+.

i The Travel Training Company, The Cornerstone, The Broadway, Woking, Surrey GU21 5AR; 01483 72732 www.tttc.co.uk

Institute of Travel and Tourism, 113 Victoria Street, St Albans, Hertfordshire AL1 3TJ; 01727 854395

Careers in the Travel Industry (Kogan Page)

TRICHOLOGIST

Trichologists treat hair and scalp disorders, the most common being hair loss. Electrical and heat treatments, massage and special lotions and ointments are used. Trichologists practise on their own behalf; some of their patients are referred to them from doctors, but trichology is not available on the NHS.

Qualifications and Training

Basic academic qualifications are necessary. Training may be by a three-year pupillage with a practising trichologist. The necessary theoretical instruction is available at technical colleges, evening classes or by correspondence. It is also necessary to have some practical experience of working in a recognised clinic.

Personal Qualities

Trichologists must understand the necessary biological principles, have a knowledge of nutrition, plus an interest in helping people. They must have high standards of personal hygiene.

£ Dependent upon number of patients, hours worked and fees charged.

i Institute of Trichologists, 20–22 Queensberry Place, London SW7 2DZ; 020 7491 7253

Truck Driver,* see *Lorry Driver

U

Undertaker, **see** *Funeral Director*

Underwriter, **see** *Insurance*

UPHOLSTERER

(see also Furniture and Furnishing)

Upholsterers measure up, prepare and fit the fabric components in all kinds of furniture. It is highly skilled work and includes not only the visible top coverings (which can vary from velvet to leather), but also the preparation and supports below, such as padding, stuffing, springing or webbing. Large furniture manufacturers employ upholsterers in their factories and there are also a fair number of smaller, often family-run, businesses which specialise in certain types of upholstery work. The job may entail anything from providing modern chairs, sofas and so on for large hotel chains to the restoration of unique pieces of antique furniture in private homes or museums.

Qualifications and Training

No specific academic qualifications are required. Training combines on-the-job apprentice work with day-release courses, leading to the City and Guilds diploma.

Personal Qualities

Upholsterers need to have nimble fingers and infinite patience and must enjoy working on individual projects.

£ A 16-year-old trainee can expect to earn around £75 a week. A trained upholsterer would receive about £175.

i Local Jobcentres and Careers Offices
London Guildhall University, Old Castle Street, London E1 7NT; 020 7320 1000

V

VALUER

(see also Auctioneer, Estate Agent, Land Agent, Surveyor/Surveying Technician)

Valuers are employed by a wide variety of firms to assess the worth of goods and property (including land, buildings, fine arts, chattels, machinery and livestock). They may work for building societies, estate agents, insurance companies, property companies or any commercial, financial or industrial organisation that has to know true commercial values for selling, renting, investment or taxation purposes. Some valuers are also surveyors, auctioneers or land agents.

Qualifications and Training

Professional qualifications are awarded by ISVA (Professional Society of Valuers and Auctioneers). ISVA asks for five GCSE passes at A to C, including English and maths, three of which must have been gained at the same time. Training combines practical work with appropriate studies in a variety of available part-time, full-time and sandwich courses. The ISVA examinations are only available via a distance-learning mode. The University of Central England (*see* below) offers an NVQ level 4 in Valuation.

Personal Qualities

A valuer needs discretion combined with aptitude to understand the various economic factors involved in commerce.

£ Trainees £8,000–£13,000 depending on age and qualifications, with higher salaries in London; £13,000–£19,000 when qualified.

i ISVA (Incorporated Society of Valuers and Auctioneers), 3 Cadogan Gate, London SW1X 0AS; 020 7235 2282 www.educ-memb.isva.co.uk

Built Environment Education Development Services (BEEDS), Faculty of Built Environment, University of Central England, Perry Barr, Birmingham B42 2SU; 0121 331 5174

VEHICLE TECHNICIAN

(see also Garage Work, Road Transport)

Apart from working in garages, maintaining and repairing cars belonging to the general public, vehicle technicians are also employed to maintain heavy goods vehicles, buses and coaches owned by large road transport operators, motorcycles, agricultural machinery or 'performance' cars. The areas of work are varied, and also include the maintenance of aero engines and a number of jobs in industry, involved with machinery of all kinds.

Industry

Categories include: metal-working machine tools, industrial pumps, valves and compressors, textile machinery, construction and earth-moving equipment, office machinery, refrigeration machinery, industrial plant and steelwork. The machinery is designed by the mechanical engineer, and maintained by the technician.

Agriculture

As farming becomes increasingly mechanised, technicians are more in demand for the maintenance of such equipment as tractors, crop harvesters of all kinds, seed drills, even automated revolving milk parlours.

Qualifications and Training

16 to 17-year-olds may embark upon a training scheme whereby different skills are learnt and tested. NVQs are now available for a range of vehicle technician occupations. There is an Edexcel (BTEC) higher national certificate in mechanical engineering, and City and Guilds offers a course in three parts for mechanical engineering technicians.

Candidates for the Edexcel (BTEC) HND course in mechanical and production engineering should be 18 and hold either the

Edexcel (BTEC) certificate or an A level in maths, chemistry or physics. Courses are for two years full-time, or three years sandwich.

Personal Qualities

Mechanical aptitude, the ability to diagnose faults with the aid of a workshop manual and to work responsibly without supervision and undertake routine tasks.

£ £65–£70 a week at the start of training (Stage 1), £130+ at Stage 3.

i Bus and Coach Training Ltd, Regency House, 43 High Street, Rickmansworth, Hertfordshire WD3 1ET; 01923 896607

The Institution of Mechanical Engineers, 1 Birdcage Walk, London SW1H 9JJ; 020 7222 7899

RTITB Services Centre, York House, Empire Way, Wembley, Middlesex HA9 0RT; 020 8902 8880

VETERINARY NURSE

Nurses assist vets during operations and X-rays, sterilise instruments, look after animals recovering from surgery and keep the animals and their cages clean. After qualification, the work of a veterinary nurse can include practice management, staff supervision, teaching and training other nurses or support staff. Some VNs choose to work outside veterinary practice in, for example, research establishments, colleges, zoos and breeding or boarding kennels.

Qualifications and Training

Entry requirements are five GCSEs at grade C or above, including English language and two passes in a physical or biological science and maths. Equivalent qualifications are accepted at the discretion of the RCVS VN Review Officer. Alternatively, the BVNA's pre-veterinary nursing course, approved by the RCVS, enables the holder to enrol on to the veterinary nursing scheme without other GCSEs. A qualified VN can go on to study for an advanced diploma in veterinary nursing (surgical and medical).

Personal Qualities

A love of animals is essential, plus patience, a calm manner and good health.

£ £3,000 for students; £5,000–£9,000 when qualified.

i British Veterinary Nursing Association (BVNA), Level 15, Terminus House, Terminus Street, Harlow, Essex CM20 1XA; 01279 450567; fax 01279 420866

The Royal College of Veterinary Surgeons, Belgravia House, 62–64 Horseferry Road, London SW1P 2AF; 020 7222 2001

Careers Working with Animals (Kogan Page)

VETERINARY SURGEON

Most vets work in private practice, usually starting out as a veterinary assistant and working their way up into a partnership or into their own business. Some specialise in small-animal treatment (including pets such as dogs, cats, cage birds, and so on), while others work with particular kinds of animals (such as farm animals, racehorses or the more exotic zoo animals). Other vets go into research or industry. The Ministry of Agriculture, for instance, employs a substantial number to work on disease control (monitoring such epidemics as foot and mouth or swine vesicular disease for instance). Others are employed by animal welfare organisations, such as the PDSA, in animal hospitals. Vets are also needed in the food-processing industries where their job is concerned with checking that conditions are humane and hygienic.

Qualifications and Training

A veterinary surgeon must hold a degree from one of the six veterinary schools in the UK. The six universities offering the course set their own entrance requirements but all demand an extremely high standard, with good A levels. Chemistry is essential, and other useful subjects are physics, maths, biology or zoology. The course lasts five years (six at Cambridge), and covers a formidable amount of academic and practical work, comparable to that involved in training to be a doctor.

Personal Qualities

Vets need sympathy combined with detachment, endless patience and physical fitness (particularly if dealing with larger animals). They must also be self-reliant and prepared to work anti-social hours. Some business sense and the ability to keep accounts are also important.

£ Assistants (less than five years qualified) in general practice start at £14,000–£15,000, more than five years qualified £18,000–£25,000 (with a car and accommodation generally provided); partners earn £32,000–£37,000; Government vets start at £20,000+.

i The British Veterinary Association, 7 Mansfield Street, London W1M 0AT; 020 7636 6541

The Royal College of Veterinary Surgeons, Belgravia House, 62–64 Horseferry Road, London SW1P 2AF; 020 7222 2001 www.rcvs.org.uk

'A Career as a Veterinary Surgeon' (£4.00 including postage and packing from the Royal College of Veterinary Surgeons)

Vision Mixer, **see** *Broadcasting*

W

Waiting, see *Catering and Accommodation Management, Hotel Work*

Warden, see *Caretaker, Conservation (Environmental), Leisure, Traffic and Amenity Management*

WATCH AND CLOCK MAKER/REPAIRER

Watch and clock makers make timepieces by hand, sometimes to a design of their own.

Repairers receive watches and clocks from customers for servicing and repair. They must be able to examine a timepiece thoroughly for worn-out parts, clean and regulate a watch or clock, and repair or replace faulty parts. The work involves the use of precision tools and electronic equipment. Restoration is carried out on antique clocks and watches.

Qualifications and Training

A good general education is advisable, to include English, maths and physics. Preferably training is by five-year apprenticeship, some of which may be spent on full- or part-time courses, leading to the examinations of The British Horological Institute (BHI). These courses are held at a number of colleges. It is also possible to study for the BHI examinations by correspondence course. NVQs will be available in the future.

Personal Qualities

Applicants must have good eyesight, the physical skill and patience to do the intricate work required, and be able to work alone.

£ About £60 a week at 16, and £110+ when qualified.

i The British Horological Institute, Upton Hall, Upton, Newark, Nottinghamshire NG23 5TE; 01636 813795

Water Engineering, **see** *Engineering*

Web site Designers, **see** *Computing*

Web site Programmers, **see** *Computing*

WELDER

Welders join pieces of metal together by applying intense heat and melting the edges so that two pieces become one. The sorts of items welded are metal sections of aeroplanes, ships, oil rigs and power turbines. Welders work in light- and heavy-engineering firms, in foundry work and in shipbuilding. Some plastics are also welded.

Qualifications and Training

Formal academic qualifications are not necessary but GCSEs in English, maths and a science are preferred. Training is on the job by three-year apprenticeship, with time off to attend courses leading to NVQs. Welders engaged in work for the Ministry of Defence are required to take quality tests every six months.

Personal Qualities

A welder must have a steady hand and excellent powers of concentration. Workers must be careful and follow safety instructions, as the work is potentially dangerous.

£ About £80 a week at 16, £260 with experience.

i Engineering and Marine Training Authority (EMTA), 41 Clarendon Road, Watford, Hertfordshire WD1 1LB; 01923 238441
www.emta.org.uk

Welding Institute, Granta Park, Abington Hall, Abington, Cambridge CB1 6AL; 01223 891162
www.twi.co.uk

Engineering Construction Industry Training Board, Blue Court, Church Lane, Kings Langley, Hertfordshire WD2 8JP; 01923 260000

WHOLESALING

Wholesalers buy in goods from manufacturers then sell them to a number of smaller customers (or retailers). In this way, the manufacturer only has to deliver to a few specific points. Wholesalers tend to specialise in particular types of goods, such as books, garden equipment and costume jewellery.

A variety of staff are employed in wholesaling, including clerks, accounts staff, buyers, managers, storekeepers and drivers.

Qualifications and Training

These vary depending on the type of job. Many of the managerial positions are filled by people who have worked their way up. Entrants may work towards NVQs levels 1 and 2.

Personal Qualities

Staff employed in wholesaling must be speedy, efficient and reliable.

£ Salaries are commensurate with those paid for similar work in other industries: £5,000+ for a junior clerk, and about £11,000 for managerial staff. London salaries are generally higher.

i Local Jobcentres and Careers Offices

WINDOW DRESSER

Window display covers window arrangements as well as displays inside a big store – an arrangement in the ladies' fashion department, for example. Display managers and buyers (*see* Buyer) have considerable authority in deciding what is to be displayed.

Junior window dressers start by assisting seniors and will probably be assigned periodically to different kinds of merchandise, from household goods and china, to clothes. Freelancers may also be employed part-time to dress windows. In small specialist shops, members of staff will probably be responsible for all the window displays.

Qualifications and Training

Three GCSEs (grades A, B or C), including English and art, are necessary for a two-year full-time course leading to the British Display Society's advanced diploma; or a one-year full-time course may be taken, leading to the general certificate. There are Edexcel (BTEC) awards in vocational art and design. Some companies have their own training schemes, which are intended to supplement the college training but not to replace it. A degree in art and design is valuable for the top jobs.

Personal Qualities

Dressers must have an interest in art and fashion and skill in handling materials, as well as an appreciation of colour, design and texture. They must have an understanding of sales techniques, be resourceful and have the ability to produce scale drawings.

£ £7,500–£9,000 with training.

i Local Jobcentres and Careers Offices

WINE TRADE

The wine trade has grown beyond the small merchant or importer and most opportunities are now with large companies which import, retail and deal with the licensed trade, hotels and catering, off-licences, supermarkets and multiple stores. There are posts in marketing, advertising, packaging, promotion, market research, buying and quality control.

Qualifications and Training

Opportunities exist at GCSE, A and degree level for entry into the wine trade. The Wine and Spirit Education Trust (a registered educational charity set up by the drinks industry) offers courses and qualifications.

Personal Qualities

These depend on the area entered, but a love and knowledge of wine are obviously important, plus relevant knowledge about the chief wine-growing areas, and their type of soil and climate.

£ Dependent upon position and experience, but commensurate with salaries in other industries for a similar job, such as in advertising or quality control.

i Wine and Spirit Education Trust, Five Kings House, 1 Queen Street Place, London EC4R 1QS; 020 7236 3551; fax 020 7329 8712

Harpers Wine and Spirit weekly, Harling House, 47 Great Suffolk Street, London SE1 1RQ (job advertisements)

Wine and Spirit Association
www.wsa.org.uk

WRITER

(see also Journalist)

Some authors exist solely on the proceeds of their writing, but for many it is a part-time occupation, additional to a full-time job. The field of creative writing is probably the most difficult in which to succeed. It is also the area which contains some of the best-known writers, the authors of popular fiction bestsellers. It is probably slightly easier to make a living by non-fiction writing, producing text on a specialist or technical subject, or writing for textbooks.

There are a few posts as writer in residence, where writers work for regional authorities developing writing projects with people living in the region. There are also opportunities of a journalistic nature for non-journalists. Writers may contribute to specialist journals or submit short stories to magazines interested in fiction.

Qualifications and Training

Generally, writers are born, not made. However, it is possible to take courses in both creative and technical writing.

Personal Qualities

Writers must be self-disciplined, able to work on their own, highly motivated and persevering.

£ Earnings vary enormously, but the majority of writers do not support themselves by their writing alone. Writers in residence can expect about £10,000–£12,000.

i Society of Authors, 84 Drayton Gardens, London SW10 9SB; 020 7373 6642
www.writers.org.uk/society
Writers' and Artists' Yearbook (A&C Black); *The Writer's Handbook* (Macmillan)

Y

YOUTH AND COMMUNITY WORKER

(see also Social Work and Social Care – Children and Young People)

Youth and community workers work in a range of settings including youth clubs, schools, colleges, community centres and specialist agencies such as those offering information, advice and counselling. Some workers also work in mobile centres and with young people on the streets and in cafés. The majority of youth and community workers are either part-time or unpaid.

The aim of youth workers is the informal education and social development of those with whom they work. This is accomplished through work with individuals, work with and in groups, and with communities.

In Scotland, youth and community work is combined with adult education under the generic term 'community education'.

Qualifications and Training

Various routes, including full-time and part-time courses, postgraduate courses and employed-based apprenticeship schemes currently exist. NVQs in Community Work are also available at levels 2, 3 and 4. Detailed information on courses can be obtained from the National Youth Agency, directly or via their Web site. Details of training and employment in Scotland and in Wales can be obtained from Community Learning Scotland and from the Wales Youth Agency, respectively.

Applicants are normally at least 21 years old, although some institutions set higher and lower age limits, and applicants are usually expected to have substantial experience of work with young people or adults. This can be paid or unpaid. Mature entrants may be accepted without formal academic qualifications.

Personal Qualities

An interest in and understanding of the issues that affect people's lives, plus patience, stamina and a sense of humour are all qualities demanded of youth and community workers.

£ Ranges from £12,500 to £25,000.

i The National Youth Agency, 17–23 Albion Street, Leicester LE1 6GD; 0116 285 3700

'The National Youth Agency Guide to Initial Training Courses in Youth and Community Work' (National Youth Agency, £3.95)

'NYA Guide to Becoming a Youth Worker' (National Youth Agency, £1.00)

'What is the Youth Service?' (National Youth Agency, £1.00)

Community Learning Scotland, Rosebery House, 9 Haymarket Terrace, Edinburgh EH12 5EZ; 0131 313 2488

Wales Youth Agency, Leslie Court, Lan-y-Llyn, Caerphilly; 01222 880088

Z

ZOO KEEPER

Keepers look after animals in zoos, mucking out their living quarters, preparing their food and feeding them. They work long hours – from 8am to as late as 7pm – much of the time outdoors and the work is often physically demanding.

Qualifications and Training

No specific school-leaving qualifications are asked for and training is on the job and by a correspondence course followed by a City and Guilds qualification. So far, the NVQ qualifications in animal care have not been adopted by zoos. Unfortunately, applications for such jobs far exceed the number of places available, and zoos prefer people to enquire only when a vacancy is advertised.

Personal Qualities

Affection and respect for animals, combined with an unsentimental approach, are essential.

£ Applicants should apply to individual zoos. Salaries range from about £5,000+ to £12,000+.

i The Association of British Wild Animal Keepers, 12 Tackley Road, Eastville, Bristol BS5 6UQ (send sae)
Careers Working with Animals (Kogan Page)

ZOOLOGIST

Zoologists work in either research or teaching. A very small number find jobs in industry, mainly in pharmaceutical and animal foodstuff companies. Research zoologists will probably work in one of the many Government-backed centres on a variety of projects including animal behaviour, pest control and the population ecology of birds.

Qualifications and Training

A degree in zoology, available at some universities, is needed for a career as a zoologist. Postgraduate training in specialisations such as entomology or nematology is also available.

Personal Qualities

Zoologists should have a scientific mind and a bent for research.

£ £12,000 upwards.

i The Institute of Biology, 20–22 Queensberry Place, London SW7 2DZ; 020 7581 8333
www.iob.org.uk
'Careers in Biology' (send £4.50 to Institute of Biology)

INDEX

INDEX OF ADVERTISERS